STOIC AND EPICUREAN

'Αλλ', ὦ φίλε, ἦν δ' ἐγώ, μέτρον τῶν τοιούτων ἀπολεῖπον καὶ ὁτιοῦν τοῦ ὄντος οὐ πάνυ μετρίως γίγνεται· ἀτελὲς γὰρ οὐδὲν οὐδενὸς μέτρον.—PLATO, *Republic*, VI, 504, C.

EPOCHS OF PHILOSOPHY

STOIC AND EPICUREAN

BY

R. D. HICKS, M.A.

FELLOW AND FORMERLY LECTURER OF TRINITY COLLEGE, CAMBRIDGE

NEW YORK

RUSSELL & RUSSELL · INC

1962

L. C. CATALOG CARD NO : 61–13090

PRINTED IN THE UNITED STATES OF AMERICA

PREFACE

THE philosophical systems of Zeno and Epicurus may profitably be studied together. For, in spite of obvious differences, over which their adherents for centuries waged internecine warfare, it is easy to discern the fundamental similarity between them. Both schools sought by devious paths one and the same goal. Both exalted practice above theory, and conceded to sense and experience their full right. Both, in short, were crude forms of realism, which for the time (and not for that time alone) had come into its inheritance and held full sway over the minds of men. The temper of the age favoured such a reaction from extreme intellectualism. The success of the new schools, if not immediate, was assured from the first, reaching its height when Hellenistic culture was taken up by the practical Romans. My exposition of these two parallel systems of thought is primarily based on independent study of the original authorities. In this department of the history of philosophy much good work has been done in the last quarter of a century. I have made it my business to compare the results of recent investigation with the sources themselves, now rendered accessible, as they never have been before, through the labours of such competent scholars as Diels, Wachsmuth, Usener, and von Arnim. Even with these welcome aids, the task of research is by no means easy, owing to the scantiness and the peculiar nature of the materials which time has spared. To take the early

v

Stoics, Zeno and Chrysippus; much of the evidence
is derived from opponents who were naturally more
alert to detect and expose inconsistencies than careful to state impartially the doctrines they impugned.
When ampler means of information become available,
new difficulties arise; for while it is certain that the
Stoics of Cicero's time had diverged from the standards of orthodoxy prescribed by their predecessors,
it is not equally certain wherein precisely this divergence consisted. Thus Cicero puts into the mouth
of Cato a lucid exposition of Stoic ethics, but what
particular Stoic was Cicero's authority, and how far
this authority reproduced or modified the original
doctrine of Zeno and Chrysippus, is matter of dispute. Nor are these difficulties removed by con-
sulting Seneca, Epictetus and Marcus Aurelius, the
authors whom we know at first hand and in fullest
detail. It is difficult to see how, from a mass of
precepts, exhortations and moral reflections the underlying structure of dogma can be inferred with
such clearness and precision as readily to serve for
comparison with other authorities. The most careful inquiry must, therefore, leave room for doubt, on
questions of grave importance. In the first three
chapters of this work the reader will find a nucleus
of fact, well attested by documentary evidence, and
my constant endeavour has been to bring him, wherever possible, face to face with the utterances of the
Stoics themselves, so that he may judge for himself
of the correctness of my interpretation.

In the fourth chapter I have followed substan-
tially the same course, availing myself of the excellent versions of Epictetus and Marcus Aurelius by
Long and Rendall. Seneca, on the other hand,
though still popular in France, has with us of late

fallen into neglect. Even of his epistles we have no standard translation, a fact which well deserves the attention of English and American scholars.

The rival school of Epicurus has been more fortunate. Not only have we the summaries of its founder, but the task of reconstruction is rendered comparatively easy by the poem of Lucretius, which the English reader can study for himself in the admirable prose version of H. A. J. Munro. Here, while reserving the right to form my own judgment from the evidence, I have, in the main, followed the guidance of Munro and Giussani. Some points of detail are obscure, but on the whole no ancient system is more easily comprehended or appraised. In my sixth chapter I have tried to render adequately one valuable Epicurean document, the letter to Herodotus, and occasional illustrations and parallels have been added to make its meaning clearer. In dealing with Epicurean theology in the seventh chapter, we quit the region of ascertained fact for dubious speculation and ingenious conjecture. Caution is therefore necessary, since the promised exploration of Herculaneum may some day bring to light the missing clue to this puzzling riddle.

Not the least noteworthy feature in these two philosophies is the long duration of their exclusive, if divided, supremacy. In the school of Epicurus there are no changes to record. Everything goes to show that the doctrine of the founder was guarded intact as he had left it. Even the genius of Lucretius did but enshrine it in an imperishable memorial. It was far otherwise with Stoicism, which provoked fierce opposition and was continually modified by pressure from without and within. No narrative of its rise and development would be complete which failed to take account of these conflicts. It has, therefore, been incumbent upon me to linger awhile over the adversaries and critics of the Stoics, to describe the successive phases of Academic Scepticism and Eclecticism, and above all, to emphasise the influence of Carneades. In this way the eighth and ninth chapters may be regarded as forming an integral portion of my plan. For the last chapter a similar excuse may be tendered. After permitting the other opponents of the Stoics to state their objections it would have been inconsistent to pass over Ænesidemus and not to allow Sextus Empiricus and the Pyrrhoneans to say the last word. For the use of students a select bibliography has been appended, as well as a chronological table of the more noteworthy thinkers and writers. A historical sketch ranging over five centuries stands in need of some such aid, if it be no more than the merest framework of names and dates.

The proprietors of the Encyclopædia Britannica have courteously granted me permission to use for my present purpose the article on Stoics, which I contributed to the Encyclopædia some twenty years ago. I gratefully acknowledge my obligations to Mrs. Adam for allowing me to include in this volume a verse translation of the Hymn of Cleanthes, which her husband, the late Dr. James Adam, had privately printed. I am further indebted to Prof. H. N. Gardiner for his kindness in reading through the proofs and suggesting various improvements.

CONTENTS

CHAPTER IV

THE TEACHING OF THE LATER STOICS . . 113

CHAPTER V

CHAPTER VI

CHAPTER VII

CHAPTER VIII

criticism, 323; of Stoic epistemology, 324: theology, 326;
and the doctrine of Providence, 334; his limitations as a
critic, 337; positive side of his teaching, 341; his calculus
of probability, 342; his defence of human freedom, 344;
his formal classification of ethical theories, 347; general
estimate of Carneades as a thinker, 351.

CHAPTER IX

CHAPTER X

CHRONOLOGICAL TABLE[1]

[1] The Roman civil year began, like our own, in January. The Attic civil year began after the summer solstice, say in July: hence the occasional double dating. Moreover, a Greek Olympiad covers a space of four years.

RISE OF THE NEW SCHOOLS

B.C.

310. **Epicurus** teaches at Mitylene and Lampsacus.

307/6. **Epicurus** at A t h e n s opens his school in the garden.

300/299. **Epicurus** completes Book XV of his work *On Nature.*

296/5. **Epicurus** c o m p l e t e s Book XXVIII *On Nature.*

c. 294. **Zeno** lectures in the Stoa Pœcilē at Athens.

277. Death of **Metrodorus.**

276. **Zeno,** invited to the Court of Macedonia, sends **Persæus** in his place. **Aratus** of Soli at the same court.

270/69. Death of **Epicurus.** **Hermarchus** succeeds.

264/3. Death of **Zeno. Cleanthes** succeeds. **Aristo, Herillus** and **Dionysius** secede and found independent schools.

CONTEMPORARY EVENTS

B.C.

307. D i o d o r u s Cronus and Stilpo famous in the Megarian School.

294. Siege of Athens and consequent famine.

288/4. Death of Theophrastus. Strato of Lampsacus succeeds.

277/6. Antigonus Gonatas, now King of Macedonia. The kingdoms formed out of Alexander's conquests (Egypt, Syria, etc.) permanently established.

276/5. D e a t h of P o l e m o. Crates of Athens succeeds, followed a few years later by Arcesilas of Pitane.

c. 275/70. Death of Pyrrho at Elis.

275 (or later). Timon settles at Athens, where he writes his philosophic satires or *Silli.*

270/68. Death of Strato. Lyco succeeds.

241/0. Death of Arcesilas.

232/1. D e a t h of **Cleanthes.**	
Chrysippus third head of the Stoa.	c. 230/225. Death of Timon.
208/4. D e a t h of **Chrysippus.**	
Zeno of Tarsus fourth head of the Stoa.	202. Zama. Rome victorious over Carthage.

CONFLICT OF THE SCHOOLS AND DEVELOPMENT OF DOCTRINE

190/85. Birth of **Panætius** at Rhodes.

? 180. Death of **Zeno** of Tarsus. **Diogenes** the Babylonian fifth head of the Stoa.

168. Pydna. Macedonia crushed by Rome.

166. Polybius arrives at Rome. (Returned to Greece 150.)

155. **Diogenes** the Stoic, **Carneades** the Academic and **Critolaus** the Peripatetic, at Rome as envoys from Athens.

? 152. Death of **Diogenes** the Babylonian. **Antipater** of Tarsus sixth head of the Stoa.

146. Destruction of Corinth and Carthage.

144. **Panætius** and Polybius at Rome. Scipio the Younger a patron of Greek learning and philosophy.

141. **Panætius** completes two books *On Duty*. He accompanies Scipio to the East (returns 139).

135. Birth of **Posidonius** at Apamea.

129. Death of Scipio the Younger.

129/8. Death of **Carneades**. **Clitomachus** (Hasdrubal) of Carthage the next head of the Academy.

? 128. Death of **Antipater** of Tarsus. **Panætius** seventh head of the Stoa. **Hecato** and **Posidonius** pupils of **Panætius**.

? 111. Death of **Panætius**. **Mnesarchus** and **Dardanus** his successors.

106. Birth of Cicero.

100–90. **Posidonius** travels in the West.

99. Approximate date of the birth of **Lucretius** [94 Jerome].

87/6. Mithridatic War. Visit of **Posidonius** to Rome. **Philo** of Larissa, now head of the Academy, removes to Rome. **Antiochus** of Ascalon protests in his *Sosus* against Philo's innovations. Triumph of Eclecticism over Scepticism in the Academy.

78. Cicero studies at Athens and Rhodes; attends lectures by **Antiochus** of Ascalon and **Posidonius**.

69. **Antiochus** of Ascalon present at the Battle of **Tigranocerta**, not long before his death.
55. Death of **Lucretius** on the Ides of October, in his 44th year. His poem *De Rerum Natura* subsequently edited by Cicero.
  Philodemus of Gadara, the author of numerous Epicurean treatises, severely censured, though not by name, in Cicero's speech against his patron Calpurnius Piso.
54. Cicero, *De Republica*.
52. Cicero, *De Legibus*.
c. 50. Death of **Posidonius** at Rhodes.
46. Death of Cato at Utica.
45. Cicero, *Academica, De Finibus, Tusculan Disputations*.
44. Cicero, *De Natura Deorum, De Divinatione, De Officiis*. Assassination of Cæsar.
43. Death of Cicero.
? 42. **Ænesidemus**, Pyrrhonean Hypotyposes.

PHILOSOPHY UNDER THE EARLY ROMAN EMPIRE

A.D.
34. Birth of the poet **Persius**.
41. **Seneca** writes *Consolatio ad Marciam*. He is banished to Corsica.
49. **Seneca**, recalled from exile, becomes tutor of Nero, the future Emperor. He writes *De Ira, De Tranquillitate Animi*, and *De Brevitate Vitæ*.
54. Accession of Nero. Seneca becomes his minister.
54-59. Quinquennium Neronis. Seneca in power.
55. **Seneca**, *De Clementia*.
c. 56. **Seneca** commences his Epistles to Lucilius.
62. **Seneca** attempts in vain to retire from the court. He writes *De Otio Sapientis*.
  Death of **Persius**.
63. **Seneca** writes the last four books of his *Naturales Quæstiones*.
65. Conspiracy of Piso betrayed, in which Lucan is implicated. Many eminent Stoics, including **Seneca**, put to death. Others are exiled.
66. Death of **Pætus Thrasea** and **Soranus Barea**.
69. **Musonius Rufus**, the teacher of Epictetus, intervenes in the civil war between Vitellius and Vespasian.
75. Expulsion of philosophers from Rome. **Helvidius Priscus** is banished and afterward forced to commit suicide. **Musonius Rufus** is excepted from the decree.

A.D.

c. 90. **Plutarch** lectures at Rome during the reign of Domitian.

93. **Arulenus Rusticus** put to death for eulogising Thrasea. Domitian issues a second edict for the expulsion of philosophers. **Epictetus** retires to Nicopolis, where he afterward worked successfully as a teacher for many years.

117. Accession of Hadrian. **Epictetus** still living, if, as is said, he was favoured by Hadrian.

130. **Arrian,** who had committed to writing the *Discourses* and *Encheiridion* of his teacher **Epictetus**, while resident at Athens, becomes Consul Suffectus under Hadrian.

131. Birth of Galen.

161. Accession of **Marcus Aurelius Antoninus**; the philosopher on the throne.

164. Galen comes to Rome, where he resided for the rest of his life.

172–175. Campaigns of the Emperor Marcus on the Danube against the Quadi and Marcomanni. In the intervals of these campaigns he seems to have commenced his *Meditations*, or at least Books I and II, which are subscribed "among the Quadi" and "at Carnuntum."

176. Four chairs of philosophy at the University of Athens endowed by the Emperor for (1) Stoics, (2) Epicureans, (3) Academics, (4) Peripatetics.

180. Death of **Marcus Aurelius**.

180 (or shortly afterward). Lucian writes his *Alexander*.

180–200. Approximate date for the writings of **Sextus Empiricus,** the seventh in the Sceptical succession from Ænesidemus.

c. 200. Approximate date of the inscription set up at Œnoanda by **Diogenes,** an Epicurean teacher.

201. Death of Galen.

221–235. Alexander Severus, Emperor. Approximate date for the *Lives of Philosophers* compiled by Diogenes Laërtius, who ends his list of the Sceptics with Saturninus, the pupil of **Sextus Empiricus.**

STOIC AND EPICUREAN

STOIC AND EPICUREAN

CHAPTER I

THE EARLIER STOICS AND PANTHEISM

It is not often that a turning point in the history of thought synchronises with some great social or political change. But the age of the Diadochi, that period of stress and storm in which the Stoic and Epicurean systems took their rise, is severed by a wide gulf from the previous course of Greek civilisation. Alexander's conquests, while extending Hellenism to the farthest East, had rudely shattered the old order of the Greek world and made way for the new order of wide territorial kingdoms destined eventually to be swallowed up in the Roman empire. The city-states, which had played so honourable a part in the past, retained as a rule the control of their municipal affairs, but the virtual loss of independence tended inevitably to loosen the ties of civic and local patriotism in the fatherland itself. The change in the political system involved a corresponding change in the position of the individual. The very foundation of political theory, even to Plato and Aristotle, had been the life of a small civic community, and when this was undermined the alert Greek intelligence recognised the significant consequences for ethics. As the old, outworn sanctions disappeared, they were replaced by new social

3

obligations at once more individual and more universal. The conception of the narrow canton-state enlarged to that of the nation, and in the process of time nationality tended to become cosmopolitan.

Already the course of philosophic inquiry had been profoundly changed. The earliest Greek thinkers started with the study of nature: as we might say in modern phrase, they set out to discover the constitution and properties of matter. Then in that age of enlightenment which we associate with the name of the Sophists there came a reaction, and attention was directed to literature and culture—in a word, to humanism. Socrates confined his inquiries to human conduct and to man, emphasising, as no one had done before him, the importance of opinion for determining action. Henceforth the main interest of speculation embraced the subject as well as the object, the problem of knowledge even more than the problem of nature. Socrates had declared knowledge, or correct opinion, the sole basis for moral conduct, and his commanding personality combined with the schools which sprang from him to perpetuate this untenable position. It is in Stoicism, and not in the schools founded by the immediate disciples of the master, that we find the Socratic tradition most faithfully represented. Accordingly, from this point of view we proceed to consider the historical antecedents of Stoicism.

Zeno, the founder of the school, was a native of Citium, a Greek colony in Cyprus. In that island the Greek settlers had a checkered history and found it difficult to make headway against men of alien, especially Semitic nationality. Possibly Zeno himself, in spite of his Greek name, may have been of mixed descent, for he was often taunted with being a Phœnician. The chronology is not quite certain, but we have the testimony of his disciple Persæus that Zeno was twenty-two when he came to Athens, and died at the age of seventy-two. The year of his death may be fixed at 264 B. C., and, reckoning backward, we obtain 336 B. C. for his birth and 314 B. C. for his arrival at Athens. There he studied under Crates the Cynic, Stilpo and Diodorus Cronus of the Megarian school, and Polemo the Academic. After a long time spent in study (the precise statement of twenty years seems a round number), he opened a school of his own not later than 294 B. C. He selected for the scene of his lectures a public place in Athens memorable for the beauty of its decoration. This was the Stoa Pœcile, a colonnade or cloister rather than a porch, on the north or south-east side of the Agora or market-place, which the genius of Polygnotus and Micon had adorned with magnificent paintings or frescoes, among them one representing the battle of Marathon. From the place of instruction the school derived its name—called at first Zenonians, they were ever afterward known as Stoics, men of the porch. The personal appearance of Zeno is minutely described for us. He carried his head on one side, was lean, flabby, delicate, short in stature, with swarthy complexion and stout calves. After Demetrius, the besieger of cities, became king of Macedonia, he and his son, Antigonus Gonatas, made repeated visits to Athens, in consequence of which the latter became Zeno's pupil and remained his friend until his death. The personal relations of Zeno and Antigonus are honourable to both. By the Athenian people, also, Zeno was held in the highest esteem for the nobility of his character. The statement

that they deposited the keys of their citadel with
him is doubtless an invention, but the request of
Antigonus that he should receive a public funeral
may well have been granted, even if the decree to
this effect preserved by our authority [1] be not genuine.   The excessive frugality and even parsimony of
his life impressed observers no less than his moral
earnestness, dignity, and affability, and some may
be disposed to see in them Semitic traits of character.
Among his pupils Persæus, also from Citium, lived
in the same house with Zeno, who sent him as his
substitute to the court of Antigonus when he declined the king's invitation for himself.   Next may
be mentioned Aristo of Chios, Herillus of Carthage,
and Dionysius of Heraclea, in Pontus, all three of
whom diverged in various ways from their master's
teaching.   Other pupils were Aratus of Soli, in Cilicia, the author of an extant astronomical poem,
Sphærus of Bosporus, the friend and adviser of the
reforming Spartan king Cleomenes, and lastly Cleanthes of Assos, who succeeded to the headship of the
school and held it from 264 to 232 B. C.   The story
goes that Cleanthes had been a pugilist; for nine-
teen years he attended the lectures of Zeno by day,
while earning a frugal livelihood by toilsome occupations at night.   To some he was known as the
second Hercules, but others gave him the nickname
of the Ass, on account of his patience and endurance and a certain slowness and dulness of intellect,
of which he was himself painfully conscious.   His
was, in truth, a reflective, brooding nature not devoid
of political imagination, a fact to which the extant
fragments of his verse bear witness.   The Stoics
held that under certain circumstances suicide was

[1] Diogenes Laërtius, VII, 10-12.

justified, and, as our historical sources are both scanty and imperfect, this doctrine may be the only ground-work for the tradition that not only Cleanthes but also his master Zeno and his pupil Chrysippus, ended their days by suicide. We are told of Cleanthes that, when taunted with old age, he replied: "Yes, I am willing to be gone, but when I see myself sound in every part, writing and reading, I am again tempted to linger." At last, however, when he was suffering from an ulcer on the tongue, his physician advised him to abstain from food for a while as a means of cure. After two days of abstinence he was completely cured and advised by the physician to return to his ordinary way of life. But he said: "Since I have gone so far on the road, it would be a pity not to finish the journey." Accordingly, he continued his fasting and died.

At the time of Cleanthes the outlines of the system were still plastic. With all his reverence for his master, Cleanthes did not hesitate to introduce many modifications. In particular, he made the system more rigorously monistic and pantheistic, and we now meet with the doctrine of tension, which distinguishes Stoic materialism from all conception of matter as dead and inert. Under Cleanthes the school did not exactly flourish. In controversy it was pressed hard, not only by the Epicureans, from the first its uncompromising foes, but from another side by the Sceptics of the New Academy. But if the qualities of Cleanthes were not fitted to shine in polemic, the next head of the school made up for all such deficiencies. This was Chrysippus of Soli, in Cilicia, who lived till after 208 B. C. Of this extraordinary man the saying ran: "Had there been no Chrysippus, there had been no Porch"; which probably means, not that he saved the school from extinction, though this may well have been the case, but that he reduced its doctrine to a final and unalterable form. In doing so he exercised a moderating influence, mediating between extreme utterances, reconciling conflicting opinions, removing inconsistencies, obviating objections, and rounding off the whole with numerous contributions of his own. His aim was avowedly to interpret Zeno's utterances, but occasionally, to avoid all risk of misunderstanding, he had to restate them. His ingenuity and acumen were unequalled. "Give me the doctrines," he is reported to have said to Cleanthes; "I will find out the proofs for myself." He was short of stature, so much so that a jesting Epicurean, seeing a statue of him in the Ceramicus eclipsed by a neighbouring equestrian figure, remarked that a more appropriate name than Chrysippus, "Gold-Horse," would have been Crypsippus, or "Horse-hidden." He was the most voluminous of all ancient writers, being credited with seven hundred separate rolls. He was not averse to padding, and made huge citations from other authors, if we may trust the anecdote that some one, being asked what he was reading, replied, "The *Medea* of Chrysippus," so largely had the Stoic drawn upon the drama of Euripides for illustration of his argument. The logic of Stoicism is almost entirely his creation, and he contributed much to recast its psychology and epistemology.

These, then, were the men who moulded into shape the Stoic system, and in the form in which it was fashioned by them it endured for centuries. Its adherents grew and multiplied, and, although they always had to contend with powerful rivals in the Epicureans, Academics, and Peripatetics, they gradually extended their influence until in the first century of the imperial era their claim to be recognised as the dominant school of philosophy passed almost unchallenged. Stoicism owed this success, in the first place, to the strength and earnestness of its moral teaching. Every one knows that they regarded virtue as the only good, the one thing in life worth striving for; but this had already been proclaimed to the world by those earlier followers of Socrates, the Cynics. It is by comparing the basis of their moral teaching with that of the Cynics that the distinctive features of the Stoics can best be understood. The Cynics were revolutionists who would willingly dissolve the ties of the family and political society and reduce men to the state of nature. They were individualists and carried their contempt for convention—and, we may add, for decency and order—to lengths which shocked the sentiments of the average man. Zeno for a time imbibed and reproduced the doctrines of the Cynics, and wrote at least one celebrated work while under their influence. This was his *Republic*, most probably intended as a correction and criticism of Plato's great dialogue bearing the same title. In it Zeno imagined a universal state with one government and one manner of life for all mankind, in which there should be no organisation of separate nationalities under their several laws and no distinctions, such as had hitherto prevailed, between Greek and barbarian, bond and free. Here the Cynic teaching finds complete expression and full development. The breaking down of existing barriers is merely a step toward the realisation of a more perfect society, the abrogation of the discordant laws from separate states and nations, but the preliminary to the promulgation of the one universal law which holds this more perfect society together. But what is this law? The Cynic interpreted the precept "Follow Nature" negatively and destructively by ridiculing the institutions of his country and the very idea of patriotism and by making a violent protest in his daily life and behaviour against the traditional code and the established order. Thus nature became almost another name for anarchism and unparalleled license was permitted to individual caprice. To Zeno, on the contrary, the natural was the rational and the first mark of reason was self-consistency. A rational life must follow a single harmonious plan, whereas the paths of folly are many and various, but always stamped with inconsistency and contradiction. In this postulate of a rational law the Stoics had a precursor in Heraclitus. His term for it was Logos, sometimes rendered into English by Word, as in the introduction to the fourth gospel, more often by Reason. Heraclitus emphasised, as no previous thinker had done, the universal change and mutability of all things that we know, and yet he maintained as stoutly that all change obeys reason or law. To him the Logos is not only a sovereign ordinance which nature invariably obeys, but also the divine reason, immanent in nature and man, which possesses intelligence and thinks—nay, is itself intelligence.

This, at any rate, seems to follow from his fragmentary utterances concerning it. The most relevant are: "Having hearkened not unto me, but to the Logos, it is wise to confess that all things are one." [1] "This Logos is always existent, but men fail to understand it both before they have heard it and when they have heard it for the first time. For, although

[1] Fragment 1, Bywater.

all things happen through this Logos, men seem as if they had no acquaintance with it when they make acquaintance with such works and words as I expound when I divide each thing according to its nature and explain how it really is. The rest of mankind are unconscious of what they do when awake, just as they forget what they do when asleep." [1] "There is but one wisdom, to understand the knowledge by which all things are steered through all." [2] "Intelligence is common to all things. Those who speak with understanding must strongly cleave to that which is common to all things, even as a city cleaves to law, and much more strongly. For all human laws are nurtured by the one divine law; for this prevails as much as it will, and suffices for all and has something over." [3] "Although the Logos is universal, most men live as if they had a private intelligence of their own." [4] "Men are at variance with the Logos, which is their most constant companion." [5] It is also clear that, since Heraclitus had not learned to separate the material from the spiritual, he identified his Logos with that which he conceived to be the ultimate reality, the primal element of fire. Of this he says that "it is everliving, always was, is, and shall be"; [6] and the Logos, too, is, as we saw, eternal. And again, using "Thunderbolt" as a semi-oracular term for fire, he says "the thunderbolt steers all things," [7] language which suggests an intelligent helmsman, such as is his Logos. Thus the Logos on its material side is Fire, and Fire on its spiritual side is the Logos.

[1] Fragment 2.   [2] Fragment 19.   [3] Fragment 91.
[4] Fragment 92.   [5] Fragment 93.   [6] Fragment 20.
[7] Fragment 28.

But this Fire Heraclitus expressly affirms to be one
with the universal order or the universe. "This
world-order, the same in all things, no one of gods
or men has made; but it always was, is, and shall
be ever-living fire, kindled in due measure and extinguished in due measure." [1] "God is day and
night, winter and summer, war and peace, satiety
and hunger. But he is changed, just as fire, when
mingled with different kinds of incense, is named
after the savour of each." [2] "To God all things are
beautiful and good and right, but men consider
some things wrong and others right." [3] God, then,
is the unity in which all opposites are reconciled,
the one unchanging ground of all change and plurality. It makes no difference whether we name Him
Zeus, or Fire, or Logos. As Logos, He brings all
things to pass, for He is the Wisdom which steers
all things; as Fire, He is the substance which creates,
sustains, and in the end, perhaps, reabsorbs into itself
the world.

The exact interpretation of the Heraclitean fragments is a matter of controversy, and it may
readily be conceded that the above conclusions
are strongly tinctured with Stoic dogma. Some
scholars deny that in the time of Heraclitus the word
Logos had acquired the signification of Reason.
It meant no more, they say, than "word" or "discourse." But on the other hand there is strong and
explicit testimony that Zeno and Cleanthes studied
Heraclitus and derived from him many of their
cardinal doctrines. The function of Zeno, as of
almost every contemporary philosopher, was not
to originate, but to combine. Greece had long out-
lived the first fresh ardour of speculation and dis-

[1] Fragment 20.   [2] Fragment 36.   [3] Fragment 61.

covery. Moreover, since the time of Socrates the practical needs of the individual had become the paramount consideration. The question: "What must I do?" was more pressing even than that other: "What can I know?" Judged superficially, the Stoic account of the universe has nothing new about it. Some parts could be traced to Heraclitus, others to Aristotle. But even in appropriating the results of previous philosophers the Stoics imparted to them a new and fuller meaning by their whole mental attitude. Aristotle's dualism of matter and form, the two principles into which he analyses individual and particular existence, they transformed into the antithesis of matter and force or energy, which they united in the single conception of body. They fastened upon the pantheism everywhere underlying the utterances of Heraclitus and presented it in its most mature and unambiguous form. Whether Zeno himself took this decisive step the remains of his writings do not sufficiently indicate. It may be that he never went beyond recognising God and formless matter as the two distinct principles, coexisting in all that is. But in the view of Cleanthes and Chrysippus, so far as we can judge from the evidence, not only do these two factors coexist, but ultimately they are regarded as one and the same. We thus arrive at a conception of the universe as one Being endowed with life and reason, one whole to which all living and all intelligent creatures are related as members, a conception which is most familiar to English readers from Pope's lines:

> All are but parts of one stupendous whole,
> Whose body Nature is and God the soul.[1]

[1] *Essay on Man*, I, 267.

It is a fortunate accident that in the wreck of the entire literature of the early Stoics the famous hymn to Zeus by Cleanthes has been preserved. Short as it is, this is the only document of any eminent Stoic which we possess at first hand and in full. It cannot be too often remembered that we are cut off by unkind fortune from direct access to all the other original authorities. For our knowledge of Stoicism we depend either upon scanty fragments of the masters' own writings laboriously collected by modern scholars from the whole range of classical literature or upon the diligence of compilators who, centuries after the foundation of Stoicism, put together for their own purposes and in their own language the main outlines of the system as it appeared to them. Other writings, it is true, have come down to us from Stoic authors, but in some cases they have small philosophical importance, e. g., Aratus, Cleomedes, Heraclides; in others they belong to the Roman age, and no one will maintain that Persius or Seneca, Epictetus or Marcus Aurelius committed themselves to a single statement of doctrine on their own authority. The hymn of Cleanthes has been thus translated by the late Dr. James Adam:

> O God most glorious, called by many a name,
> Nature's great King, through endless years the same;
> Omnipotence, who by thy just decree
> Controllest all, hail, Zeus, for unto thee
> Behoves thy creatures in all lands to call.
> We are thy children, we alone, of all
> On earth's broad ways that wander to and fro,
> Bearing thine image wheresoe'er we go.
> Wherefore with songs of praise thy power I will
>   forth shew.
> Lo! yonder heaven, that round the earth is wheeled,

Follows thy guidance, still to thee doth yield
Glad homage; thine unconquerable hand
Such flaming minister, the levin-brand,
Wieldeth, a sword two-edged, whose deathless might
Pulsates through all that Nature brings to light;
Vehicle of the universal Word, that flows
Through all, and in the light celestial glows
Of stars both great and small.   O King of Kings
Through ceaseless ages, God, whose purpose brings
To birth, whate'er on land or in the sea
Is wrought, or in high heaven's immensity;
Save what the sinner works infatuate.
Nay, but thou knowest to make crooked straight:
Chaos to thee is order: in thine eyes
The unloved is lovely, who did'st harmonise
Things evil with things good, that there should be
One Word through all things everlastingly.
One Word—whose voice alas! the wicked spurn;
Insatiate for the good their spirits yearn:
Yet seeing see not, neither hearing hear
God's universal law, which those revere,
By reason guided, happiness who win.
The rest, unreasoning, diverse shapes of sin
Self-prompted follow: for an idle name
Vainly they wrestle in the lists of fame:
Others inordinately Riches woo,
Or dissolute, the joys of flesh pursue.
Now here, now there they wander, fruitless still,
For ever seeking good and finding ill.
Zeus the all-bountiful, whom darkness shrouds,
Whose lightning lightens in the thunder clouds;
Thy children save from error's deadly sway:
Turn thou the darkness from their souls away:
Vouchsafe that unto knowledge they attain;
For thou by knowledge art made strong to reign
O'er all, and all things rulest righteously.
So by thee honoured, we will honour thee,
Praising thy works continually with songs,

As mortals should; nor higher meed belongs
E'en to the gods, than justly to adore
The universal law for evermore.

The first thing which strikes us is the religious tone. The great Stoic dogmas are presented, not as physics or metaphysics, but as theology, the truths of natural religion in poetic form. The Stoic's attitude to God is that of a child to his father, dependent and yet responsible. It is his duty, but also his privilege and reward, to praise God, and his one prayer is for knowledge, whereby alone he can be saved from the miseries of sin. The next thing to note is the remarkable blending of characteristics which to us seem utterly opposed. Zeus is addressed as a personal God, and yet by the whole tenor and by certain Heraclitean echoes—"the levin," that is fire, like the thunderbolt, "one Word" (Logos) "through all things everlastingly, one Word whose voice alas! the wicked spurn"—we are forced to believe that He is not only the author of all things, but also in essence identical with all things, save only the works of wicked men in their folly.[1] But, seeing that this same Zeus "did harmonise things evil with things good," is in fact the unity of opposites, the one seeming exception vanishes from the higher stand-point. Again, while all the universe is ruled by Zeus and all things everywhere are wrought by His purpose, yet it is evident that man holds a privileged position. It is our bounden duty to requite God with honour because we have been honoured by Him. In other words, man is the only rational creature on earth and the possession of reason stamps him with the divine image. The result has

---

[1] "Save what the sinner works infatuate" in the translation above.

been called by a quite permissible oxymoron a
curious personal kind of pantheism. Something of
the same sort is to be found not only in Heraclitus,
but earlier still in Xenophanes, who affirmed the
unity of God as a Being possessed of perception and
intelligence not less strongly than he proclaimed the
unity of the world, of all that exists.

Centuries afterward in modern England a writer
wholly unacquainted with ancient philosophy, either
blending two phases of belief or making the transition from one to the other, embodied the very
essence of Stoicism in lines which deserve a place beside the hymn of Cleanthes.

> O God, within my breast,
>   Almighty, ever-present Deity!
> Life, that in me has rest,
>   As I—undying life—have power in thee.
>
> With wide-embracing love
>   Thy spirit animates eternal years,
> Pervades and broods above,
>   Changes, sustains, dissolves, creates, and rears.
>
> Though earth and man were gone,
>   And suns and universes ceased to be,
> And thou wert left alone,
>   Every existence would exist in thee.
>
> There is not room for Death,
>   No atom that his might could render void:
> Thou—Thou art Being, Breath,
>   And what Thou art may never be destroyed.[1]

The hymn of Cleanthes strikes a note of ex-
ultant joy, of serene and unwavering optimism.

[1] Emily Brontë, *Poems.*

This temper is assuredly not that which is usually
associated with the Stoics, conceived too often in
the popular imagination as severe, morose, apathetic
persons, stifling all emotions with pride, or else, on
the lines of Cicero's famous delineation of Cato, as
stern, unbending, impracticable precisians—in short,
moral prigs, the Pharisees of the pagan world. It is
matter of history that in their dealings with their
fellow-men they often presented these unamiable
traits, but from the few glimpses we have of their
inmost feelings and that attitude to the universe
which constitutes the essence of religion, what is
most clearly distinguishable is joy and gratitude,
serene confidence and unwavering submission. Here
again is a marked divergence from popular conception, which has seized upon apathy as a prominent
trait of the Stoic without comprehending the term
aright. It will hereafter be seen that the suppression of all emotion never was and never could be
a Stoic tenet. The religious tone of cheerful optimism is as conspicuous in Epictetus as in Cleanthes.
Not more firm is the conviction of the Hebrew
Psalmist that all things must go well, since the Lord
reigneth.

It is now time to examine more closely the nature of this pantheism and, if possible, to determine
its exact relation to other modes of Greek thought.
It bears a superficial resemblance to more than one
tendency or current of previous speculation. The
Ionian natural philosophers in search of a single
principle by which they could explain the manifold
variety of nature are usually described as hylozoists, a
term which implies that, overlooking the distinction
between organisms and inorganic substances, they
endowed all matter with the qualities of living things

by supposing it capable of self-determination.[1] But, as system after system developed, the inquiry became more complicated and a cause of motion, life, and consciousness was postulated, in contradistinction from the things which exhibited motion and life. Nowhere is this dualism more prominent than in Aristotle, who defined God as an immaterial essence. Aristotle's deity by the attraction which he exerts upon the world is the cause of motion, the ultimate cause of all the ordered regularity and life of nature. In framing such a system Aristotle was confessedly influenced by Anaxagoras, who, in order to explain the progress from chaos to universal order, introduced his unique element of Nous or Intellect, without definitely determining its exact nature, so that it is still matter of controversy whether he intended by it a spiritual principle or merely a material substance, fluid or gaseous, of greater purity and fineness than the rest and endowed with the power of ordering and knowing. The point to notice is that both Anaxagoras and Aristotle diverge from the beaten track of Ionian speculations by postulating a transcendent cause or first principle. And this is still more true of Plato. For him the highest reality existed in a world of ideas set over against the phenomenal world in which, however, the ideas were somehow immanent. On the other hand, Democritus, the apostle of materialism, had declared that all the phenomena of motion and life followed by natural necessity, when once immutable

[1] Hylozoism has left its mark on language. Take the term "body." Both in Greek and in English it is applied, not only to animate things, the organisms of the biologist, but quite as freely to such as are inanimate. In the latter signification it is firmly established as a scientific term. Thus Newton's laws of motion are enunciated of "bodies," and astronomers talk of the heavenly "bodies."

atoms, devoid alike of reason, consciousness, sense, and instinct, were conceived as moving, colliding, and combining in infinite space. Thus Democritus put an end to hylozoism without resorting to transcendence. When compared with the theory either of Democritus or of Aristotle cosmic pantheism exhibits a retrograde tendency. Conceptions which it had been the business of philosophers to separate are again confused and the world interpreted on the analogy of the individual organism, or, more precisely, of a rational human being. This analogy may be traced back to Thales, if his apothegm, "All things are full of gods," is rightly interpreted by Aristotle to imply a belief in a world-soul.[1] Anaximenes, a later Milesian philosopher, is much more explicit. "Even as our soul, which is air," says Anaximenes, "holds us together, so breath and air encompass the whole universe."[2] As man inhales from outside the breath which constitutes his soul, so the world, a similar living, breathing whole, respires into the sea of air which Anaximenes conceived to surround and support it. Some such process of cosmical respiration into the circumambient infinite was also a Pythagorean tenet. Pythagorean, too, in origin is the conception of the world-soul in Plato's *Timæus*, endowed with motion and intelligence, the sole cause in virtue of which the body of the universe, and therefore the universe as a whole, possesses life and motion. There is, then, ample evidence that the Greeks were familiar with conceptions of which pantheism would be the natural outgrowth and the names of Heraclitus, Xenophanes, and Parmenides suffice to prove that pantheism

---

[1] Aristotle, *De Anima*, I, 5, 411, a. 8.
[2] Fragment 2, Diels[2] (*Fragmente der Vorsokraliker*, ed. 2).

of some sort, though distinct from Stoic pantheism, did arise on Greek soil. On the other hand, it has been conjectured that Zeno's Semitic origin is the clue to this tenet of his system. Undoubtedly, there are many passages in the Old Testament ascribing the operations of nature directly to God, which favour the notion of divine immanence and omnipresence. Any one who reads certain of the Psalms [1] or the finale of the Book of Job,[2] or certain passages in the second Isaiah,[3] can hardly escape this conclusion. "Whither," says the Psalmist, "shall I go from thy spirit? Or whither shall I flee from thy presence? If I ascend up into heaven, thou art there; if I make my bed in Sheol, behold, thou art there; if I take the wings of the morning, and dwell in the uttermost parts of the sea, even there shall thy hand lead me, and thy right hand shall hold me. If I say, Surely the darkness shall overwhelm me, and the light about me shall be night, even the darkness hideth not from thee, but the night shineth as the day: the darkness and the light are both alike to thee."[4] Further, the whole series of events in the world of nature, organic and inorganic, all celestial phenomena, all atmospheric conditions, all vital processes, so far as known to these Hebrew writers, are attributed to the immediate agency of God. That very order and regularity which Democritus and Epicurus found incompatible with divine interference in the world the Hebrew writers adduce as irrefragable testimony that God is manifest in all His works. "He appointed the moon for seasons: the sun knoweth his going down."[5] And

---

[1] E. g., Pss. 104, 107, 139.   [2] Especially chapters 36 to 41.
[3] E. g., c. 45.   From later Jewish writings may be cited *Ecclesiasticus*,
c. 43.   [4] Ps. 139, 7–12.   [5] Ps. 104, 19.

again, "He saith to the snow, Fall thou on the earth; likewise to the shower of rain."[1]   So far, therefore, as the unity and immanence of God are concerned, the conjecture appears very plausible.   Again, the exclusion of wickedness and sin from divine agency is as conspicuous in the writings of the Hebrew prophets as in the hymn of Cleanthes. From this last point of agreement, however, no cogent inference can be drawn, in view of Plato's equally emphatic pronouncement that God is the author of good, of good alone and never of evil.[2]   But however great the similarity, however strong the case for Semitic elements in Stoicism, it would be in vain to seek any Biblical parallel for the final step to monism.   Man and his Maker, God and the world are everywhere kept distinct, even in the analogy of the potter and the clay.[3] Jahveh is no Brahma, consubstantial with all that is.   On the whole, then, it seems more reasonable to attribute this retrograde step by which the hylozoism of the Ionians was revived in an altered form to purely Greek influences.

Contemporary Greek thought was not more inclined to tolerate the idealism of Plato and Aristotle than the mechanism and atomism of Democritus. The Cynics, under whom Zeno studied, were nominalists and denied the separate existence of any reality corresponding to a general notion, such as the Platonists found in the ideas. The school of Zeno was not nominalist, but conceptualist, and expressly affirmed that the Platonic ideas were notions in our minds, in modern phrase, universals. Even among Aristotle's own immediate followers the conception of a transcendent, immaterial deity was surrounded with difficulties, and it is not sur-

---

[1] Job, c. 37, v. 6.   [2] *Republic* II, 379 C.   [3] Isaiah, c. 45, v. 9.

prising that Strato of Lampsacus, who succeeded to the headship of the school on the death of Theophrastus (circa 288 B. C.) dropped this tenet. He saw no need for an external supernatural cause and renounced the idea of God as a Being separate and distinct from the world as a whole. For him, as for Aristotle, nature is impersonal, a necessary force, operating without consciousness or reflection. The favourite argument with all the later schools ran as follows. Whatever exists must act and be acted upon. Action implies contact and therefore body, since only corporeal things can touch and be touched. From this it follows that such corporeal things or bodies alone have real existence and everything incorporeal is non-existent. The argument is worthless, action and passivity being strictly limited to the kind of action and the kind of passivity occurring between bodies in contact, but it is useful as determining for us more precisely what is meant by the terms existence, body, and causation. Body is defined as that which is capable of extension in three dimensions. Such bodies exist: our own bodies, external things. This mode of existence is given and it is the only mode which the Stoics recognised. Body is that which acts and is acted upon, such interaction being a special case of causation. By cause the Stoics always mean efficient cause, which implies the communication of motion from one body to another. All bodies can be moved and modified. For all that is or happens there is an immediate cause or antecedent, and as "cause" means "cause of motion," and only body can act upon body, it follows that this antecedent cause is itself as truly corporeal as the body upon which it acts.

Such a conception of the world as made up

of particular bodies acting and reacting upon each other might suffice for Epicurus, but it is only the husk of the Stoic doctrine, unless to activity we add soul, life, and mind. Let us see where and how the two materialistic systems differ. To Epicurus the atoms are unchangeable, both quantitatively and qualitatively. They never waste away, they never pass from one state to another. They always remain perfectly inelastic solids. They move everlastingly with the same ceaseless motion and the same uniform velocity. Epicurus was not aware that he had here combined incompatible attributes. The Stoic primary matter, on the contrary, though quantitatively constant, indestructible, incapable of increase or diminution, is not qualitatively constant, but capable of transformation. It becomes by turns all the four elements. The difference between these states of the primary substance depends upon the greater or less degree of tension. Matter being infinitely divisible, in whatever state it is, whether solid, liquid, or gaseous, it must be in virtue of its own inherent force that it possesses any continuity or coherence whatsoever. In a rarefied condition the exceedingly fine particles of air and fire are subjected to the greatest strain. In earth and water continuity and coherence are attained by the exertion of less force: in other words, the tension of the primary substance is slackened. The same variety of tension is presented when inorganic substances are compared with organic. In the vital principle of animals or the principle of growth in plants, technically known as "nature," primary matter exhibits a degree of tension far greater than is necessary to give coherence and numerical identity to stones or metals. Again, to the Stoics the sum of being, the totality of particular bodies is a whole and a unity which is living and conscious, while the atoms of Epicurus are a mere aggregate without unity, an infinite aggregate, but no true whole and devoid of life, which belongs only to particular things. This view of the world, however, as an infinite aggregate the Stoics rejected as unsatisfactory and fell back upon the alternative conception of the universe as a living whole or, in modern phrase, a single organism. If, again, the world is a living being, like other living beings, it has a soul and we may distinguish the rational world-soul from the world itself, as we distinguish the human soul from the man himself. All particular things within the world must be its parts and members or, more precisely, particular determinations of its one substance, which is in eternal activity. The determination of the particular by the universe and of the part by the whole was a fundamental doctrine of the Stoics. The single substance is at once both force and matter; or rather, though we can distinguish in it that which acts and that which is acted upon, there is ultimately no difference between these two phases or aspects of the one same substance. It alone conditions and determines all particular things and processes and, according to its variable relations to particulars, it may be variously described. The divine Word or Reason (Logos) is the power to produce and create, to mould and form particulars, present in each thing as its own germinal reason, i. e., as its formative force or vital principle. But, since all organic processes fulfil some purpose and have a rational end, this same universal Reason must be regarded as an overruling Providence in relation to all particular occurrences. The course of the world, then, is a rational order, an ordinance by which all individuals should be guided in the development of their activity. But this all-determining ordinance is likewise all-compelling power, and in the unalterable succession of causes and effects every event is necessary and predestined. The universe would cease to fulfil its purpose as a coherent whole, if any event took place without an antecedent cause. There is no such thing as chance: what appears to happen through chance really happens from a cause which we cannot discern. The Divine Providence extends even to the smallest details of life; there are no exceptions to the working of natural necessity. This assumption had first been made by Leucippus and Democritus, but the Stoics were the only school that carried out the thought in all its completeness, and with them the natural necessity of every event follows, not from the motions of single parts, the separate atoms, but from the living activity of the whole. Thus God, Nature, Reason, World-Soul, Germinal Reason, Law, Providence, Necessity, Destiny are but expressions of the different relations in which the one universe, the sum and whole of existence, stands to particular things and events within it.

We have said above that the universal substance is at once both force and matter, and the statement seems on the whole to offer the best solution of certain difficulties inherent in the system. At the same time it must be conceded that while this is the logical consequence of the pantheistic spirit of Stoicism, it is at first sight at variance with the letter of its teaching. The orthodox Stoic account of nature starts with the recognition of two principles, the one active, the other passive: in other words, the one is God, the other is matter devoid of quality. If this were an absolute distinction, the account given above would be erroneous. It is worth while, then, to inquire within what limits the assumption of two principles is legitimate and how these two are related to each other.

"We Stoics, as you know," says Seneca, "distinguish in nature (*in rerum natura*) cause and matter as conditions for all becoming. Matter is inert, indifferent to all determinations, and will remain in a state of rest unless it be moved. Cause or reason shapes matter and turns it at will in any direction, producing out of matter a variety of objects. In other words, that *out of which* all things are made must be distinct from that *by which* all things are made and this is what is meant by matter and cause." [1] Seneca, be it observed, is speaking of the world as we know it, in which particular things are already formed or in process of formation and the active causal principle, force, inseparable from the passive principle, matter. The latter is conceived as indeterminate, but capable of determination, as in itself devoid of any quality, yet capable of assuming all qualities. As such, it is the germ or seed of all Becoming and of the ordered universe of particular things. And this is equally true of the contrasted principle, reason or force or God. He also is capable of becoming all things and His eternal substance contains the seeds of all Becoming. And here there is a difficulty. Plutarch objects: "If God is identified with matter, why is matter called irrational? If, again, they are ultimately distinct, if matter and reason separately exist, God is no single supreme principle, but a composite being, reason in matter." [2] So far as this difficulty is

[1] Seneca, *Epistles*, 65, 2.   [2] Plutarch, *De Communibus Notitiis*, 48.

inherent and fundamental in every pantheistic system, it does not immediately concern us. Holding as we do, that the two principles were ultimately identified, if not by Zeno, at any rate by Cleanthes and Chrysippus, we should rather be disposed to ask another question: What led Zeno to assume two distinct principles and why did Chrysippus retain the distinction? The problem admits of no authoritative solution, from the scantiness of the evidence. Indeed, we have not even the explicit testimony of any Stoic writer to the ultimate identity of the two principles in the mature system. But the most probable explanation is based upon historical considerations and is in perfect accord with the Stoic practice of incorporating and assimilating the teaching of other schools. Thus Zeno's two principles were suggested by Aristotle's analysis of the particular thing into form and matter. For incorporeal form, however, which he would regard as non-existent, Zeno substituted real and corporeal cause or force. From the inherence of attributes in a substratum he passed to the conception of the universal intermingling of corporeal qualities in things.

This last distinctive tenet calls for further explanation. Let us endeavour to trace the steps by which the Stoics were led to an explicit denial that matter is impenetrable, that two bodies cannot simultaneously occupy the same place. All that really exists is body. But souls exist and qualities exist, whence they infer that souls and qualities are corporeal things. But the soul pervades the whole body, as all the facts of animal life go to prove; and when two inorganic substances are mixed, the qualities of the one pervade the whole substance of the other. Suppose wine poured into water, whether in a bowl or in a pond. The wine will gradually extend over and permeate the whole of the water until finally it is lost in the mixture in which each fluid interpenetrates the other. This is not a case of mechanical mixture, as when sand is mixed with sugar and each particle of sand, as also each particle of sugar, retains its distinctive qualities; for, according to the Stoics, every part of the one substance is interpenetrated by every part of the other. Nor, again, is it analogous to chemical combination, in which the constituent elements part with their distinctive properties when the new compound is formed; for, according to the Stoics, soul and body, substance and attribute retain each its own distinctive qualities when interpenetrated, as do wine and water when intermingled. The clue to this astonishing doctrine is found in another Stoic conception, that the parts or faculties of the soul and the attributes of bodies were currents, were matter, but highly rarefied matter. At a time when there was scarcely any scientific knowledge of matter in the fluid, much less in the gaseous state, the fact that heat expands and cold contracts gave rise to an ingenious theory. The colder a substance, the more it coheres and the less the tension of its parts. Increase the heat and the tension is increased, until in fluids and gases a high degree of tension is reached. Currents of air, then, currents of heat, present that condition of matter, fine, rare, and subtle, which to the Greek mind seemed most akin to the incorporeal because, as intangible and invisible, it escaped the observation of the senses. When, therefore, the attributes and qualities of bodies, or the parts and faculties of soul, were declared to be corporeal things, permeating more solid bodies, it was in this guise that they were imagined. Hence a curious inversion of Platonic idealism. Plato said that a man is just and musical by partaking in the ideas, the objective realities, of justice and music: the Stoics said that a man was just when he had the material of justice, musical when he had the material of music within him. While we justly condemn this wild speculation as crude and baseless, we must remember that even in modern science there is a region of unverified hypotheses in which speculations on the nature of electricity and the properties of ether play their part.

The statement that the universal substance is at once both force and matter, and therefore that the distinction between them is only transitory and relative, is strongly confirmed by the Stoic cosmogony. In the world as it is we resolve each particular thing into form and matter, but let us go back to the time before there was a heaven and earth and review the work of creation. Here again the analogy of the macrocosm and the microcosm is all-important. The germination of a plant, the birth of an animal implies a seed or ovum, moisture being one indispensable condition. So, too, with a world, which is evolved, attains maturity, and again perishes by a process of orderly sequence stretching over an immense period of time. Before the birth of the world God alone existed, having absorbed into His fiery substance all nature at a general conflagration. At this stage the distinction between the soul and the body of the universe, between the active principle, God, and the passive principle, matter, is merged in complete identity. In the words of Chrysippus, "the universe is then its own soul and its own controlling mind," [1] and yet at the same time it never ceases to

[1] Plutarch, *De Stoicorum Repugnantiis*, 41.

be material substance with extraordinary physical properties of temperature and tension. The nebular theory of modern astronomers requires us to imagine at some point of time anterior to the formation of the solar system a vast mass of gaseous vapour at a high temperature. This might serve as a picture of the primary substance of the Stoics. The tension throughout was enormous. From this ignited condition the primary substance passes through the stage of vapour or "air" to that of water or moisture. Here we pause to remark that the Stoics are following Heraclitus, who reduced the constant transformation of the sensible world to a formula, the way downward from fire to water and earth and the way upward from earth to water and fire. There was this difference, however, that to Heraclitus air was a transition, not a state, whereas the Stoics, like Aristotle, recognised air as one of their four elementary bodies. Later Stoics date the birth of the world from the stage when the primary substance is in the moist or watery condition. Thus Seneca says: "We maintain that it is fire which takes possession of the universe and transforms all things into itself. This fire dies down gradually, and when it is extinguished there is nothing else left in nature but moisture. In moisture lies hidden the promise of the world that is to be. Thus the universe ends in fire and begins from moisture." [1] The seed, whether of vegetable or animal life, is fostered by moisture: the seed of the world that is to be is the primary substance itself under the aspect of germinal reason. In the next stage all the four elements are developed out of this moisture. One part is precipitated in the form of earth, another remains as water, a third

[1] Seneca, *Naturales Quæstiones*, III, 13, 1.

part, evaporating, constitutes atmospheric air, and air, again, enkindles fire out of itself. These four elements not only account for the world of particular things, in which they are combined in varying proportions, but also by their relative positions massed round the earth as centre they give the universe its spherical form. A belt or sphere of air surrounding land and sea is itself surrounded by the spherical heaven or ether made of the purest fire and containing the heavenly bodies.

The picture of the one universe consisting of these concentric spheres dominated imagination from Eudoxus and Aristotle down to Dante and Copernicus. It is, then, by no means peculiar to the Stoics. They merely followed in the beaten track. The science of that day had a huge admixture of unverified hypothesis and consequent error. The Stoics took over from Plato and Aristotle the outlines, not only of astronomy, but also of natural history with the stereotyped division of organic life into plants, animals, and rational beings. In these departments their contributions call for no special notice. The two elements, air and fire, situated further from the centre of this Stoic universe and higher, if we look upward, represent active force, the soul of the world; the other two elements, earth and water, play the part of passive matter, or the body of the world. Thus primal unity is differentiated into force and matter, soul and body, as well as into the variety and multiplicity of individual things. As these distinctions, however, had their origin in time, so also will time put an end to them. The parts undergo a perpetual transformation; each individual thing that has come into being by the combination of elements ceases to be when they separate, and when the present cycle has run its course all matter will be absorbed once more into primary substance or deity and the world be consumed in a general conflagration. This restoration of all things becomes again the starting-point for a new cycle, in which every phase of the world's existence and every particular event is exactly repeated with unfailing regularity. Not many Stoic dogmas lend themselves to poetic handling, but the idea of a new era, of a fresh start in universal history, has sunk deep into the heart of mankind. Sometimes it is presented as the return of a weary world to the happy innocence of a far-distant past, sometimes as a deliverance from the intolerable evils of a worn-out state of society, but always as a consummation devoutly to be wished and heralded with eager anticipation. To such hopes and aspirations Virgil gave a splendid setting in his Fourth Eclogue. Who the particular child was whose birth is there foretold is a question which has greatly perplexed the learned,[1] but in his glowing picture of the blessings to follow its advent the poet has skilfully interwoven the old belief in the golden age and the reign of Saturn with the Stoic doctrine of a restitution of all things. Virgil sings of better, brighter times to come, and yet for the realisation of this dream he reverts to a primeval past. The age of the heroes will in due course return, another Jason will go in quest of the golden fleece, another Achilles will start for the siege of Troy. The glamour with which the poet's imagination invests the new order of things tends to conceal the fundamental inconsistency: for, if the new is but the repetition of the old, how can

---

[1] See the recent volume, entitled *Virgil's Messianic Eclogue: Three Studies*, by J. B. Mayor, W. Warde Fowler, R. S. Conway. Also the review by H. W. Garrod, in *Classical Review*, XXII, 149.

the future be any improvement upon the experience
of the past? According to the Stoics, as we have
seen, there is no advance. Both morally and
materially and in every exact detail the new is a
faithful reproduction of the old; whence it inevitably
follows that all the evil, as well as all the good, is
everlastingly perpetuated. This consideration comes
out more prominently in Shelley, whose adaptation of
the same theme in the final chorus of his *Hellas* is so
beautiful that I make no apology for quoting it at
length:

> The world's great age begins anew,
>   The golden years return,
> The earth doth like a snake renew
>   Her winter weeds outworn:
> Heaven smiles, and faiths and empires gleam,
> Like wrecks of a dissolving dream.
>
> A brighter Hellas rears its mountains
>   From waves serener far;
> A new Peneus rolls his fountains
>   Against the morning star.
> Where fairer Tempes bloom, there sleep
> Young Cyclads on a sunnier deep.
>
> A loftier Argo cleaves the main,
>   Fraught with a later prize;
> Another Orpheus sings again,
>   And loves, and weeps, and dies.
> A new Ulysses leaves once more
> Calypso for his native shore.
>
> Oh, write no more the tale of Troy,
>   If earth Death's scroll must be!
> Nor mix with Laian rage the joy
>   Which dawns upon the free:
> Although a subtler Sphinx renew
> Riddles of death Thebes never knew.

Another Athens shall arise,
    And to remoter time
Bequeath, like sunset to the skies,
    The splendour of its prime;
And leave, if nought so bright may live,
All earth can take or Heaven can give.

Saturn and Love their long repose
    Shall burst, more bright and good
Than all who fell, than One who rose,
    Than many unsubdued:
Not gold, not blood, their altar dowers,
But votive tears and symbol flowers.

Oh, cease! must hate and death return?
    Cease! must men kill and die?
Cease! drain not to its dregs the urn
    Of bitter prophecy.
The world is weary of the past,
Oh, might it die or rest at last!

Shelley, even in the moment of writing these lines, obviously hesitates between two conflicting ideals. His ardent vision embraces on the one hand the moral regeneration of mankind, whereby the future will be better than the past, and on the other hand the Stoic idea of a restitution of all things, whereby the future becomes a mere repetition of the past and must therefore bring with it all the old attendant evils. The theory of recurrent cycles in the history of the universe is incompatible with the conception of unending progress; rather it rests ultimately upon that of permanence and fixity, of destiny working by the same laws under the same unalterable conditions to all eternity, the consummation of a moral order which is adapted to secure uninterruptedly the good of the whole, but not necessarily that of its several parts.

The monotony of life, the weary round of human existence, has been a favourite theme with moralists of every age. In the weighty words of the Preacher: "that which is hath been already; and that which is to be hath already been: and God seeketh again that which is passed away. . . . That which hath been is that which shall be; and that which hath been done is that which shall be done: and there is no new thing under the sun." [1] But we must be careful not to confuse the daring speculation sketched above with such generalities. Sombre reflections of this kind have, for the most part, an ethical tendency; they correct the eager anticipation of youth by an appeal to larger experience, to a wider, though still limited, observation. The doctrine we have just considered is of far-reaching cosmical import, transcending all experience. How, it may be asked, did this singular conception gain such a hold upon the Greeks? It certainly did not originate with the Stoics. A fragment of Eudemus attributes to the Pythagorean school the identical doctrine. "If," says that contemporary and pupil of Aristotle, "we are to believe the Pythagoreans, numerically identical conditions will be repeated, and I with this little rod in my hand shall some day once again be addressing you my class sitting round me precisely as you sit now, and everything else in like manner will recur precisely as before." [2] But there is no reason to father it upon the Pythagorean school. More probably it is an inevitable corollary from the Heraclitean doctrine of flux—at least for those who accept the latter in its entirety. That doctrine, which

---

[1] *Eccles.* 3:15; 1:9.

[2] Eudemus apud Simpl. *In Phys.*, 732, 26. This interesting fragment (Diels[2] *Vors. Fr.*, p. 277) is taken *verbatim*, Simplicius informs us, from the third book of the *Physics* of Eudemus, *cf.* 732, 23 *sqq.*

has already engaged our attention, postulates everlasting change governed by an immutable law of
change. But, if we look at the conception more
closely, whether as presented by Heraclitus or the
Pythagoreans or the Stoics, the ancients, so far as
we can see, made no attempt to arrive at their conclusion by any logical process. It comes as an orac-
ular utterance; it would be unkind to call it a mere
guess. We should be inclined to doubt whether the
contemporaries of Heraclitus understood the scheme
of causality in nature as we understand it; most certainly they were unacquainted with the mathematical
notion of probability which a modern exponent of the
theory has employed in its support. Within the last
decade a posthumous work of that great but erratic
genius Friedrich Nietzsche[1] has again revived this
curious speculation. The doctrine there expounded
is known as "eternal recurrence," *Die ewige Wieder-
kunft;* and one little passage which contains the gist
of Nietzsche's conception is here presented in a literal
translation by my friend, Mr. G. Ainslie Hight.

"If the world may be conceived as a definite magnitude of force, and a definite number of force-centres
—every other conception of it is wanting in definite-
ness, and therefore useless—it follows that it has to
go through a calculable number of combinations in
the great game of chance[2] of its existence. In the
eternity of time every possible combination would,
at some time or other, have been reached. More, it
would be reached an infinite number of times. And
since between each combination and its next return
every possible combination will have occurred, and
since each of these combinations determines the en-

---

[1] *Werke*, Bd. XV. *Der Wille zur Macht* (Leipzig, 1901).

[2] Lit. "game of dice." Heraclitus calls it a child's game of draughts.

tire sequence of combinations in that series, we must assume a cycle (Kreislauf) of absolutely identical series; the world as a cycle which has already repeated itself an infinite number of times and plays its game *ad infinitum*." [1] Whether this amounts to a demonstration and whether we must accept the premisses on which the conclusions are based are questions for the students and critics of Nietzsche to determine. But there can be no reasonable doubt of the identity of his conception with that of the ancients. That which he set himself to prove had been formulated by them long before, and, as the fragment of Eudemus shows, in precise terms. Of orthodox Stoicism it became a fundamental tenet, defended, tooth and nail, against the rival Peripatetic doctrine that the existing order of things as we know it now is eternal. None but heterodox Stoics like Panætius ever expressed doubts on this head or were seduced into accepting Aristotle's alternative hypothesis.

Such then is the sketch which Stoicism affords of the world's history. If all difficulties are not cleared up, at any rate we understand from it why the leading terms, such as God, nature, matter, are applied in what appears to be an inconsistent manner. God is sometimes regarded as a spiritual power working upon and in the material universe, and similarly matter sometimes assumes an independent place beside Him. Such language is appropriate to the world already constituted, in which the active and passive principles are set over against each other.

---

[1] *Der Wille zur Macht*, Bk. IV, chap. 1, § 384, p. 410. The entire exposition includes § 375–§ 385. It is as sober and logical as anything ever written by the author. The editor states in the preface (pp. xviii–xix) that Nietzsche intended to treat the idea more fully in poetical form.

Perhaps this is the more habitual attitude of Seneca, Epictetus, and Marcus Aurelius, our fullest authorities, in ethical discussions or wherever Providence and the moral order of the world come up for treatment.   At other times God is spoken of as embracing in Himself the totality of being, no longer identified with the spiritual part of the world, but with the world itself, embracing soul and body alike.   From this point of view the question, "What is God?" is answered by the question, "What is God not?" or by Lucan's line: "All that thou seest, yea, all that moves is God."[1]

From the one point of view physics passes over into natural theology.   Socrates had discoursed on the wisdom and goodness of the gods and their special care of men.   Aristotle was the first to demonstrate from his own premisses the being and attributes of the deity whom he conceived as the first cause and immobile mover of the physical universe.   The Stoics approached the subject with a far stronger conviction of its importance and a determination to carry to its legitimate consequences the teleological conception of nature, which to a greater or less extent was inherited by all the schools deriving from Socrates.   They undertook, not only to prove that gods exist, but also to explain their nature. But these inquiries were preliminary to their main thesis that the universe and all its parts are ordered and administered by divine Providence and that all events subserve the highest end, the welfare and advantage of rational beings.   In taking up this position they found themselves in direct hostility to

[1] Jupiter est quodcunque vides, quodcunque movetur, *Pharsalia* IX, 580. *Cf.* prope est a te Deus, tecum est, intus est, Seneca, *Epist. Mor.* 41, 1. Also *Acts of the Apostles*, XVII, 27, I *Cor.* III, 16, 17.

Epicurus, who denied the interference of the gods in the world of nature, and not less at variance with the Peripatetics, who attributed the adaptation of means to ends throughout the natural world to the unconscious agency of an immanent power, without explaining the relation in which this unconscious power, nature, stood to the deity. To the popular religion the Stoics were in reality as much opposed as Aristotle or Epicurus. They denounced what they called superstition, myths unworthy or immoral, trivial or mischievous rites. Zeno declared images, shrines, temples, sacrifices, prayers, and worship to be of no avail. The best and holiest worship is to reverence the gods with a mind and voice sincere and free from the stain of guilt. A really acceptable prayer can only come from a virtuous and devout mind. At the same time it was their task to cherish and foster all the elements of the orthodox faith which could be pressed into the service of their system. They took religion under their protection and felt at liberty to defend and uphold the truth in polytheism. The universe is God, the one supreme Being, who may be addressed as Zeus. But, further, divinity must be ascribed to his manifestations, the heavenly bodies, sun, moon, and stars, the forces of nature, the blessings and advantages of life, such as corn and wine, the qualities which tend to the welfare of the individual and society—even to deified men. When the world was thus peopled with divine agents, it was necessary to turn to account myth and legend, especially the poems of Homer and Hesiod, by extracting from them or reading into them physical explanations and moral truths. Thus some moral significance was discovered in almost every incident in the career of the two favour-

ite heroes, Hercules and Ulysses.   But the popular
religion had a strong hold on men's minds by means
of divination and oracles.   To these the Stoics
lent the sanction of their system.   But how, we may
ask, could this be reconciled with the doctrine
of natural necessity by which every event in the
physical universe has its fixed and predetermining
cause?   The reconciliation was effected by the re-
course to another doctrine of the mutual coherence
and interconnection between all the parts in the
whole universe.   Omens and portents are thus
produced in sympathy with those events of which
they are precursors and indications, so that by natural
aptitude or acquired art the connection between
them may be empirically observed and noted.   If
it were objected that divination was superfluous since
every event was unalterably fixed, the reply was that
both divination and our behaviour under the warn-
ings thus afforded were included in the chain of
causation.

In establishing the thesis that there is a moral
government of the world, the Stoics started from
all those phenomena which, in the judgment of
Socrates and the Socratics, especially Plato and
Aristotle, implied an intelligent adaptation of means
to ends.   That there is an abundance of such phenomena was a matter of general agreement, and on
this common ground Plato, Aristotle, and Zeno were
united in opposition to Epicurus and Carneades.
The teleological conceptions of the Stoics often sank
to a low level, and they inferred purpose from very
questionable premises of supposed utility resulting
to mankind at large or to a few favoured individuals.
On the whole, however, their use of the physico-
theological argument, or argument from design,

did not greatly differ from that of their successors on the same lines. Even Hume and Mill attributed to it a certain degree of probability, and until Darwin revolutionised biological science it was not seriously shaken. The Stoics, however, were not content with the conclusion to which Hume gave a halting assent, that on the balance of probabilities the world as we know it does exhibit the work of intelligence. They made the further assumption, which Hume stoutly resisted, that purpose in nature is working for the benefit of rational beings, *i. e.*, of gods and men, to whose welfare that of the rest of particular beings is subordinated. They held that in this world, the common habitation of all living things, everything had been ordained by perfect reason for the general good; everything, therefore, happens in the best way possible. This conclusion was directly challenged as conflicting with actual facts. It is at first sight a glaring contradiction of the admitted existence of evil in the world. Unlike their philosophic predecessors, Zeno and Chrysippus could not attribute this evil to any power or agency in the world external to the godhead; they could not take refuge in chance or spontaneity or necessity or intractable matter. In handling this question they displayed the utmost acumen, and it may be doubted whether any subsequent attempt to justify the ways of God to man will ever be more successful than theirs. With physical evils, such as calamity, disease, and pain, their task was comparatively easy, for these to them are not evils in themselves; it is we who by our assent to a false opinion make them so. In themselves they are things indifferent which can be put to a right or a wrong use and so turned to a blessing or a curse.

Moreover, it was easy to show that advantages to mankind at large resulted from some of them. Thus disease and the like had a moral effect, partly as deterrent or reformatory punishments, partly as a stimulus for the exercise of our powers. The scourge of cholera may lead to the destruction of slums and to improved sanitation; the sleeping-sickness may result in fresh discoveries of medical science. But, supposing all this to be granted, what of folly, sin, and wickedness, whose existence in the world no Stoic could deny when he divided all mankind by a sharp line into wise and fools, sheep and goats?

The first and weightiest reply to this objection is drawn from the metaphysical distinction between the whole and the parts. Epicurus inquired whether it was because he could not or because he would not that God refrained from banishing evil from the world. The Stoic reply is in effect that of the Hebrew prophet: God's thoughts are not our thoughts, neither are our ways His ways. He must by the necessity of His nature allow evil and baseness among men. The Stoic emperor frequently uses this argument when exhorting himself to take a more tolerant and charitable view of his fellow-men. This leads to the further inquiry: why must evil be tolerated in the universe? The answer is that good and evil are relative. Destroy the one and you also destroy the other. Only by opposition to evil is good brought about: were there no sin or folly, there would be no virtue and wisdom. Lastly, it was not difficult to follow up this train of thought by pointing to actual instances in which good had resulted from evil and deducing the conclusion that God can overrule even evil and make it subservient to His own ends.

The reader must not expect to find these separate lines of argument clearly distinguished in the extant fragments of Chrysippus or in the writings of the later Stoics. In the passages to which we now draw his attention stress is laid first on one and then on another of the considerations above adduced. In all the extracts, however, the general intention is to show why evil, whether physical imperfection or moral defect, is not only consonant with, but actually indispensable to, the scheme of a rational universe under providential government (*cur mala fiant, cum sit providentia*). To begin with Chrysippus, whose doctrine is summed up in the pithy sentence, "Vice cannot be removed, nor is it well that it should be removed." [1] As Gellius informs us, [2] Chrysippus in his fourth book on Providence dealt with the objection that if the world had been made and was now governed in the interests of men, there would have been no evils in it, and his answer was as follows: "It is the height of absurdity to suppose that goods could have existed without evils. For, since goods are the contraries of evils, both must of necessity coexist in mutual opposition; indeed, of any pair of contraries neither can exist without the other. How could justice be known apart from injustice? What is justice, in fact, but the negation of injustice? Or how could courage be understood except by its opposition to cowardice? Or temperance apart from intemperance? Or wisdom apart from folly? Nay, why do not these foolish people go on to wish for truth to exist apart from falsehood? Goods and evils, good fortune and evil fortune, pain and

---

[1] Plutarch, *De Stoicorum Repugnantiis*, 1051 B: Von Arnim, *Stoic. Vet. Fragm.*, No. 1182.

[2] *Noctes Atticæ*, VII, 1; Von Arnim, No. 1169.

pleasure are just as inseparable from one another as are truth and falsehood. For these are pairs, in which each member is bound to the other with opposing fronts, in Plato's phrase: if you take away the one, you take away both."

In the same book Chrysippus went on to the particular inquiry whether disease is natural to man. He allows that it was not the primary purpose of the Creator to create men subject to disease. But in the production of much that was serviceable and advantageous to mankind he could not prevent the intrusion of kindred disadvantages closely bound up with the advantages, and the former stand to the latter as their natural concomitants. For instance, in the construction of the human body considerations of reason and utility required the head to be fashioned of very small and thin bones. But this superior utility involved a disadvantage, viz., that a head so constructed is easily broken and exposed to risk from ever so slight a blow. Hence disease and trouble date their birth from the birth of health. Similarly it is nature's design to produce virtue among mankind, and vice sprang up in the same soil because vices are related to the virtues as their contraries.[1] In the second book on the gods, as we learn from Plutarch,[2] he laid down that discomforts, by which are meant material evils, befall the good, not for punishment, as in the case of the wicked, but by a different dispensation as happens in states, and this is further explained by the statement that evils are distributed according to the rational will of Zeus, either for punishment or by some other dispensation which

---

[1] *Noctes Atticæ*, VII, 1 § 7 *sqq.*; Von Arnim, No. 1169.
[2] *De Stoic Repug.*, 1050 E; Von Arnim, No. 1176.

has its importance to the universe at large. Again, in a perfect universe there is nothing calling for censure or blame; and yet Plutarch complains [1] that Chrysippus was sometimes disposed to attribute the external misfortunes of good men to causes which imply a reflection on the course of Providence, as when he speculates whether such misfortunes are due to oversight, on the analogy of the trifling accidents due to neglect in a large household otherwise well administered, or to the mismanagement of evil spirits to whom has been intrusted a share in the government of the universe. So in another context he says: "Vice is determined in relation to the rest of the accidents. For it also in some sort comes into being according to the law of nature and is not, so to say, wholly unprofitable to the universe at large; for without it there would be no goodness." [2] And again, "As comedies have in them ludicrous verses which, though bad in themselves, nevertheless lend a certain grace to the whole play, so, while in and for itself vice is to be blamed, it is not without its utility for the rest." [3]

Marcus Aurelius turns again and again to the problem of evil. In the first of the following passages he is obviously alluding to the last citation from Chrysippus.

"One and all we work toward one consummation; some knowingly and intelligently, others unconsciously; even as Heraclitus, was it not, said of those who sleep that they too are at work, fellow-workers in the conduct of the universe. One works in one way, another in another; and not least he who finds fault and who tries to resist and undo what is

---

[1] De Stoic. Repug., 1051 C; Von Arnim, No. 1178.
[2] Plutarch, De Communibus Notitiis, 1065 B.   [3] Ib., 1065 D.

done. Even of such the world has need. It remains then to make sure in which ranks you range yourself; he who disposes all things will in any case make good use of you, and will receive you into the number of his fellow-workers and auxiliaries. Only do not you play foil to the rest like the coarse jest in the comedy, to use the figure of Chrysippus." [1]

"Be the world atoms or be it nature's growth, stand assured—first, that I am a part of the whole, at nature's disposition; secondly, that I am related to all the parts of like kind with myself. First, then, inasmuch as I am a part, I shall not be discontented with any lot assigned to me from the whole; for nothing is hurtful to the part which is good for the whole. The whole contains nothing which is not for its own good; this is true of all nature's growths, with this addition in the case of the world-nature, that there is no external cause compelling it to generate anything hurtful to itself. Thus in the thought that I am a part of such a whole, I shall be content with all that comes to pass. And, secondly, in so far as I own my relation to the parts of like kind with myself, I shall do nothing for self-seeking, but shall feel concern for all such parts, directing every endeavour toward the common good, and diverting it from the contrary. So long as I pursue this course, life must perforce flow smooth, smooth as the ideal life of one ever occupied in the well-being of his fellow-citizens, and contented to accept whatever the city assigns to him." [2]

"He gives me the impression of wrong-doing, but after all how do I know whether it is wrong? or supposing it was, that he did not upbraid himself for it—like the mourner defacing his own visage? He

---

[1] *Marcus Aurelius To Himself*, VI, 42.   [2] *Ib.* X, 6.

who would not have the vile do wrong is like one who would not have the fig-tree bear juice in her figs, or infants scream, or the horse neigh, or anything else that is in the order of things. What else can result, his bent being what it is? If it aggrieves you, amend it." [1]

"That from such and such causes given effects result is inevitable; he who would not have it so would have the fig-tree yield no juice. Fret not. Remember, too, that in a little you and he will both be dead; soon not even your names will survive." [2]

"Think of being shocked at the fig-tree bearing figs! you have just as little right, remember, to be shocked at the world bearing the produce proper to it. Shame on the physician or the pilot who is shocked at a case of fever or a contrary wind!" [3]

"Evil-doing does not hurt the universe at large; evil to one part does not hurt another. It is hurtful to the evil-doer only, and release from it is within his reach as soon as he so wills." [4]

"To my moral will my neighbour's will is as completely unrelated as his breath is or his flesh. Be we ever so much made for one another, our inner selves have each their own sovereign rights: otherwise my neighbour's evil might become my evil, which is not God's good pleasure, lest another have power to undo me." [5]

"When some piece of shamelessness offends you, ask yourself, Can the world go on without shameless people? Certainly not! Then do not ask for the impossible. Here, you see, is one of the shameless, whom the world cannot get on without. Similarly, in any case of foul play or breach of faith or any other

[1] *Marcus Aurelius To Himself*, XII, 16.   [2] *Ib.*, IV, 6.
[3] *Ib.*, VIII, 15.   [4] *Ib.*, VIII, 55.   [5] *Ib.*, VIII, 56.

wrong fall back on the same thought.   When once
you remember that the genus cannot be abolished you
will be more charitable to the individual.   Another
helpful plan is at once to realise what virtue nature
has given to man to cope with the wrong.   For
she provides antidotes, such as gentleness to cope
with the graceless, and other salves for other irri-
tants.   You can always try to convert the misguided;
for indeed every wrong-doer is really misguided and
missing his proper mark.   Besides, what harm has
he done to you ?   For look—none of the objects of your
ire has done anything that can inflict injury upon
your understanding;   yet there, and there only, can
evil or hurt to you find realisation!   What is there
wrong, pray, or shocking in the clown acting the
clown ?   See that the fault does not lie rather at
your own door for not expecting him to go wrong
thus.   Reason supplied you with faculties enabling
you to expect that he would go wrong thus; you forgot, and then are surprised at his having done so.
When you complain of some breach of faith or gratitude, take heed first and foremost to yourself.
Obviously the fault lies with yourself, if you had
faith that a man of that disposition would keep
faith, or if in doing a kindness you did not do it upon
principle, nor upon the assumption that the kind act
was to be its own reward.   What more do you want
in return for a service done ?   Is it not enough to
have acted up to nature without asking wages for
it ?" [1]

Hence the attitude of resignation to and acquiescence in the course of events so characteristic of
Marcus Aurelius beyond all other Stoics.   "All that
befalls the individual is for the good of the whole.

[1] *Marcus Aurelius To Himself*, IX, 42.

That might suffice. But, looking closer, you will perceive the general rule, that what is good for one man is good for others, too. But 'good' or 'interest' must be regarded as wider in range than things indifferent."[1]

"We talk of doctors' orders and say: Æsculapius has prescribed him horse exercise, or cold baths, or walking barefoot. It is the same with nature's orders, when she prescribes disease, mutilation, amputation, or some other form of disablement. Just as doctors' orders mean such and such treatment, ordered as specific for such and such state of health, so every individual has circumstances ordered for him specifically in the way of destiny. Circumstances may be said to fit our case, just as masons talk of fitting squared stones in bastions or pyramids, when they adjust them so as to complete a given whole. The adjustment is a perfect fit. Just as the universe is the full sum of all the constituent parts, so is destiny the cause and sum of all existent causes. The most unphilosophical recognise it in such phrases as ' So it came to pass for him.' So and so then was brought to pass, was 'ordered' for the man. Let us accept such orders as we do the orders of our Æsculapius. They are rough oftentimes, yet we welcome them in hope of health. Try to think of the execution and consummation of nature's good pleasure as you do of bodily good health. Welcome all that comes, perverse though it may seem, for it leads you to the goal, the health of the world-order, the welfare and well-being of Zeus. He would not bring this on the individual were it not for the good of the whole. Each change and chance that nature brings is in

[1] *Marcus Aurelius To Himself*, VI, 45.

correspondence with that which exists by her disposal. On two grounds, then, you should accept with acquiescence whatever befalls—first, because it happened to you, was ordered for you, affected you as part of the web issuing from the primal causation; secondly, because that which comes upon the individual contributes to the welfare, the consummation, yea, and the survival, of the power which disposes all things.   As with the parts so is it with the causes; you cannot sever any fragment of the connected unity without mutilating the perfection of the whole. In every act of discontent, you inflict, so far as in you lies, such severance and, so to say, undoing." [1]

"Either all things spring from a single source possessed of mind, and combine and fit together as for a single body, and in that case the part has no right to quarrel with the good of the whole: or else, it is a concourse of atoms, a welter ending in dispersion.   Why, then, perturb yourself?" [2]

"When offended at a fault in some one else, divert your thoughts to the reflection: What is the parallel fault in me?   Is it attachment to money? or pleasure? or reputation? as the case may be. Dwelling on this, anger forgets itself and makes way for the thought—'He cannot help himself—what else can he do?'   If it is not so, enable him, if you can, to help himself." [3]

"Claim your right to every word or action that accords with nature.   Do not be distracted by the consequent criticism or talk, but, if a thing is good to be done or said, do not disclaim your proper right. Other men's minds are their own affair; they follow their own impulse: do not you heed them, but keep the straight course, following your own nature and

[1] *Marcus Aurelius To Himself*, V, 8.   [2] *Ib.*, IX, 39.   [3] *Ib.*, X, 30.

the nature of the universe, and the way of both is one." [1]

"Tenth and lastly — a gift, so please you, from Apollo, leader of the Choir. Not to expect the worthless to do wrong is idiocy; it is asking an impossibility. To allow them to wrong others, and to claim exemption for yourself, is graceless and tyrannical." [2]

"Always be clear whose approbation it is you wish to secure and what their inner principles are. Then you will not find fault with unintended blunders; neither will you need credentials from them, when you look into the well-springs of their views and impulses." [3]

" 'No soul,' says the philosopher,[4] 'wilfully misses truth'; no, nor justice either, nor wisdom, nor charity, nor any other excellence. It is essential to remember this continually; it will make you gentler with every one." [5]

"The immortal gods do not lose patience at having to bear age after age with the froward generations of men, but still show for them all manner of concern. Shall you, whose end is in a moment, lose heart?—you, who are one of the froward?" [6]

"How is it that the gods, who ordered all things well and lovingly, overlooked this one thing: that some men, elect in virtue, having kept close covenant with the divine, and enjoyed intimate communion therewith by holy acts and sacred ministries, should not, when once dead, renew their being, but be utterly extinguished? If it indeed be so, be sure, had it been better otherwise, the gods would

---

[1] *Marcus Aurelius To Himself*, V, 3.   [2] *Ib.*, XI, 18, *sub finem.*
[3] *Ib.*, VII, 62.   [4] Plato, as twice quoted by Epictetus, I, 28, 2 and 22.
[5] Marcus Aurelius, VII, 63.   [6] *Ib.*, VII, 70.

have had it so.   Were it right it would be likewise
possible; were it according to nature, nature would
have brought it to pass.   From its not being so, if
as a fact it is not so, be assured it ought not so to be.
Do you not see that in hazarding such questions you
arraign the justice of God ?   Nay, we could not thus
reason with the gods but for their perfectness and
justice.   And from this it follows that they would
never have allowed any unjust or unreasonable neglect of parts of the great order." [1]

[1] *Marcus Aurilius To Himself*, XII, 5.

CHAPTER II

STOIC PSYCHOLOGY AND EPISTEMOLOGY

In considering the body of Stoic doctrine due weight must be attached to the pantheistic spirit which, as we have seen, has its outcome in the view of the universe as a rational whole. In the last resort purely physical inquiries and ethical generalisations tend to become merged in the problems of natural theology. But in accordance with the needs and ideas of the time the Stoics regarded philosophy itself in the first instance as a practical concern. If wisdom be the science of things human and divine, philosophy or the pursuit of wisdom should be defined as consisting in the exercise of a serviceable art. The pre-eminently serviceable art is the art of living. We study philosophy in order to live and act. Conduct is the one thing of supreme importance. In a well-known passage of the *Ethics*, Aristotle had exalted speculative over practical activity. Chrysippus objected that the life of the student, when closely examined, turns out to be but one more variety of hedonism. It is true, the student leads a refined and leisurely existence, but it is a life of pleasure all the same. The question always recurs: To what use do we put our knowledge? Right conduct or moral excellence is, after all, the end, and, in order to attain it, training and discipline are needed even more than correct views. So complete is the fusion of theory and practice with the Stoics that logic, physics, and ethics, the three current divisions of philosophy, are actually held to be the three most comprehensive and universal virtues. Each is a manifestation of wisdom, and wisdom is only properly attained when it is realised in action and life. We must exercise ourselves to form right judgments and to choose proper objects of endeavour. In spite of this threefold division of philosophy, wisdom is at all times and under all conditions essentially one. The Stoics were fond of using illustrations which well bring out this unity. They compared philosophy to an animal organism, logic being the bones and sinews, ethics the flesh, physics the soul. Or it may be likened to an egg, of which logic is the shell, ethics, the white, and physics the yolk. Or, again, to a fertile field, or fruitful garden, logic being the wall or fence, ethics the fruit or produce, physics the soil or the trees. All definitions are conveniently summed up in the simple formula—"The rule of life and conduct." For such a rule of life all the three divisions are equally indispensable. The man must know his place in nature or else he cannot adopt the proper attitude either to the universe at large or to his fellow-men. Hence the need for physics and ethics. He is in a world of sense and sensible things are incessantly craving his attention. Moreover, he is a rational being capable of judging; in fact, he must exercise his judgment at every moment of his waking life. Hence he needs to have his faculties braced if he is to form right judgments and make a right use of the data of sense. This is the work of logic.

Under the department of logic the Stoics included a variety of studies, among them grammar and rhetoric, poetry and music. The link of connection is that they all have somehow to do with thought and speech. Of this whole branch of philosophy there were four main subdivisions. Dialectic embraced what we now know as formal logic, rhetoric was made co-ordinate with dialectic, and there followed two subsidiary inquiries, one into definition and the other into the standard or test of truth. Formal logic, *i. e.*, the doctrine of the notion, the judgment, and the syllogism, had been systematically investigated by Aristotle, and the Stoics were content to appropriate his results with some not very important additions. Thus, besides categorical judgments, Chrysippus treated hypothetical and disjunctive judgments with especial fulness and elaborated the corresponding hypothetical and disjunctive syllogisms. He declared the hypothetical syllogism to be the normal type of reasoning, of which the categorical syllogism is an abbreviation.

Again, the Stoics were dissatisfied with Aristotle's table of ten categories or *summa genera* and attempted to frame a new table of their own under four heads, in which subordination and not co-ordination was the guiding principle. These are, roughly: (1) substance; (2) essential attribute, called form or quality; (3) mode or accident; (4) relation or relative mode. If we think of something, it must be something which exists. The most universal and all-comprehensive general term for such an existent thing, and at the same time the most indeterminate, is Being or Something. Again, when we differentiate the particular something we are thinking of and determine it more closely, we recognise it as the substratum of certain essential attributes. These, according to the Stoic view, are forms or qualities which, in themselves

corporeal, permeate and pervade its entire substance or matter. This gives the second category,
less universal and more determinate than the first,
since the various existent things have various qualities and are determined by various and mutually
exclusive forms. Next, a further determination
ensues when we take into account the unessential
or accidental attributes, which distinguish particular
things belonging to the same class and exhibiting
the same forms or qualities. Again, as some of these
depend upon the relation of one thing to another, in
such cases a fourth category must be added.

Here seems an appropriate place to remark that
the Stoics were the first to grasp and formulate the
principle of individuality, as it is called (*principium
individuationis*), which has since played no small part
in the history of thought. No two particular things,
they maintain, are entirely and in all respects similar,
no two hairs of the head, no two leaves of the forest
exactly reproduce each other. Each and every existent particular is absolutely unique. But a full description will always specify that it is (1) a thing, (2)
of a certain quality, (3) modified in a certain way, (4)
in a certain relation to something else. In comparing
with the Aristotelian table the main point to seize is
that the second, third, and fourth categories imply
the first, the third, and fourth, the second and the
fourth all the rest.

Of the other contributions to formal logic made
by the Stoics, as indeed of many similar improvements upon Aristotle, it may be said that
they were for the most part of no great value or
were even pedantic and useless. But there is one important point which, though properly psychological,
requires to be cleared up in advance and may claim

our immediate attention. In what light was the subject-matter, with which this whole branch of logic deals, regarded by the Stoics? What precisely, in their view, is the content of notions, judgments, and syllogisms? Not external things, not spoken words, nor, again, processes of thought so far as they are modes of the mind itself. Three things may be distinguished: (1) the external thing which a word symbolises, of which a word is the name, e. g., the really existent moon; (2) the spoken word "moon"; (3) that of which the spoken word is significant. To us the word "moon" calls up something, because we know its meaning, while to a savage totally ignorant of the language, even if he hears the spoken word, it either has no meaning or calls up something different. It is this last with which logic deals, according to the Stoics, and which they designate Lekton. They held that the first and second, the external object and the spoken word, are corporeal, but that the last, the meaning of the word, was incorporeal. If this meaning had been identical with the external object or with the processes of thinking, recollecting, or conceiving the external object, it would, according to them, have been corporeal and therefore real. But here they were bound to make an exception and recognise something incorporeal, something fictitious, interpolated as it were, between language and thought, between the objective spoken word and the equally objective modification of corporeal mind. Here is a strange inconsistency in a system avowedly materialistic, and it naturally provoked a shower of objections, taunts, and reproaches from adversaries belonging to different schools. The meaning of a term, then, the subjective idea which it excites, is incorporeal, and so are all the judgments in which it plays a part and all the logical constructions obtained by combining these judgments in inference. This anomalous position is not assigned to Lekton alone; it is shared by space, whether full or empty, and by time. Space, time, and the subjective idea or meaning of terms, according to the Stoics, have no counterparts in objective reality. Let Seneca explain. "There are corporeal things, such as this man, this horse. Next follow movements of thought conveying an assertion respecting bodies. These movements of thought have a sort of content peculiar to themselves and incorporeal. For instance, I see Cato walking. Sense has shown this; my mind has believed it. That which I see, that to which I have directed my eyes and my mind is a body. Thereupon I say: 'Cato is walking.' The thought which I express in these words is not corporeal, but by it an assertion is made respecting body, and some call it a judgment, others an assertion, others a predication." [1]

Plato had already distinguished between the thought or meaning and the words or language in which the thought is clothed, between judgment and proposition. The judgment is an *unspoken* proposition, the proposition a judgment *expressed in words*. How was this distinction to be retained in a system which allowed reality to corporeal things alone? There are none such corresponding to general terms: and yet there are general terms and general propositions. Moreover, even a particular judgment, "Cato walks," is distinct from the perception which gives rise to it. The percept is presented to sense, the concept or judgment to intellect, and the concept is the counterpart of the percept.

[1] *Epist. Mor.*, 117, 13.

It is held by the Stoics to be a mental fiction, an unreal addition, as it were, a reflection or duplication of reality; whereas the act of perceiving, the act of judging they regard as activities or modes of the corporeal mind.

In dealing with the problems of psychology the Stoics and Epicureans stand on common ground. Both agree that whatever appears to have independent existence as spirit can be resolved into a mode or function of matter, which is the sole ultimate reality. They must be prepared, then, to combat the opposing arguments of idealism and in particular to explain what mode of existence they assign to mental phenomena. When Plato in the *Sophist* asked: "Do you pronounce that qualities like virtue and justice and the soul in which they inhere are corporeal or incorporeal?" the answer which he anticipated from the materialists of his own time, viz., that the soul was a corporeal thing, was precisely the answer subsequently given by Stoics and Epicureans alike. Both schools argued that, unless the soul were corporeal, it could neither act nor be acted upon, and both held that mental qualities were hereditary and must therefore be connected with a corporeal substratum; while in the passage in question Plato admits that capacity to act and be acted upon is a valid test of real existence. The soul, then, according to the Stoics, is a corporeal thing, a part of universal substance or primary being in its purest condition of heat or fiery breath. It may be more exactly described as warm, vital breath (Pneuma) fed by exhalations from the blood. The distinctive characters of vital and mental phenomena were referred to the fact that the human soul was an offshoot or isolated fragment of the world-soul.

The later Stoics sometimes describe this divine element within the man, this *particula divinæ auræ*, as his dæmon or genius. The relation between the soul of the whole and the soul of the part, or, in other words, the divine origin of the human soul, is plainly recognised in the hymn of Cleanthes. Soul is the unifying principle which holds the organic body together. It is diffused all over the body, since sensation can be localised at any point of the periphery.

The conception of soul as something corporeal present in the organism was nothing new in Greek philosophy, and in ignoring the difficulties inherent in such a theory the Stoics were at one with their predecessors, the hylozoists, and with almost all their contemporaries. Here also a comparison between the macrocosm and the microcosm had free play. As the soul of the universe, or universal soul, is one, so also the unity of the human soul is the fundamental tenet of the Stoic psychology and the key to many of its problems. The doctrine of interpenetration was used to explain the diffusion of soul all over the frame. This diffusion was rendered compatible with the essential unity of the soul by means of the favourite assumption of breath-currents. The heart is the seat of the central or governing part of soul (Hēgemonikon), which for our purpose it will be best to designate the mind. The blood-vessels start from the heart, from the breast come the voice and the breath. The five senses, with the faculties of speech and propagation, are merely channels of communication, breath-currents, which connect the centre with various points of the circumference. Parts of this theory bear a strong family resemblance to the views of Strato the Peripatetic. The sense-impressions, he said, are conveyed by currents from the periphery to the central organ. It is in the central organ that an affection of sense is transformed into a sensation of the subject. The central organ of soul, however, was located by Strato, not in the heart, but in the brain. Herein he agreed with Alcmæon and partly with Plato, while the Stoics reverted to Aristotle, who located it in the heart. The sense-organs, according to Strato, have no more than a capacity for receiving and transmitting impressions. So, too, the Stoics held that, when sensation takes place, the currents connecting the peripheral sense-organ with the central organ play the part of a mechanism for keeping up communications. They may be compared to the arms or tentacles of a polypus. It is with the central organ alone that we are conscious.

The Stoics, then, agree with most materialists in considering the phenomena of mental life to be functions of organic matter, and in assimilating 'them to those ordinary cases of physical action and reaction between external bodies which are usually held, so far as our present knowledge goes, to be unattended by consciousness. The soul cannot be broken up into different parts or faculties. There is no such distinction as Aristotle made between intellect and the rest of soul, which would justify us in calling the latter irrational. Even the irrational soul of animals must be credited with perception and desire. Man is parted from the brutes by the possession of that which is variously termed reason, thought, or intellect. Under this all other functions of a human soul must be subsumed, as also that vital principle which man shares with the irrational brute. For it may be said that the same force, which in the centre of the soul is reason, is present throughout the organism, though it appears merely as a principle of coherence in bones and sinews, as a principle of growth in hair and nails. The operations of the distinctively human soul may be classified under the heads of sensation, presentation, assent, desire, thought. All alike have their seat in the central or governing part of soul, the mind, which is the corporeal substratum to which they must all be referred. Take the case of external perception. When the bodily organ, the eye or ear, is affected by an external object either by direct contact or through a medium, that object, in the view of the Stoics, is presented to the mind. "Presentation" is a fair equivalent for the Stoic term, which Cicero renders by *visum*. The more literal translation, "appearance," would be misleading, in so far as it suggests an erroneous contrast with reality. Objects, then, are presented to the mind through the senses. But not all presentations are of this kind. There are rational presentations, such as those of moral and æsthetic general notions, of space and time and, as explained above, of the abstract content of thought or the meaning of terms. With all of these the mind or reason is conversant, but they are not, as such, revealed by sense, *i. e.*, as good and evil, as beautiful and ugly, as space or time or Lekton.

The relation of the other "parts" of soul recognised by the Stoics to the whole soul and to the governing part has given rise to some controversy. On the whole it seems probable that the term "part" is misleading. It is better to speak of diverse functions than of diverse parts, for clearly the seven diverse parts have no independent psychical function of their own; on the contrary, the eighth or governing part is active in them. The comparison to the arms of a polypus must be taken to convey that the other seven are branches or ramifications of the central or governing part and make up with it a single whole. They are, in fact, nothing but its peculiar functions attached to some definite organ. Since force and matter are inseparable, there can be no opposition between function and substance. Wherever there is a function of soul, there must be the substance or substratum of soul as well. The assumption of parts is only needed to explain the various effects of soul upon the body and its organs. Even when these parts are described as breath-currents connecting the peripheral sense-organs with the centre of soul, this description is qualified by ascribing to such currents intelligence or consciousness. The main fact is that the human soul, like the world-soul, is active. It thinks, perceives, desires, and wills in virtue of the same living force. Thus difference of function rests on and implies essential identity.

Since, as we have seen, all processes in the soul are functions of the governing part, the Stoics recognised only one faculty, the rational faculty. From Socrates they inherited the intellectualism which converted all mental processes into, or interpreted them as, opinions or judgments. It may also be pointed out that this denial of different faculties tended to confuse different functions. The barriers between judgment and will, between what is rational and what is irrational, seemed to break down, when every operation of the human soul was pronounced rational. Feeling was merged in knowing, and under the elastic term assent or approval were combined sense-perception, intellectual judgment, and volition. The fault usually alleged against

Aristotle's psychology is that he views the soul as a bundle of distinct faculties, an incongruous assortment held together by a purely external tie. A superficial reading of his treatise favours this assumption, though he himself is sometimes most anxious to guard against it. The Stoics, whose dependence upon Aristotle is direct and obvious, escaped this error only to rush to the opposite extreme. In the endeavour to unify all phases of mental life the intellectual factor was their starting-point. The mind is active when it judges, and if judgment be interpreted as assent to a proposition, such an act of assent forms a link uniting sensation and perception to desire and will. He who perceives implicitly assents to the perception as true; he who desires implicitly assents to the proposition that the thing desired is good. The presentation of an object is the part-cause, in the one case of perception, in the other case of impulse or desire. The mind has free play for its activity in giving or withholding its assent to such presentation. All mental states, then, however similar, agree in this, that they are reactions of the individual subject when he is affected by an external object. The presence of the object gives rise to the presentation, and I become aware of it. My taking note of it is assent or affirmation of the form "This is A." Further, it is impossible to be aware of the object without taking up a certain attitude toward it, and from this point of view every phase of conation and emotion, whether desire, will, or purpose, love or hate or fear, is but another interpretation of the judgment "This is A." Movement of soul toward (or away from) the object is the general definition applied by the Stoics to all the conative or emotional states, which they crudely collected under the term impulse (Hormē; Latin: Cicero, *appetitus;* Seneca, *impetus*).

On this psychological basis rests the Stoic theory of knowledge. The current belief is that the Stoics derived all knowledge from sensation, but this requires very careful qualification before it can be endorsed. The mind of a man at birth, we are told, is a *tabula rasa*, a blank tablet, on which he records each successive idea or notion. The first written characters come through the senses; past sensations are retained by memory and, when accumulated, constitute experience. From single sensations of particular things or particular qualities arise general notions, which fall into two great divisions. The first are known as preconceptions or intuitions, such as that of God or those of good and evil. They arise naturally and spontaneously in much the same way in all men. The second class are methodically and artificially framed and depend upon instruction. Such are the notions which a student acquires when he learns any particular art or science, such as painting or astronomy. Reason, in virtue of which men are called rational beings, is developed out of these notions. Chrysippus defined reason as a store of preconceptions and notions. Different accounts are given as to the exact period when reason is developed. Whether the accumulation began with the seventh year or the fourteenth, it must have been a gradual process. The point to decide is how we come by preconceptions. Our authorities furnish particular information as to various ways in which notions are formed by abstraction and generalisation. Some are manufactured out of the facts of experience by comparing and combining the materials of sense, others by analogy, transposition, and contrast, others, again, by privation and by transcending experience. Instances are the notion of Socrates formed from his picture, of a centaur from the separate notions of horse and rider, of the earth's centre from those of small spheres, of death by contrast with life, and so on; lastly, there is the notion of the incorporeal, which transcends experience. The empirical origin of most of these notions is quite evident, but not of all; and this does not conflict with the statement that the earliest records inscribed on the *tabula rasa* come through the senses. But, as sense-material is accumulated, there is also a corresponding development of reason, and there is no ground for disbelieving the plain statement that the origin of some notions is to be sought in reason itself. This will become clearer if we consider the class of preconceptions, the distinctive possession of rational beings, and therefore widely, if not universally, distributed among mankind. To these preconceptions the Stoics appealed in their favourite argument from universal assent, from instinctive beliefs and intuitions unconfined to any age or country. They are general notions, but a special class of general notions. The standing instances are the practical ideas, the just, the good, the beautiful. They are said, as we have seen, to arise naturally and spontaneously in all men, which implies that no special training or instruction is necessary for their acquisition, but does not exclude the possibility that reason and experience are needed to render them explicit and precise.

Such a preconception, then, differs from the innate idea, in the sense in which Locke used the term, for it is certainly not knowledge ready-made, but only the germs out of which knowledge grows up. For some species of knowledge, for moral truth, in particular, we are favourably disposed by nature. While most empirical general notions are painfully collected and require skill in comparison, others suggest themselves in the absence of methodical investigation. Even children can form them; they are the same everywhere. The vague inkling which by nature we have of good and evil, is subsequently verified by experience and strengthened by the exercise of reason. Epictetus certainly affirms that all men by nature have elementary moral notions. For example, their notion of good is that it is beneficial, of evil that it is hurtful. They use these terms in a definite sense, even when they do not understand their full import and content. Epictetus makes this the starting-point of his discourse. It is the task of man, he maintains, by reflection to work out and elaborate these vague preconceptions and make them articulate and distinct, in order that these moral notions may be applied as the standard by which to judge the things of actual experience. By such steps, for example, from the vague conception of evil as something to be avoided and of that which is necessary as something which cannot be avoided, we are led to the conclusion that death is no evil. When this clarified and articulate notion is applied to actual things, we come to have synthetic knowledge and to estimate outward things by their moral worth. But not every one who has the vague notion of evil has developed it so far as to realise that death is no evil. Indeed, this could hardly be done without the aid of philosophy and that development of reason which it insures. Moreover, if good and evil were empirical notions derived wholly from experience, men would not differ so widely in the application of these notions to things, i. e., in their

moral judgments. As it is, since the things themselves tell us nothing of their value for us, there is
room for divergence and conflict. Experience practically never shows us the ideal of virtue.

But to return to sensible experience. Through
the sense-organs the mind has contact, directly
or indirectly, with external objects. The reaction
technically known as the presentation, *visum*, of an
object was defined as an impression in the soul or in
the governing part of the soul, and compared by
Cleanthes to the imprint of a seal reproducing
faithfully protuberances and depressions in the wax.
Chrysippus substituted the term "alteration" for
"impression." The rejection of the crude comparison does not affect the attitude of the soul,
which remains more passive than active. For an
act of perception many things are required. The
presence of the object and the possession of sound
senses do not depend upon the percipient, but he
on his part must direct his attention to the object
and observe it if he would escape from hallucination.
For the evidence of the senses is not always to be
trusted, and it lies in his power by an act of judgment
or decision to accept as true a presentation of sense
or to reject it as false or even in doubtful cases to
withhold judgment. In the process of assent the
mind's activity is evident. If we assent to a true
presentation, the result is simple apprehension; if
to a false or unconvincing presentation, the result
is opinion, a mental state which is always disparaged
as akin to error and ignorance unworthy of the
sage.

There remains the practical question, How is the
percipient to be sure which of his presentations
are true, affording him the means of knowing real

external objects, and how are they to be distinguished from untrustworthy presentations, which are before his mind when he makes a mistake or is subject to hallucination or madness? This inquiry, so important to all schools after the time of Aristotle, is generally described as the inquiry for a criterion of truth, a standard of knowledge. Our authorities report that the older Stoics made right reason (Logos) the standard, that Chrysippus interpreted this by declaring sensation and preconception to be the twofold test or criterion of truth, while the school in general, especially the later Stoics, ultimately settled on a particular character of certain presentations as affording a valid test of truth and guarantee of reality. Such a presentation was technically known as the "apprehending" presentation. It was recognised that none but true presentations have this particular apprehensive character, though it does not follow that it is possessed by all true presentations, for an opinion may be correct and yet not certain to its possessor. When we compare these three answers: (1) right reason, (2) sensation and preconception, (3) a particular kind of presentation, it is important to remember that the question what is the criterion is ambiguous. It may mean (1) who distinguishes, (2) what means does he use to distinguish, or (3) by what sign does he distinguish truth from error? In an inquiry for the standard of truth we are certainly asking by whom is truth distinguished from error, and it would be an adequate answer to say, "By the sage, in so far as he possesses right reason." But we may want to know more precisely what means does he use, what function is he exercising when he so distinguishes. The answer of Chrysippus is here to the point, viz., that this is done by sensation and preconception, the one being his guide for sensible things, the other for moral and æsthetic ideas. Even this is not enough. We go on to inquire, How does the sage apply this twofold criterion to any particular case in order to distinguish truth from error ? His procedure is exactly like that of the carpenter when he applies his rule to a surface in order to measure it, or like that of one who employs a balance to determine weight. He brings his faculties to bear upon the object, and, provided his sense-organs are normal and healthy, provided a real external object be present, the result is a presentation of the particular kind known as apprehending. He has then an immediate certainty of conviction that he is apprehending a real object through its real qualities. His immediate certainty is the subjective counterpart of objective reality.

The precise force of the adjective "apprehensive" as applied to a presentation has given rise to some uncertainty. Etymologically it ought to be active in meaning, although the corresponding negative adjective is apparently not active but passive in form, as if the Stoics divided presentations into those which can apprehend and those which cannot be apprehended. It has been supposed that the adjective "apprehensive," at least upon occasion, was taken in a passive sense or was purposely rendered ambiguous and taken in a sense partly active, partly passive. This I now believe to be an unfounded assumption. Through the presentation the mind of the percipient apprehends the real qualities of the real object. The fact that a similar word is used to describe the irresistible force of conviction engendered by such a presentation, which, in the words of Sextus, "seizes upon the subject, as it were, by the hair and extorts his assent," is a mere coincidence and nothing to the point. Again, the feeble and unreal presentations of mere opinion or hallucination are sometimes called, not inapprehensive, but inapprehensible—as Cicero expresses it, *visa quæ comprehendi non possunt.* For presentation is here interchanged with object presented; when I experience a feeble or false presentation the external thing objectively presented, the content of the presentation, is apprehended by me either imperfectly or not at all.

To proceed. The presentation thus obtained, immediately certain because faithfully reproducing a real object, has an important part assigned to it in the development of knowledge. All empirical science is merely a system of apprehensions of this kind strung together and closely connected; and similarly in the world of moral and æsthetic ideas, we start each with the same presentments, whether of the good, the beautiful, or of God, and all ethics is but a system by which they are linked together and further developed, the discursive reason being the great instrument by which they are manipulated and extended. But the systems of science and morality, however vast they grow, are after all but accretions built up and developed from single isolated cells or atoms of certainty, each a separate, irrefragable presentation, whether to sense or to reason, and capable of verification at every step by experience. The relation between the elementary constituents and the perfected whole or system Zeno sought to make clear by his celebrated simile. We follow Cicero's version of the story: "Showing his hand open to view with the fingers stretched out, 'presentation,' said Zeno, 'is like this.' Then, closing his fingers slightly, 'assent is like this.'   Next, when he had entirely pressed his fingers together and clinched his fist, he declared this position to resemble the act of mental apprehension.   Again, when he had brought up his left hand and had enclosed the other fist in its tight and powerful grasp, that position he declared to resemble knowledge or science." [1]

[1] Acad. Pr., II, 145.

CHAPTER III

MORAL IDEALISM

The two preceding chapters have made clear the practical tendency of the Stoic system. Logic, psychology, and physics—indeed, the whole of science, the entire theory of man and the universe, serve as a basis for morals. The outcome of all study is a rational life, a virtuous life, a happy and successful life, which to the Stoic are but different names for one and the same thing. Even the study of ethics deserves consideration only so far as it promotes this life. But first a word upon the form taken by ethical inquiries. To us the rightness or wrongness of conduct is its fundamental attribute. A right action is an action which ought to be performed, where the notion expressed by 'ought' is too elementary for definition. But this is not the way in which the Greeks approached the subject. They raised the more comprehensive question, What is the good? By right actions they meant those which lead to the attainment of the good. Reflection and discussion revealed a hopeless diversity of opinion as to what the good really was. Some identified it with pleasure, some with interest or utility; some allowed a variety of goods, mental, bodily, and external, others argued that from its very nature there could only be a single supreme good. The antithesis between what we now call moral and material good was only gradually developed. No Greek denied that judgments of praise and blame attached to specific actions or, in other words, that virtue was a good, vice an evil. The disagreement arose when the attempt was made to assign virtue its place in relation to the other things ordinarily recognised as good, such as pleasure, knowledge, health, or even external advantages like wealth, fame, and honour. All these things were conceived to exert an attraction upon the individual and to invite pursuit. The choice of an end of course regulated the means for its attainment: success or failure afforded an empirical test of the rightness or wrongness of conduct relative to the ulterior end pursued. All Greek ethical systems appear to us more or less prudential, self-regarding, or, as it is sometimes expressed, eudæmonistic. Socrates declared that he had never heard of a good which was not good for some one, and when the main problems of ethics take the form of asking what things are good in themselves and what conduct is the right means to good results, we are tempted, however unfairly, to interpret good as good for me, ignoring the fact that the inquirer is seeking a rule of objective validity and universal application.

For convenience of instruction the Stoics treated of scientific ethics under six heads: (1) impulse natural and rational, (2) the end of action, (3) virtue, (4) the classification of things as good, evil, and morally indifferent, (5) a similar classification of actions, and (6) emotion. Of these sections the first and last largely consist of psychological inquiries. The distinctive points in their ethics, upon which they were involved in controversy with other schools, concerned the determination of the end and the relation to virtue of those external things which ordinary men reckon among goods. To understand this controversy, however, we must revert to the fundamental points of doctrine already established, particularly the relation of man as a rational being to the universe. If the universe is essentially rational, then the good is perfectly realised in it, and in this realisation all rational beings, as citizens of the one city of Zeus, co-operate, for reason is the common tie which binds all its members in the closest association, and the course of the world is regulated by a law of inner causality, working always and everywhere for the best. This is a necessary conclusion, if we fix our gaze upon the whole universe, and the hymn of Cleanthes, as we have seen, has given it adequate expression. Let us now turn from the whole universe to its parts and consider the individual man. He is a part, but a rational part. He stands, then, in a certain relation to this organic whole and to other similar parts of it. His attitude is determined by the knowledge of these relations. As a part, he is subordinate and, like all parts, he must obey the universal law, which by the reason within him bids him do certain things and refrain from others. In this way Epictetus declares that the highest aim is to follow God and please Him, to live in His service and obey His commands. The same thought appears in a poetical fragment [1] of Cleanthes, which may be thus rendered:

> Lead me, O Zeus, lead Thou me, Destiny,
> By whatsoever path ye have ordained.
> I will not flinch; but if, to evil prone,
> My will rebelled, I needs must follow still.

With this may be compared the words of Seneca: "Ducunt volentem fata, nolentem trahunt." [2] Resig-

---

[1] Fragment 91, p. 313, Pearson.   [2] Seneca, *Epistles*, 107, 10.

nation to the course of destiny, submission to the
divinely appointed order of the world is the proper
attitude for man. This would be an exact definition
of the ethical end as conceived by Cleanthes. There
is but one way to happiness and freedom, and that
is to will nothing but what is in the nature of things,
nothing that will not be realised independently of
us. In this way success is insured beforehand.
Our wishes cannot be balked or disappointed. Our
rational freedom is a willing co-operation with destiny, instead of a reluctant submission under compulsion. Chrysippus, by the express testimony of
his critic Plutarch, whenever he laid down any moral
precept, started with a long preamble about Zeus,
Destiny, and Providence, in conformity with his
general principle that all ethical inquiries must
start with considering the universal order and arrangement of the world.[1]

Let us proceed to the line of argument by which
the Stoics sought to justify their conclusions. They
had somehow to arrive at virtue starting either from
nature or from reason. They required to prove
that moral good or virtue is the natural object of a
rational man's desire and pursuit. The all-embracing end which is never a means they found in
life itself, a life consistent and harmonious, the
smooth flow of existence unchecked by eddies and
cross-currents. Of such a life activity and energy,
not feeling or emotion, are the constituent elements.
To live such a life the individual man must be in
harmony with himself and with reason, that reason
which is his own individual nature and at the same
time the nature of the whole universe. In the formula "Follow nature," the word 'nature' may mean

[1] *De Stoicorum Repugnantiis*, c. 9.

the nature of the universe or our human nature, but since we are organic parts of the universe, the two interpretations come in the end to the same thing. We must be guided by experience of the course of nature. This formula points in two directions: (1) to submission to the divine will, the course of Providence, the inevitable, and (2) to the perfecting and full development of the divine within us, the guardian genius or dæmon, our human reason, intelligence, and mind. But this development is a process in time. Man is born into the world a non-moral being, and though he has natural, uncorrupted impulses, he is not much better off during his helpless minority than the brutes. The primary impulse in the human infant, as in the brute, is toward self-preservation. Let us quote the words of Diogenes Laërtius,[1] whose summary of Stoic ethics is on this point universally held in the main to follow Chrysippus:

"The first instinct which the animal has is the impulse to self-preservation with which nature endows it at the outset. The first possession which every animal acquires is its own organic unity and the perception thereof. If this were not so, nature must either have estranged from itself the creature which she has made or left it utterly indifferent to itself, neither of which assumptions is tenable. The only alternative is that she should have designed the creature to love itself. For in this way it repels what harms it and welcomes what benefits it. It is not true, as some say, that the first instinct of animals is toward pleasure. For pleasure, if it is an end at all, is a concomitant of later growth which follows when the nature of the animal in and by itself has sought and found what is appropriate to it.

[1] Diogenes Laërtius, VII, 85.

Under like circumstances animals sport and gambol
and plants grow luxuriant. Nature has made no
absolute severance between plants and animals: in
her contrivance of plants she leaves out impulse and
sensation, while certain processes go on in us as they
do in plants. But when animals have been further
endowed with instinct, by whose aid they go in search
of the things which benefit them, then to be governed
by nature means for them to be governed by instinct.
When rational animals are endowed with reason, in
token of more complete superiority, in them life in
accordance with nature is rightly understood to
mean life in accordance with reason. For reason
is like a craftsman shaping impulse and desire.
Hence Zeno's definition of the end is to live in conformity with nature, which means to live a life of
virtue, since it is to virtue that nature leads. On
the other hand, a virtuous life is a life which con-
forms to our experience of the course of nature, our
human natures being but parts of universal nature.
Thus the end is a life which follows nature, whereby
is meant not only our own nature, but the nature of
the universe, a life wherein we do nothing that is
forbidden by the universal law, i. e., by right reason,
which pervades all things and is identical with Zeus,
the guide and governor of the universe. The virtue
of the happy man, his even flow of life, is realised only
when in all the actions he does his individual genius
is in harmony with the will of the ruler of the universe. Virtue is a disposition conformable to reason,
desirable in and for itself and not because of any
hope or fear or any external motive. And well-
being depends on virtue, on virtue alone, since the
virtuous soul is adapted to secure harmony in the
whole of life. When reason in the animal is per-

verted, this is due to one of two causes, either to the persuasive force of external things or to the bad instruction of those surrounding it. The instincts which nature implants are unperverted."

The unknown Stoic whom Cicero follows puts the matter thus: "Immediately upon its birth a sentient creature is attracted to its own being and is impelled to maintain its own existence and to feel affection for its own constitution and for all that tends to maintain that constitution, while it recoils from death and from all that seems to induce death. One consideration is sufficient to prove this. Children, before pain or pleasure has touched them, crave for what is wholesome and refuse what is hurtful; this would not be so unless they felt affection for their own constitution and shrank from death. They could by no means yearn after anything, unless they had consciousness of their own personality and so felt affection for themselves. From this we are bound to understand that the earliest impulse proceeds from love of self. Moreover, among the earliest objects of natural impulse pleasure has no place. Its inclusion among them would involve many immoral consequences. Our affection for the objects above mentioned needs no further proof than this, that no one with both alternatives open to him would not prefer that all parts of his body should be symmetrical and sound, rather than dwarfed and warped, even if their usefulness remained the same." [1] The common quality which makes objects of this class to be preferred to their opposites by unreasoning instinct is termed value. "In order to have value, a thing must either be itself in harmony with nature or else be the means of procuring something which

[1] Cicero, *De Finibus*, III, §§ 16, 17.

is so. All objects, then, that are in accordance with
nature are relatively choiceworthy on their own account, while their opposites have negative value and
call for rejection. The primary duty is that the
creature should maintain itself in its natural constitution; next, that it should cleave to all that is in
harmony with nature and spurn all that is not; and
when once this principle of choice and of rejection
has been arrived at, the next stage is choice, conditioned by inchoate duty; next, such a choice is
exercised continuously; finally it is rendered unwavering and in thorough agreement with nature;
and at that stage the conception of what good really
is begins to dawn within us and be understood.
Man's earliest attraction is to those things which are
conformable to nature, but as soon as he has laid
hold of general ideas or notions and has seen the
regular order and harmony of conduct, he then values
that harmony far higher than all the objects for
which he had felt the earliest affection and he is led
to the reasoned conclusion that herein consists the
supreme human good. In this harmony consists
the good, which is the standard of action; from
which it follows that all moral action, nay, morality
itself, which alone is good, though of later origin in
time, has the inherent value and worth to make it
the sole object of choice, for none of the objects to
which earlier impulses are directed is choiceworthy
in and for itself." [1]

Here the main tenets stand out sharply: the prior-
ity in time of the non-moral instinctive impulses
directed to self-preservation and the attainment of
external things conformable to the economy of nature;
the steady growth of firmness and constancy in the

[1] Cicero, *De Finibus*, III, §§ 20, 21.

actions of choice and rejection to which these impulses give rise; the dawn and development of reason, as the harmony of nature begins to be understood, as general notions are successively framed and vague preconceptions made more definite by experience, until the greatest of these, the conception of moral good, emerges clear and precise. Five stages in the performance of duty are distinguished by Cicero. The first four are not yet moral: they fall within the competence of the child and mark a continual progress on the road to virtue not yet reached. In the last stage, when invariable consistency and conformity to nature has been reached, we recognise the ethical end as previously defined.

At this point the exposition may be profitably interrupted by a few general criticisms. It has been well said that in all ancient systems the attempt to construct ethics on a philosophic basis easily lends itself to reasoning in a circle. With the Stoics the circular demonstration is the neatest and the most easily detected of any. The semblance of cogent deduction is illusory. The plain man is told that to live according to nature is the end. But "nature" is ambiguous. Sometimes the term denotes that which is, sometimes that which ought to be, on the one hand that which actually exists everywhere or for the most part, as when natural impulse is said to be directed to self-preservation, and on the other hand that which would exist if the original plan of man's life were fully carried out, as when to live in conformity with nature is identified with a life of virtue. A similar ambiguity in the term reason did not escape the Stoics themselves, for they sometimes contrasted mere reason with right reason. This by the way. Let us pass on to inquire in what life according to nature consists. The answer is, in a life at one with reason, in a harmonious, consistent life, tending to realise a single, self-consistent aim. If so, the life according to nature must be followed because it is the reasonable life or life according to reason. Here the circle is complete. It is reasonable to live according to nature and natural to live according to reason, and as to the content of virtue, the particulars of conduct, we have no more information than at the outset. Nor is the case better if we call to our aid the conception of knowledge. The Stoics insist that the life which both reason and nature demand is a virtuous life, and they agree with Socrates that virtue is identical with knowledge. But how are the particulars of good conduct determined? What is the content of this knowledge? Surely the good: and, as they also hold that only virtue is good, not pleasure nor merely theoretical cognition, the circle is again complete.

Fresh difficulties arise over the distinction drawn by them between natural instinct and rational impulse, for both turn out, after all, to be concerned with the same class of objects, viz., the things indifferent which are according to nature. Reason, it is true, desires the good, but this supreme end is realised by the immediate choice of things not in themselves good. As Cicero urges, what can be more illogical than to assert that, after acquiring a knowledge of the supreme good, we turn back to nature and seek from her a principle of right conduct? For it is not our views of conduct which impel us to seek the objects that are in agreement with nature: on the contrary, it is by these objects that all impulse and all activity are called into being.[1]

[1] Cicero, *De Finibus*, IV, § 48.

It may, perhaps, be fairer to regard the assumption that virtue is the sole good as a postulate which can only be justified when the results following from it are tested by experience. The test applied is that of success or failure. The Stoics are entitled to argue that to desire the unattainable is futile and stands self-condemned, and that, as certain things are not in our power to command, our efforts must be withdrawn from them and concentrated upon those things which are in our power, our volitions, purposes, moral character—in short, our inner life. By confining our attention to these we can insure success. This brings us to the conception in which success is embodied as happiness or welfare. Neither of these English equivalents of the Greek term Eudæmonia is free from misleading associations. It is not primarily a state of feeling, still less does it connote enjoyment of external prosperity, but rather corresponds to the objective condition established when the end is attained. If so, it is something more akin to perfection or self-realisation, as these terms are used by modern theorists. To be happy on the rack is unintelligible unless by this so-called happiness is understood the consciousness of an objective relation. "When the mind," says Hume, "by Stoical reflections is elevated into a sublime enthusiasm of virtue, and strongly smit with any *species* of honour or public good, the utmost bodily pain and sufferance will not prevail over such a high sense of duty; and 'tis possible, perhaps, by its means even to smile and exult in the midst of tortures. But how," Hume pertinently asks, "can the philosopher support this enthusiasm itself?" [1]   As I

---

[1] Hume, *Dialogues Concerning Natural Religion*, Part I (II, 383, ed. Green and Grose).

conceive it, the answer becomes clearer from the analogy of the arts. The poet, the painter, the musician have made their way into a new world of beauty, where their creative impulse finds free play, and they exercise their art for art's sake alone. Similarly the dawn of reason opens a new world to the Stoic, where he also is awake and alive to the symmetry and harmony and charm of moral ideas. There his creative impulse finds free play in disinterested conduct, and, as with the artist, so with him, the gratification of this impulse, or, as Hume calls it, enthusiasm, absorbs all his energies. In both alike the impelling motive is the attractive force of beauty, in the one case æsthetic, in the other moral.

To resume. In the view of the Stoics a rational life, in conformity with the general course of the world, is the highest good. Virtue alone is good and welfare or happiness consists exclusively in virtuous action. Virtue is the fountain or source from which particular actions flow. It is a permanent disposition, when the soul is set or bent to realise harmony and consistency in the whole of conduct. Such a condition of soul is to be chosen for its own sake and not from the expectation of good or fear of evil, for no external results following upon it could possibly increase or diminish its absolute and unconditional value. Hence Chrysippus ridiculed the Platonic myths of rewards and punishments in a future life as bugbears intended to frighten children. The life of the bad man upon earth is the true hell. Whether the virtuous disposition be interpreted as a state of the will or of the intellect, the Stoics were bound by their psychology to maintain its unity. Their definition of prudence, one of the virtues, viz., that it is the science of what should be done and what should be left undone and of things indifferent, would stand *mutatis mutandis* for any of the others. At the same time they were entitled to recognise, not only the four cardinal virtues, prudence, temperance, courage, and justice, but also to subordinate to these a number of others generally recognised as commendable qualities. They merely explained that by a plurality of virtues is only meant the different manifestations in action of the virtuous disposition in various relations to different objects, in all of which relations it is essentially the same. Thus the same priceless knowledge or science which becomes courage when directed to objects inspiring fear or confidence or a neutral attitude is known as temperance when it is directed to objects of choice or avoidance or to those indifferent things which call for neither of these attitudes. It is also justice in so far as it assigns to each man his deserts. "Virtue," says Aristo, "when it considers what should be done and what should not be done, is called prudence; when it controls desire and defines what is moderate and seasonable in pleasures, it is called temperance; when it is concerned with dealings and contracts with other men, it is called justice."[1] In any case these several particular virtues mutually accompany each other. A man cannot be perfect unless he possesses all the virtues, nor can an action be perfect unless it is done in accordance with all the virtues, so that, virtue being one and indivisible, it is impossible to possess a single virtue without possessing all. This holds of altruistic conduct, for the Stoics believed that self-regarding virtues cannot exist without the social virtues. The good of society is best attained

[1] Plutarch, *Virt. Mor.*, 441 A.

by each individual pursuing his own good. The permanence of this virtuous disposition implies that, once attained, it can never be lost, so long as man is a rational being, and it becomes a minor question of casuistry whether the circumstances which tend to impair the supremacy of reason, such as intoxication or hypochondria, involve a temporary lapse from virtue.

Another consequence which follows directly from the definition was often presented in an offensive paradoxical form, viz., that there can be no degrees in virtue and no middle point between virtue and vice. A man's disposition either is virtuous or it is not. As there are no degrees in straightness, so one virtue is equally virtuous with another and all sin and vice, by the mere fact that it falls short of this absolute perfection, is on the same footing of equal depravity. This conclusion, so repugnant to common sense and the ordinary conventions of human society, can be rendered intelligible by a comparison with New Testament teaching, as when St. Paul maintains that whatever is not of faith is of sin, or when it is laid down that he who offends in one point is guilty of the whole law. Such teaching, whether Christian or Stoic, is bound to divide the world of existing men into two opposing classes, saints and sinners, the wise and the foolish, between whom there is a great gulf fixed. Popular Christianity admits that an individual man may pass from the one class to the other by conversion, and there are traces of a similar belief among some of the Stoics. But, on the whole, Stoicism was chary of bestowing the appellation "wise" upon any actual man. To the question, Who, then, are the wise? the Stoic probably of any age, and certainly the later

Stoics, would point either to legendary heroes, like
Hercules and Ulysses, or among historical men
to famous names of an earlier and far-off time.
To the founders of the school Socrates, Antisthenes,
and Diogenes served as examples; at a later date,
Zeno and Chrysippus.   By the Stoics of the Empire,
Cato was, so to speak, canonised.   But we have
every right to infer that just as Epictetus does not
claim to be himself wise and perfect, so neither did
any of the eminent Stoics who preceded him make
a similar claim in their own lifetime.

It comes to this, then, that the wise man is an
ideal and Stoicism a system of moral idealism.
But this was never fully recognised because the
Stoics at the same time held this ideal to be capable
of complete realisation here and now by any man
who followed the dictates of reason.   Instead of re-
nouncing the task of attaining an impossible wisdom,
the school introduced the conception of progress
toward virtue.   Life on this view becomes a grand
experiment.   Teacher and pupil alike are engaged
in one common endeavour.   They set out as ad-
venturers in quest of well-being or, like Bunyan's
pilgrims, on a long and toilsome journey.   The
Stoic cherishes no illusions as to the moral condition
of those in this state of progress or probation; he is
conscious that they have not yet attained to virtue
and, *ipso facto*, must still be reckoned among the
unwise and sinful.   The rigid demands of ideal
morality are never one jot abated.   On the high seas,
he who is one foot below the surface is drowned
as surely as if he were five hundred fathoms down.
And so Chrysippus lays down firmly that he who has
almost completed his progress toward virtue, who
discharges all moral duties in every way, without

omitting any, has, nevertheless, not yet attained the life of well-being and happiness.[1] One thing is still lacking. Yet, as the Stoics were honestly bent upon the moral improvement of mankind, they came to concentrate their energies more and more upon the effort to initiate, encourage, and continue in every one, however ignorant and sinful the idea, the hope and ardent desire of making progress. Indeed, this is the chief content of philosophy to later Stoics, such as Seneca and Epictetus. But it would be an error to suppose that this was an innovation or that it had been neglected by the founders. We have express testimony to the contrary. Zeno claimed that dreams furnished an easy test by which any one might discover whether he were making progress. If he found upon examination that even in sleep his imagination never ran on impure delight, evil thoughts or actions, this was a sure sign.[2] Cleanthes says in a striking passage: "Man walks in wickedness all his life or, at any rate, for the greater part of it. If he ever attains to virtue, it is late and at the very sunset of his days."[3] Here he evidently has in mind the state of probation and the possibility that the probationer may not have emerged from it when death overtakes him. The explicit testimony of Chrysippus to such a state has already been cited.

We pass now to that side of the system in which some[4] have seen a concession to the demands of common sense, a modification of abstract theory to meet practical considerations. The charge seems unwarranted, but it concerns the precise point on

[1] Stobæus, *Florilegium*, 103, 22; Von Arnim, Vol. III, No. 510, p. 137.
[2] Pearson, *Fragments of Zeno and Cleanthes*, No. 160, p. 196; Von Arnim, *Stoicorum Veterum Fragmenta*, Vol. I, No. 234, p. 56.
[3] Pearson, No. 51, p. 281; Von Arnim, Vol. I, No. 529, p. 120.
[4] *E. g.*, Zeller, *Stoics, Epicureans and Sceptics*, c. XI, p. 278.

which Zeno and all his school diverged from the
Cynics, whose doctrine in this particular was retained by Zeno's heterodox pupil Aristo. What is the
attitude of a perfectly wise and good man to external
things? The Cynics and Aristo maintained that,
since virtue alone is good and vice alone is evil, this
attitude should be to treat all other things as absolutely indifferent, attaching no value to one in preference to another. At this rate wealth and poverty,
health and sickness, sight and blindness, life and
death, are to the sage of absolutely no moment.
There is no rational ground why any one of them
should move his will rather than any other. Such
a view carried out strictly means the upheaval of
all society, and the revolutionary Cynics did so
carry it out. Aristo was free from the extravagances
of the Cynics, but like them, he rejected physics and
logic as useless, thus narrowing down philosophy to
the precepts of practical morality. All authorities
agree that Zeno introduced the conception of value
in the estimation of things external and coined a pair
of uncouth technical terms to designate the classes
of things which have positive and negative value
respectively, calling the former desirable and preferred, the other undesirable and unpreferred.[1] In
this connection value must be understood as a
relative term, but value for what or for whom?
Presumably for the agent, because he can put the
external things to a good or a bad use. This value
does not reside in the things themselves, but in the
judgment of the reason. Even the child, before he
develops reason, is prompted by nature to prefer
certain external things to their opposites. What,
then, is the ground alike of the rational judgment

[1] Proëgmena and Apoproëgmena.

and of the instinct? It is not that the things preferred contribute or co-operate to our well-being or
happiness. To make such an admission would be
a fatal mistake, for if health and wealth were productive of the good, it would be impossible to deny,
as all Stoics invariably do, that they are themselves
entitled to rank as goods.

There is a similar difficulty, it may be remarked,
in Aristotle's ethical theory. His end, miscalled
happiness, is a good *per se*. But, unlike the Stoics,
he admitted that there were other goods *per se* in,
and for themselves desirable, such as wisdom and
pleasure; and the relation of these latter to his
chief and highest good, his end or happiness, he nowhere clearly explains. The difficulty is far greater
with the Stoics, who recognise only one good *per se*,
viz., virtuous activity. The ultimate fact is the
judgment of preference. The external thing preferred is capable of moving the will, which must be
because it has a natural attraction. That when so
much has been admitted they should still refuse to
call it good, either *per se* or even as a means to good
per se is a strange inconsistency. Why does the
Stoic take care of his health? Because it is a re-
quirement of reason, a commandment of God,
because he has certain knowledge that *salva virtute*
health is more according to nature than sickness,
and therefore to be preferred, so far as extraordinary
considerations do not come into play. And, since
happiness consists in the attainment of what we
will, the performance of duty in this respect of taking
care of health is in itself a good *per se*, which is attained by the mere act of preference. We should
not be happy if without regard to circumstances we
refused to prefer health or deliberately rejected it for

sickness.[1] The deepest thought of Stoic ethics is that virtuous or vicious life is not to be regarded as a sum of isolated virtuous or vicious actions, but as an inward unity governed by a single principle, good or bad will, godly or worldly disposition, spirit or flesh. The class of things preferred is illustrated by such mental qualities as genius, skill, moral progress; such bodily qualities as life, health, strength, soundness of constitution and limb, beauty; such external advantages as wealth, repute, noble birth. With one exception, that of life, all the items on this list are accidents of individual men and not essential constituents of human nature. Most of them are held to be "gifts of fortune." To the Stoic they are the dispensations of Providence, results of the divinely appointed, unalterable course of nature. When they come to him, he gratefully accepts them and makes the most of them; when they do not come or are taken away, he as cheerfully dispenses with them. For he knows well that true happiness does not depend upon them; their presence or absence leaves unaffected the pearl of great price, the true and only good, which is at all times within his reach, if he so wills. But none the less he is bound to take a rational view of his environment and estimate every object at its due value. This judgment of value determines impulse and action and converts the thing so judged into material for the exercise of virtue. Or the same thing may be otherwise expressed by insisting on the importance of attending to perceptions and using them correctly. Since the term perception here includes presentations to thought as well as to sense, our entire attitude toward and judgment upon outward reality is thus summed

[1] Stobæus, *Eclogue*, Vol. II, p. 86 (Wachsmuth).

up. Sin is propagated by bad example and false instruction, but in part it is due to the deceitfulness of appearances, the false suggestions to which outward things give rise. Against this deception reason is an effectual guard only when it is trained and disciplined. Thus alone we learn to appraise each thing at its true value, for, as above remarked, things themselves tell us nothing of their true value.

We have thus unfolded the conception of a scale of value, positive and negative, to be assigned to all external things. In themselves they are neither morally good nor morally evil. Such a conception is intimately connected with the rudimentary theory of duty expressed in the technical term Kathēkon, which Cicero rendered by *officium*. Duty, in the strict imperative sense, is not a Stoic conception. Etymologically, the Greek term Kathēkon is wholly destitute of the notion of obligation or categorical imperative and might, indeed, be translated "suitable" rather than "right," where by "suitable" is meant "becoming to man," suitable to his nature and being. Such was the meaning given to the term by Zeno, who first introduced it into ethics.[1] But so much casuistical discussion took place upon what was or was not suitable that a train of associations became attached to the word, associations which were afterward inherited by the Romans. Thus the modern idea of duty grew up, fostered by the Roman character and their love of law, and ultimately borrowing its expression from the formulas of Roman jurisprudence, as the term "obligation" itself testifies.

---

[1] Cleanthes and Chrysippus sometimes use Epiballon apparently as a substitute for Kathekon. The literal meaning of Epiballon is "that which falls to or upon," of Kathekon "that which reaches to" or "arrives at," *sc.*, some particular agent.

Various definitions of the "suitable" are given by the earlier Stoics. They explain it as (1) an action adapted to the arrangements of nature, (2) the consistent or harmonious in life and conduct. And here we may pause to notice that the Stoics recognised this quality of consistency or harmony as in some measure exhibited in the vital functions of irrational creatures, in plants and the lower animals, though its highest manifestation was in the rational being, man. Lastly, Kathēkon was defined as (3) that which, being done, admits of reasonable justification. Over against the whole class of actions, suitable and consistent, was set the opposite class, actions which infringed or violated natural fitness. The instances of suitable actions cited have a wide range. They include, not only the purely selfish choice of any external things which are according to nature and have value, but also much besides, much that the ordinary consciousness and customary morality recognised as things suitable and expedient to be done. Thus such rules of conduct as to worship the gods, to honour and love one's parents, to take part in public life, to marry and rear children, had the sanction of public opinion in Greece and sometimes of positive law. But the meaning of the suitable and proper is not yet exhausted. Virtuous activity, the practice of prudence, justice, and courage, cannot possibly be excluded from the class of actions under consideration, and we are expressly told that every violation of propriety and expediency is, *ipso facto*, a sin.

What, then, is the fundamental conception of this class of action, and how is the suitable related to the right action? The perplexity of the problem is increased by two statements. The first is attributed

to Zeno and is to the effect that the class of suitable
actions and their opposites occupies an intermediate
position between moral action, which is good, and
immoral action, which is evil.[1] The inference would
seem to be that Zeno was thinking of actions in
themselves morally indifferent, and some of the
instances cited by other authorities, such as to converse, to walk, to eat, to bathe, support this inference.
The second statement comes, not from Zeno, but
from later Stoics who treated suitable conduct as
a generic conception, including two distinct species,
the one morally intermediate, the other morally complete. The contrast is no longer between the suitable and the right, for the completed performance
of the suitable is declared to be the right, to be truly
virtuous or moral conduct. At the same time the
complete performance is declared impossible for any
but the sage. Even if the external act is the same,
its performance by ordinary unwise men falls short
of the right, because it either is not done from the
right motive or has some other inherent formal
defect. Thus, if Zeno had intended originally that
the term Kathēkon, of which he was the inventor,
should be restricted to acts in themselves morally indifferent, his intention was frustrated by the subsequent development of his system. The conception
of moral progress received increasing attention,
and Chrysippus allowed that the probationer who
is nearing the end of his course performs all suitable
actions on all occasions without omitting any;
all that he needs to realise happiness is that his performance of these intermediate actions should acquire certainty, constancy, and a characteristic firmness. Chrysippus could not have written this if the

[1] Cicero, *Acad. Post*, I, § 37.

sphere of Kathēkon were a lower morality. On the contrary, it was the very material of virtuous action, for none could realise happiness but the truly wise and virtuous. It is not the external act, the seasonable thing done, which makes the difference, but the motive, the intention, the virtuous disposition of the agent and the conscious reference of the act to the supreme end of a moral life. The ordinary unwise man is, as a rule, incapable of recognising on the spur of the moment what are the actions suitable in the various relations and contingencies of life, and will therefore overlook many such actions; nor will he perform those he recognises in the proper way, e. g., duties to parents. The restoration of a deposit may be performed by an ordinary man or by the sage. In both cases it is a suitable action, but the sage alone knows how to perform it with justice; therefore, it is only in his case that the performance is virtuous and right. Moreover, the performance of suitable actions by the unwise is at all times irregular, not to be depended on, not proof against temptation. From this point of view the attempt to assign a distinct province to actions suitable and appropriate, which shall be neither morally good nor morally evil, seems to break down. The class of actions in question is a logical abstraction which it is useful to define; but as soon as we come to actual performance all actions, like all individual agents, must be ranked as either virtuous or vicious, moral or immoral. To worship the gods, to honour one's parents, stock instances of things suitable, can only fail of being moral acts through some flaw in the performance or from the absence of the right intention. When Cleanthes, at the end of his hymn, declares praise and honour of Zeus to be the highest privilege of all rational beings, the whole context shows that he regards the rendering of this praise and honour, not as a thing morally indifferent, but as absolutely right and good.

It may be urged as an objection to this account of the matter that the absolute character of moral rules is impaired by making the suitable the ground-work and subject-matter of right conduct. But this rests on a misapprehension. No moral precepts can have higher sanction than conformity to nature or reason, which are characteristics of the suitable, according to the definitions above given. The earlier Stoics emphasised the essential relativity and con-ventionality of the received precepts and conceptions, and in so doing grossly offended against good taste and natural sentiment, though, unlike the Cynics, they never attempted to put their paradoxical con-clusions into practice. But they did not propose to supersede popular morality by a new code of rules, immutable and binding apart from all reference to the end. According to them, the end is immutable, the means of attaining it are not. Conformity to virtue and reason admits of variation, according to the various circumstances in which the agent finds himself. Over and over again it will happen that the same action may be at one time suitable and expedient and at another time, under altered circumstances, unsuitable and inexpedient for the same individual agent. All particular acts, then, are relative to circumstances. Of possible or conceiv-able actions in life, some correspond to durable, others to temporary relations, some are occasional, arising out of special circumstances, others normal, without regard to special circumstances. It would be erroneous to equate the suitable with conditional, the right with unconditional duties, as Zeller seems inclined to do, for in any given case there is a line of action prescribed by the relation, whether durable or temporary, occasional or normal, and, however hard to determine, this course of conduct, as being conformable to reason, is absolutely and unconditionally binding.

Later Stoics, *e. g.*, Epictetus, have a threefold division, actions tending (1) to preservation of existence, (2) to formation of a definite character by the choice of what is in accordance with nature and the rejection of what is contrary to nature, (3) acts essentially moral.   In the last and highest class are found the duties which the unwise systematically ignore, such as universal, disinterested benevolence, renunciation of revenge, love of enemies.

The theory of appropriate action in the guise of inchoate duty admits of a very special application to the case of suicide.   That under any circumstances the school should have held suicide to be justifiable is an astonishing fact.   It seems to render their ethical optimism illusory.   But our surprise is diminished when we give closer attention to the general principles of the system and the conditions under which alone suicide was permitted.   First of all, it is a tenet of the Stoics that happiness is independent of temporal duration.   Virtue does not consist in doing the greatest possible number of good actions, but in an uninterrupted series of such acts.   Temporal prolongation, whether in this life or in a life hereafter, can add no whit to happiness, its characteristic is seasonableness.   Next we will cite the conditions as laid down on orthodox Stoic lines by Cicero, premising that death and the time of death are neither morally good nor morally evil,

but things indifferent. "Since things morally indifferent form the starting-point for all appropriate
actions, it is not without reason said that they constitute the test for deciding on all our plans, and
among them those about departure from life and
continuance in life. When the bulk of a man's
circumstances are in accord with nature, it is appropriate for him to remain in life; when the balance is
on the other side, or seems likely to be so, it is appropriate for such a man to quit life. This proves
that it is sometimes appropriate for the wise man to
quit life, though he is in possession of happiness, and
for the fool to continue in life, though wretched.
For the primary natural advantages, whether prosperous or adverse, are submitted to the wise man's
judgment and discrimination. They form, as it were,
the field for the exercise of wisdom, while good and
evil are the results of the choice. So any plan for
continuing in life or departing from it is entirely
to be estimated with reference to the primary natural
advantages. For it is not virtue that keeps a man
among the living, nor are those who are destitute of
virtue bound to seek for death. So it is often an
appropriate action for the wise man to turn his back
on life, though enjoying happiness to the full, if he
can do it seasonably, that is, consistently with a life
in harmony with nature. Wisdom herself enjoins
upon the wise man that he should leave her if need
require. Thus, inasmuch as vice has not the effect
of affording a motive for suicide, it is plain that the
appropriate course even for the unwise, who are,
ipso facto, wretched, is to continue in life if they are
surrounded by circumstances the majority of which
are in accord with nature. And seeing that the
unwise man, whether he quits life or continues in it,

is equally wretched, and long duration does not make life any more for him a matter to be avoided, it is not without reason maintained that men who can enjoy a preponderance of things in accord with nature must continue in life." [1]

This passage leaves the decision to each man's judgment, on a review of his external circumstances. The door is open; no one compels him to stay. Otherwise it could not be claimed for the sage that he was independent of external things. But later Stoics, who treat more fully of this subject, lessened considerably the freedom of choice, while at the same time they emphasised one situation in which the duty is imperative. This is often expressed by the military metaphor. The suicide acts in obedience to the call of God. How can we recognise this call? Solely by reason, not by a supernatural sign or inward admonition. When a life in accordance with nature is no longer possible, when we have no means to life, when we can only live by loss of personal honour or through dereliction of duty, then we must obey the call and go. Under such circumstances to remain in life is an act of cowardice as heinous as if we should shrink from death for country or friend; nay, more, it would render all our surviving life useless. "He who by living is of use to many ought not to choose to die," says Musonius, "unless by death he can be of use to more." [2] But the later Stoics fully recognised that suicide might be an immoral act if, for example, it proceeded from rashness, obstinancy, vanity, love of glory, ignorance of social duties. The end of Peregrinus, as related by Lucian, was clearly prompted by vanity and self-

---

[1] Cicero, *De Finibus*, III, §§ 60, 61.
[2] Stobæus, *Florilegium*, VII, 25.

advertisement. Seneca allowed the infirmities of old age, incurable disease, and a weakening of the powers of the mind to be satisfactory reasons for taking leave of life, but Epictetus reduced within very narrow limits the bodily circumstances which justify suicide. He would probably have admitted that it was foolish to bear unnecessary pains, but, as according to him, sickness forms a natural constituent of human life, disease in itself cannot furnish a moral ground for quitting it. Banishment under very oppressive circumstances might serve as an excuse, but isolation is in itself no bar to happiness. Moreover, he is earnest in recommending all possible effort to support life; at the worst, he says, you can wait till you die of hunger. The idea of a stain to personal honour, which in one instance, the death of an athlete,[1] Epictetus allows to be a valid justification, is not clearly defined and admits of dangerous extension, for, though nothing of the kind can touch the soul, yet quite trivial insults, *e. g.*, the loss of his beard by a philosopher,[2] might come under this head. Besides, personal honour and dignity vary with the individual, and, though suicide for Cato was glorious, that of another man under the same circumstances might not have been so. The casuistry on the subject is necessarily concerned with the action of good men, whether already wise or on the road to wisdom. What the unwise do in their unwisdom is a matter of less moment. This much is certain; that, so far from calling forth moral reprobation, suicide would be for them a consistent end to an immoral career. Here the reader of Scott will recall the answer received by Dugald Dalgetty from

---

[1] Arrian, *Dissertations*, I, 2, 26.
[2] *Ib.*, I, 16, 9.

his compatriot of the Scottish convent in Würtzburg, whom he consulted upon a point of conscience.

It has already been said that the Stoics dwelt upon the activity and energy of the virtuous life, and indeed in their whole psychology took little account of the element of feeling. This becomes still more apparent when we approach the subject of emotion. There are here four classes of feelings to be considered: (1) morbid and vicious emotion, which can only exist in rational beings, children and brutes being exempt from it; (2) rational emotion, confined to the sage; (3) intermediate states of feeling, natural and good, or at any rate inevitable, but in all cases involuntary, not resting on free self-determination; (4) sensuous physical feeling, necessary and involuntary. This fourth class, as belonging to the body, is opposed to all the other three, which are mental states. As to the first class, it is matter of common knowledge that the Stoics declared war against the passions of mankind, which they condemned as irrational, and therefore vicious and sinful. The wise man who is the embodiment of reason is exempt from vicious emotion, as from all the weaknesses of ordinary humanity, and this picture of the passionless sage has always caught the popular imagination. As we shall see, there is one-sided exaggeration in the picture. If vicious emotion is uprooted, there is still room for rational joy and satisfaction, rational desire, rational fear, so that the sage is anything but devoid of all feeling. But it is true that neither the virtuous emotion of the sage, nor the vicious passions of ordinary men are conceived as simply states of feeling. The Stoic psychology in its premature effort at unification does not separate clearly will from feeling or either ele-

ment from intellect. In impulse (Hormē), whether
rational in man or instinctive in brutes, the volitional side predominates. But in the four great
classes of vicious emotion, pain and pleasure, which
relate to the present, desire and fear, which relate
to the future, the element of feeling, of excessive
mental excitement, is more apparent than the element of will. Every impulse implies a presentation to sense or thought, and the impulse or movement of soul toward a thing or away from it is
conditioned by an act of mental assent, a judgment
that the object presented is of a certain character.
If it be judged good, it excites the hope of its attainment and the fear of missing it; if evil, feelings of
an opposite nature. In a rational being the judgment, and therefore the resulting impulse, is the
work of the mind (Hēgemonikon). When, therefore,
ordinary men give way to the passions of pain or fear,
their reason, the central governing principle of their
soul has, in the very act of giving way, pronounced
that which causes the pain or fear to be evil; and
similarly, the passions of pleasure and desire involve a judgment that the objects which inspire
them are good. If such judgments are erroneous,
as experience shows they often are, the consequent
impulse and state of feeling are vicious and sinful.
In other words, the Stoics admit that reason can be
perverted. At the same time they do not consider
emotions to be nothing but judgments; they regard
them as caused by judgments of a particular kind,
followed by particular mental phenomena. They are
called judgments because the real cause is the essence
of a thing. But they did not separate the judgment
from the attendant phenomena; they absorbed the
pathological side in the judgment and made the

former the immediate result of the latter. Besides, the error in this particular kind of judgment is not purely intellectual, for instruction and reproof do not make the victim of the error desist from his passion. For the particular species of judgment, belief, or opinion which generates emotion the Stoics employed a technical term, Doxa Prosphatos (*opinio recens*, to be distinguished from *opinio repentina*[1]), which is explained to mean an opinion that is fresh, vigorous, and forcible, calculated to upset the equilibrium of the reason.[2] The disturbance in any case is voluntary and self-incurred.

Every event is determined by natural necessity, but in the moment of judging the rational being is free to obey reason or to disobey it. The strength and tension of his soul, in the last resort, alone decides what he will do. An impulse may be rational in the sense that it proceeds from a rational being, and yet in another sense irrational because this being does not exercise his reason or exercises it amiss. To maintain, with Socrates and the Stoics, that virtue is essentially knowledge brings us face to face with two alternatives: either vice is involuntary, as Socrates held, or ignorance is voluntary. The Stoics certainly held that all forms of vicious emo-

---

[1] Cicero, *Tusculans*, III, 75.

[2] Galen (*De Hippocrat. et Plat. decretis*, V, p. 416, Kühn) follows the heterodox Stoic Posidonius in the opposite view, which interprets the technical term Prosphatos as referring not to the judgment itself, but to good or evil wrongly opined, and gives it an exclusively temporal meaning, "sudden" or "closely imminent." But events are in themselves indifferent, neither morally good nor morally evil, and nothing of this class can be the cause of an emotion which is vicious and sinful. It is not the unforeseenness of an event that is the cause of an emotion, nor are we better able to bear the event by dwelling upon it beforehand; the only real remedy against vicious emotion is to acquire right views respecting what is good, evil, and morally indifferent. *Cf. Cicero, Tusculans*, III, 55.

tion are voluntary. The morbid and disorderly
state of the soul in anger or fear rests on an erroneous
judgment as to what is to be sought or shunned, and
this error might have been avoided if the man had
chosen to exercise his reason. No doubt it depended
on the innate force and firmness of a man's soul
whether his reason was thus effectually exercised;
but if the act thus proceeded from the man himself,
and not from any external cause, he must be held
responsible. The specific definitions of pleasure
as irrational elation and of pain as irrational depression, to which those of desire and fear can be
assimilated, show by the materialistic terms employed that we have here another application of
the theory of tension in the primary substance of
the soul, just as virtue is sometimes defined by
strength, force, proper tension in the substance of
the material soul.

Here we may notice a point of divergence from the
ethics of all those philosophers who, like Plato and
Aristotle, admit a non-rational part or faculty in the
soul. According to the latter, some part or manifestation of virtue consists in the due regulation by the
reason of the non-rational impulses, which are themselves normal and natural products of the non-rational
element of soul. Orthodox Stoics deny the existence
of any non-rational part of the soul. They attribute
irrational impulses or instincts, not to an irrational
faculty in the soul, but to the self-perversion of the
reason, which can act as well contrary to as according to nature, and they call upon reason, not merely
to conquer and check these propensities, but to extirpate them altogether.

The confusion of processes of intellect and volition with states of feeling is obvious when we con-

sider the four ways in which morbid or vicious emotion was defined. In two of these, (*a*) a movement of soul contrary to reason and contrary to nature, and (*b*) a false or erroneous opinion and judgment by the rational soul, stress is laid on the intellectual side, since a judgment no less than an impulse is a movement of soul. Hence the more precise definition is (*c*) impulse in excess, with which agree the separate definitions (*d*) of vicious desire as an irrational appetency, of fear as an irrational avoidance, of pleasure as an irrational elation, and of pain as an irrational depression. Clearly the irrational character of the impulse is shown in its excess. Violent and morbid excitement, betraying a feverish or inflamed state of mind, predominates, at any rate, in pleasure and pain, though the latent judgments "This is a good" and "That is an evil" are even then by no means excluded. Erroneous judgment is the cause, morbid excitement, mental elation, and mental depression concomitant effects which necessarily attend upon the error; in them the self-perversion of reason manifests itself. In the Stoic conception the three factors, judgment, impulse, feeling, are inextricably blended. To judge death to be an evil, to endeavour to shun it, to be morbidly depressed at the thought of it, are but phases and aspects of the one vicious emotion, the fear of death, which, however defined, necessarily involves them all. Similarly avarice involves an intellectual judgment that money is the true good, a volitional impulse to obtain it, and a morbid, inordinate delight in hoarding it. In anger, again, the three elements are the belief that my neighbour has done me evil (which of course, on Stoic principles, is out of his power, as I can be injured by

nothing external, but only by myself in vice or sin),
the impulse to avenge this evil, and the morbid
emotional excitement of a painful nature which
accompanies the impulse. So, too, with pity.
Here the erroneous belief is that our neighbour's
external calamities are real evils, while the impulse
to wish the course of external events other than it is
ordained, is bound up with a feeling of pain and annoyance that things are as they are. The Stoic did
what he could to relieve the misfortunes of others,
but the indulgence of sentimental pity or grief was
incompatible with his cheery optimism and faith
in Providence.

Let us now turn to the second class, that of rational
emotion. The Stoic temper does not imply absolute
freedom from all emotion, but only from irrational
mental storms. The sage is not hard and unfeeling,
like a block of marble. He is subject to the normal
feelings which are necessarily bound up with rational
conduct and the right theory of life. These are as
voluntary as the vicious emotions. To the false
fear of future calamities corresponds in his case a
godly fear or circumspection, a conscientiousness
and wariness in guarding against moral failings.
He has no other fear, for sin and vice are the only
evils he can dread. Closely allied to this is the feeling
of shame which shrinks from moral disgrace and
just blame. So, too, his rational will, which is always directed to moral good, is the counterpart of
vicious desire prompted by fancied goods. Under
this head come goodwill, affection, and love to our
neighbour, which is purely disinterested, not for our
own sake but for his. This feeling inspires to
social service and universal philanthropy. Even
personal affection is not forbidden to the sage, but

the feeling is excited, not by sensuous beauty alone,
but by the capacity for virtue.   In rational fear and
rational desire, though they are mainly volitional
processes, the element of feeling is present; and this
is still more true of rational joy or satisfaction, which
is the counterpart in the sage of vicious pleasure in
the unwise.   Rational fear, rational will, rational
joy are the only forms of rational emotion.   It fully
accords with Stoic optimism that there should be no
counterpart in the sage, to the mental pain, the grief
and sorrow, the envy and hatred of the unwise.
Submission to the course of events is attended by
moral elation, by cheerfulness and confidence.
The road to freedom, the only escape from slavery,
is joy resting on a clear knowledge of man's nature
and destiny.   This joy and confidence must be
permanent and lasting, at any rate in the sage; the
constancy of his joy is one mark of his perfect well-
being.   The highest ideal is an inner harmony of
the soul, which is necessarily conjoined with feelings
of joy, contentment, and exaltation, and shows itself,
not only in the whole nature and deportment, but
even externally in the countenance.   This joy is related to virtue as an inseparable concomitant; it
stands so near to the essence of virtue that it is not
only natural but in itself a good.

Thus far emotion has been described as of two
kinds, the one vicious and morbid, the violent,
incalculable, and ever-shifting gusts of passion which
overtake the unwise, the other the constant, measured,
equable feelings which rest on rational knowledge
and rational self-determination.   But this is not an
exhaustive classification of feeling.   There are states
which are neither the one nor the other, natural
affection and joy, which arise involuntarily and

without conscious activity of the reason. Thus, affection for blood relations is natural and good, but arises without man's free-will, and unless and until it becomes goodwill and benevolence it has no power or constancy. Sexual love would at first sight answer to this description, though Seneca condemns it as madness, *insana amicitia*.[1] The attitude of the school to friendship is unsatisfactory. True friendship, they hold, can only exist between the wise. It is thereby robbed of its peculiar significance as a liking resting on personal sympathy. For, if friendship only exists between wise men, and these wise men are only made friends by reason and virtue, and all of them are friends in an equal degree, friendship is really destroyed. It is dissolved partly into universal philanthropy, partly into the intellectual communion and relation between the wise or, at any rate, the earnest strivers after wisdom. In the same intermediate class of emotions room must be found for pleasure in companionship or sociability, and for love of nature, of beauty, of knowledge. Nor could the severance of rational and permitted emotions from such as are morbid and vicious be completely carried out in practice when we extend our view to those in a state of progress or probation. They are bound to feel pain, grief, sorrow, and shame for their own faults in the moment of repentance, and sometimes also shame for the faults of others. Even Chrysippus allowed that there were gradations of emotion, and that some of them, though they hurt us, do not make us worse. Plutarch objects that the Stoics, after banishing emotions, bring them back under another name. "If, being convicted by tears and trembling and change of colour, they talk of stings and contrac-

[1] Seneca *Epistulæ*, 9, § 11.

tions, this is merely sophistry." [1] Zeno, too, spoke of the wise man exhibiting involuntary signs of anger, the scar remaining after the wound has healed. [2]

Lastly, there is sensuous bodily feeling, which the Stoics ascribed to an internal sense, an inner touch. Strictly speaking, as emotion resides in the mind and is voluntary self-determination of the reason, a bodily feeling which is involuntary is not emotion in the technical sense at all, being neither morally evil nor morally good, but a thing indifferent. It is unfortunate, then, that the same term pleasure should be employed in two distinct senses for this indifferent bodily feeling and also for the irrational elation of soul which has the bodily feeling for its cause and object. The reprehensible pleasure which the Stoics denounced and sought to extirpate was the mental state of elation at the presence of this physical feeling, which implies the erroneous belief that it is a good. The wise man will be subject, like other men, to bodily pleasure and pain, but he will never mistake bodily pleasure for real good or bodily pain for real evil, and consequently he will never be betrayed into that mental elation at the one and mental depression, grief, and sorrow at the other in which the vicious emotions of pleasure and pain consist. Even in the worst bodily agonies his soul is invulnerable. Later Stoics use the term flesh to distinguish the bodily feeling from the mental emotion. Marcus Aurelius and Epictetus agree that the gentle movement of the flesh does not influence the inmost spiritual nature of man. What, then, is the moral value of the bodily feeling? The school was agreed as against Epicurus that pleasure was in this sense not the good and pain in this sense not

[1] Plutarch, *Virt. Mor.*, c. 9.　　　[2] Seneca, *De Ira*, I, 16, 7.

the evil; both were included in the class of things morally indifferent. But the precise position of pleasure and pain in the class was debated. It has even been inferred that pain (more properly, toil and physical hardship) was regarded as entitled to preference over pleasure.[1] On the other hand the physical feeling of pleasure as distinct from the mental excitement it engenders was sometimes defined as a concomitant of certain natural wants. Thus, when we satisfy hunger and thirst, or warm our chilled limbs, the physical feeling is no part of the benefit and is so far unnecessary, and yet it is an invariable addition. If it were possible to quench thirst without pleasure, pleasure would have no *raison d'être*. We could get on just as well without it. Epictetus calls it an external appendage, and says that if it were away man's nature would be unaltered. It might have been thought that this invariable concomitance would have been regarded as proof of divine disposition, as part of the economy of nature. That the school should have held pleasure to be an invariable concomitant of natural wants and yet have refused to call it natural is a remarkable inconsistency, doubtless due to the pressure of controversy with Epicurus. Here, however, they seem to have stopped. "Not according to nature" is not identical with "contrary to nature." It cannot be taken as proved that physical pleasure was ever expressly declared to be unnatural. Sextus impartially sums up Stoic opinion in these words: "The Stoics hold pleasure to be a thing indifferent and not preferred in that class; Cleanthes held that it is not according to nature, any more than a wig or rouge, and has no value in life; Archedemus admitted it to be

[1] Stobæus, *Eclogue*, II, 58, 3.

according to nature in precisely the same sense as the hairs which grow in the armpits, but denied that it had value; Panætius distinguished between pleasures according to nature and pleasures contrary to nature." [1] It must be remembered that Panætius was on many points heterodox, and that his predecessor Archedemus showed the same tendency to eclecticism.

It will be seen that the relation of joy to virtue is reproduced in the relation of physical pleasure to natural necessities. This relation of an invariable concomitant to activity at once recalls the conception of Aristotle who, in the *Nicomachean Ethics*, similarly defined pleasure as not the end and motive of our actions, but only a necessary concomitant of activity according to nature, the natural perfection of every activity and, as such, the immediate outcome of the perfected activity. [2] What Aristotle asserted of pleasure in general the Stoics restrict to the moral satisfaction which attends upon virtue alone, the joy and confidence which they dissociated both from the physical feeling and from the morbid emotion of pleasure.

Each of the six heads above mentioned has now been passed under review. Something has been said of impulse, end, virtue, the classification of objects, the classification of actions, and the varieties of emotion. Sometimes from lack of material, sometimes from the nature of the subject, it is impossible to treat these topics adequately, and there are many perplexing problems, problems of which, under the circumstances, we can expect no more than a provisional solution. But, such as it is, the sketch of Stoic ethical theory is now complete.

[1] Sextus Emp., XI, 73.
[2] *Nicomachean Ethics*, X, c. 4, especially, 1174, b. 33.

CHAPTER IV

THE TEACHING OF THE LATER STOICS

A system of philosophy, in order to live and thrive, must win adherents. However reasonable its tenets, they cannot find acceptance until they have been presented to the notice of mankind. Some zeal must be shown in expounding them, since the competition of ideas for supremacy in the spiritual world is no less keen than the conflict between the opposing interests of individual men and peoples. Fortunately we are in a position to see how Stoicism was inculcated—we might almost say, preached—under the Roman empire in the first two centuries of the Christian era. Numerous treatises and epistles of Seneca have survived; the discourses and manual of Epictetus are preserved to us in the lecture notes taken down by his disciple Arrian; lastly, we still have the meditations of the emperor Marcus Aurelius Antoninus, written primarily for his own admonition and consolation, as is sufficiently clear from the genuine title of his work, *Marcus Aurelius To Himself.* Professional teachers like Epictetus and his master Musonius Rufus devoted their whole lives to the task of instructing all who were willing to hear them, but outside this inner circle there were many men of high position and distinction in imperial Rome, men like Pætus Thrasea and Helvidius Priscus, who took part in the philosophic propaganda and were prepared to seal the testimony of their lives with their blood.

From the nature of the case the teacher has two main tasks. He must first lay hold on those who have hitherto been indifferent to philosophy and then, when they have been roused and awakened, he must guide them on the painful path of progress toward virtue. A similar distinction has been made by the Christian preachers of every age. Sometimes they address the world, *i. e.*, the unconverted, at other times the Church, *i. e.*, the converted. Epictetus makes his appeal in the first instance to the natural capacity for virtue in every man. "Have you not received," he asks, "faculties by which you will be able to bear all that happens, such faculties as magnanimity, courage, endurance? And yet God has not only given us these faculties, but with truly regal and paternal goodness He has given them free from hinderance, subject to no compulsion, unimpeded, and has put them entirely in our power. You have received these powers free and as your own, but you do not use them." [1] "God has made all men to be happy, to be steadfast. To this end He has furnished the means, some things to each person as his own and other things not as his own; some things subject to hinderance and compulsion and deprivation; and these things are not a man's own; but the things which are subject to no hinderances are his own; and the nature of good and evil, as became His paternal care and protection, He has made our own." [2] "What, then, is a man's nature? To bite, to kick, to throw into prison, and

[1] Arrian, *Discourses of Epictetus*, I, 6, 28 *sq.*, 42 *sq.*
[2] *Ib.*, III, 24, 3.

to behead? No, but to do good, to co-operate with others, to wish them well."[1] "What is human excellence?" asks Epictetus of one of his hearers, and proceeds: "Observe whom you yourself praise when you praise without partiality? Do you praise the just or the unjust, the moderate or the immoderate, the temperate or the intemperate?"[2] Man, then, has by nature the capacity to find out and know the truth. He has on the one hand the moral intuitions technically known as preconceptions. On the other hand he has reason and intellect in order to develop these preconceptions and convert them by the aid of experience into useful standards for the judgment of reality. Even when undeveloped, preconceptions fit a man for the vague apprehension of moral truth. "There are certain things which men who are not altogether perverted see by the common notions which all possess."[3] Epictetus credits all men with modesty and a sense of shame. "Nature has given to me modesty, and I blush much when I think of saying anything base."[4] This sense of shame, however, can be hardened and deadened.[5] To be sure, preconceptions are in themselves mere germs which are brought to maturity, either by reflection and meditation or by instruction and teaching. Socrates and Zeno show how man can arrive unaided at moral truth; but the mass of men grow up with perverted views, so that in their case instruction is necessary. With the true instinct of a teacher Epictetus tries to do justice to both facts, that virtue is essentially simple and resides in man's own nature, and yet at the same time, that it is only to be attained by continual toil, effort, and self-

---

[1] Arrian, IV, 1, 122.   [2] Ib., III, 1, 8.
[3] Ib., III, 6, 8.   [4] Ib., Fragment 52.   [5] Ib., I, 5.

discipline. It is a pedagogic device to present morality to the pupil, not as something abnormal, but as something close at hand, something which he has really himself willed and often unconsciously practised. Philosophy is thus a means to a deeper knowledge of that with which all men are already familiar even without special instruction. Ordinary men are inconsistent. Some things they judge disgraceful; other things no less shameful they wrongly refuse to term so. Such a partial or superficial virtue is of no great value. It is no true virtue, since it does not rest on a right view of life. Nevertheless, it is a starting-point for moral instruction. In arguing against the Epicureans, Epictetus urges that their conduct is better than their principles. They are like their master, teaching what is bad, practising what is good.[1] "Epicurus disowned all manly offices, those of a father of a family, of a citizen, of a friend; but he did not, for he could not, disown the instincts of human nature any more than the lazy Academics can cast away or blind their own senses, though they have tried with all their might to do it. What a shame it is when a man has received from nature measures and rules for the knowing of truth and does not strive to add to these measures and rules and to improve them, but, just the contrary, endeavours to take away and destroy whatever enables us to discern the truth."[2]

Seneca is completely in agreement on this point. The capacity for virtue is found in all, though in some to a greater degree than others. Even in the bad, this natural endowment is not extinct, though weighed down and obscured.[3] All alike, even the most gifted, need philosophic instruction, if this

[1] Arrian, III, 7, 18.   [2] *Ib.*, III, 20, 20.   [3] Seneca, *Ep.*, 94, 31.

capacity is to be fully developed.[1] In practice
Epictetus treats sin as a fact needing no explanation,
as an infatuation which can be removed by instruction. He appeals to the sinner to will to be instructed
and makes this the really decisive factor in conversion. No one sins of his own free-will; you
have only to will and you are good. "How is this
to be done?" he asks. "How is the victory over
such passions as anger, lust, and avarice to be obtained?" "Will at length to win your own approval, will to appear beautiful to God, desire to
dwell in purity with your own pure self and with
God."[2] "Be well assured that nothing is more
tractable than the human soul. You must exercise
your will and the thing is done, it is set right; as
on the other hand relax your vigilance and all is
lost, for from within comes ruin and from within
comes help. Then you say, What good do I gain?
And what greater good do you seek than this?
From a shameless man you will become modest;
from a disorderly man you will become orderly;
from a faithless man, faithful; from a man of un-
bridled habits, sober."[3] It has already been stated
that to the Stoics sin, like truth and right, admits of
no degrees. The paradox that all sins are equal
means that a perverted direction of the will is manifest in every sin, however trivial. The sins may
differ in the objects to which they refer, but not from
the point of view of the moral judgment. They all
come from the same source, and in all the judgment
is the same, i. e., it is perverse. If sin is transgression, how far the transgressor goes astray makes no
difference to the guilt, which consists in transgressing

[1] *Ib.*, 95, 36; 94, 32; 90, 44.   [2] Arrian, II, 18, 19.
[3] *Ib.*, IV, 9, 16.

bounds at all. The intention, the pleasure in the contemplation of an action is just as heinous as the actual deed, and the omission of the good is equally sinful with the doing of the bad. In the task of instruction the pupil must co-operate with his teacher; he must make the instruction his own. As Epictetus says, "This only is given to you, to convince yourself; and yet you have not convinced yourself. Then I ask you, Do you attempt to persuade other men ? And who has lived so long with you as you with yourself ? And who has so much power of convincing you as you have of convincing yourself ? And who is better disposed and nearer to you than you are to yourself ? How, then, have you not yet convinced yourself in order to learn ?" [1]   "Now will you not help yourself ? And how much easier is this help ? There is no need to kill or imprison any man or to treat him with contumely or to go into the law courts. You must just talk to yourself. You will be most easily persuaded; no one has more power to persuade you than yourself." [2]   All this presupposes the existence of good impulses in the man, to which the evil impulses of his previous life yield easily.

The conception of progress dominates the writings of Seneca and Epictetus. Seneca in one passage declares that this progress on the way to virtue, which it is the aim of all instruction to promote, is virtue itself. The road cannot be dissevered from the goal. [3]   The first step is the recognition of sin, ignorance, and infatuation. This is accompanied by remorse, which, in itself a vicious, reprehensible emotion, is in the beginner relatively necessary and

[1] Arrian, IV, 6, 5.   [2] *Ib.*, IV, 9, 13.
[3] Seneca, *Ep.*, 89, 8: "ad virtutem venitur per ipsam."

wholesome. He must rid himself of his darkness, and acquire a correct standard for judging good and evil. But this is slow work and needs not only instruction, but also meditation and self-discipline. Daily self-examination is prescribed,[1] and watchfulness against evil inclinations and temptations to sin.[2] Every failure strengthens the evil habit.[3] At the same time failures and backslidings should be no ground for discouragement.[4] Persevere, says Epictetus, hold aloof from old companions, and avoid occupations and pleasures which you are not yet strong enough to resist.[5] Avoid even what is permitted, if it tend to weaken your new convictions. Lastly, be ever on your guard against the evil self that lurks within.[6] Exercise your will negatively by aversion only, and let desire fall for the present into abeyance.[7] Behave like a convalescent in dread of a relapse.[8] Set Socrates or Zeno or Cleanthes before you, and measure your conduct by that standard.[9] This is a period of wavering and wandering, yet it differs from the old evil life and it will give place to stronger convictions. If the convictions have once taken root, the worst is over, and the convert will grow stronger and make progress. It is impossible to glance at these and similar precepts without being struck by the analogy, partially in substance and still more in method, between the moral teaching of Stoicism and that of the New Testament. Both Stoics and Christians regard the life of progress as one continual struggle in which nothing short of the utmost effort, vigilance, and in-

---

[1] Arrian, IV, 6, 34.   [2] *Ib.*, III, 16, 15.   [3] *Ib.*, II, 18, 4.
[4] *Ib.*, IV, 19, 16.   [5] *Ib.*, IV, 2, 1; III, 12, 12.
[6] *Ib.*, *Encheiridion*, 48.   [7] *Ib.*, I, 4, 1; *Encheiridion*, 2.
[8] *Ib.*, III, 13, 21; *Encheiridion*, 48.   [9] *Ib.*, III, 23, 32.

sight, conjoined with courage, patience, and endurance, can insure the victory. By both the war is waged against the same enemies, the world of appearances without and the treacherous self within, and with hardly an exception the Apostle's "works of the flesh" and "fruits of the spirit"[1] can be identified with the vices and virtues of the Stoics.

Seneca acquaints us with a scheme of classification by which those who are in progress toward virtue were arranged in three classes.[2] The principle of division is the more or less complete eradication of vicious emotions. The lowest class includes those who have broken with some of their sins but not with all. Above them are ranked in the second class men who, dissatisfied with this inconsistency, have resolved to renounce evil passions in general though they are still liable to occasional relapses. Those in the highest class approximate to wisdom and perfect virtue. Nor is it easy to see where they fall short of it. They are said to have got beyond the possibility of relapse but to lack confidence in themselves and the consciousness of their own wisdom. This subtle distinction forcibly recalls the doctrine of "assurance" so widely maintained since the Reformation by various sections of evangelical Protestants. Upon closer examination it cannot be said that these distinctions are marked by any hard and fast line. The three classes tend to shade off into each other. Quite apart from the fact that the very idea of progress implies variation, wavering, and alteration, much might be said for another threefold division of which there are some traces. All under instruction would then be divided into (1) converts or novices, (2) proficients, i. e., all who

[1] Galatians, V, 19, 22.　　　[2] Seneca, *Ep.*, 75, 8.

are still making some progress, whatever grade
they have reached, (3) those whose education is
complete.[1] This last class Seneca expressly sepa-
rates from the wise. They are in port, he says, but
they have not yet landed. They are within sight
of wisdom and only a stone's throw off it, but they
are not there.

Epictetus, who is constantly urging his hearers
on and on, certainly makes no attempt like Seneca to
separate them into definite classes. Instead of
doing so, he is chiefly concerned with a course of instruction and discipline which he regards as necessary for all. In this course there are three stages,
the first relating to desire and aversion, the second
to impulse and action, the third to judgment and
assent. The novelty here is that a Stoic should
separate the species desire from its genus impulse,
under which it was ordinarily subsumed. So far
as we know, this separation was original in Epictetus,
and was probably dictated by practical considerations, for, though undoubtedly orthodox, he everywhere treats the theoretical side of his system with
great freedom. In his discourses physic, ethic, and
logic are intermingled, according to the needs of the
particular subject and occasion. Even the order of
succession of his three stages serves a purely practical and educational purpose. The first stage is
intended to secure in the pupil a right attitude of
mind toward external things and events. By it he
is taught to shape desire in accordance with reason.
The outcome is that freedom from morbid emotions,
that tranquillity which the Stoics called apathy.
In the second stage the mind so trained is directed
to action. Having learned to recognise true good,

[1] Seneca, *Ep.*, 72, 10.

which is also his true interest, the pupil is practised
in the performance of those duties which are incumbent upon him in the various relations he sustains
to the universe at large and to his fellow-creatures.
He is taught how he is to act as a devout man, as a
father, a son, a brother, a citizen, a member of the
world-commonwealth, and not only in those relationships to which he is born, but in those upon which
he has entered by voluntary association with others.
The problem is, How does the right view of life
realise itself in all these moral relationships through
action? Hence this second stage may be fairly described as dealing with the whole range of duty
(Kathēkon), duty to self, to God, to one's neighbour,
and to mankind at large. The third stage is more
advanced. Epictetus expressly recommends its post-
ponement until proficiency has been attained in the
other two. It consists mainly of such a thorough
logical training as will insure an unerring judgment,
a judgment which cannot be shaken by reasoning,
and in particular by the sophisms and fallacies of
opponents. By the first and second stages the pupil
has been taught to make his will and his action conform to certain principles, *e. g.*, he has learned not
to lie and why he ought not to lie. The third stage
is intended to confirm him in these principles, to
safeguard the reasonings on which they depend, to
render the demonstration of them secure and im-
pervious to assault, and to endow his every act of
judgment and assent with unshakable firmness.
But we will cite our author's own words: "There are
three subjects in which a man ought to exercise himself, if he would be wise and good. The first deals
with the desires and aversions, and its object is that
we may not fail to get what we desire and may never

fall into that which we would fain avoid. The second deals with the impulses or movements toward things or away from things, and generally with the performance of what is suitable" (Kathēkon). "Its object is that our conduct may be regular, reasonable, and not careless. The third deals with the elimination of deception and rash judgment and with assent generally. Of these subjects the chief and most urgent is the first which deals with vicious passions, for their sole cause is our failing to obtain what we desire and falling into that which we would fain avoid. Hence come perturbations, tumults, discomfitures, sorrows, lamentations, envyings, all of which prevent us from even hearing the voice of reason. The second subject is the suitable or duty. I ought not to be unfeeling like a statue, but I ought to cherish my relationships, whether natural or voluntarily formed, as a pious man, as a son, as a brother, as a father, as a citizen. The third subject begins to be incumbent when some progress has been attained. Its aim is to make the other two secure, so that even in sleep, intoxication, or hypochondria we may not let any presentation pass untested." [1]

That the aim of the third subject or topic is not theoretical, but directly moral and practical, may be seen from the censure passed upon those who would engage in it before they have mastered the first and second. "As if all your affairs were well and secure, you were busy with the final subject, that of unshakable firmness. But what would you make unshakably firm? Cowardice, mean spirit, the admiration of the rich, futile desire, avoidance which fails of its end. These are the things about whose security you have been anxious." [2] The result of

<hr>

[1] Arrian, III, 2.   [2] *Ib*., III, 26, 14.

this hurrying on to the last stage before the desires and impulses have been properly disciplined is neatly satirised thus: "Therefore we lie, but the demonstration that we ought not to lie we have at our fingers' ends." [1]

It is remarkable that in several passages Epictetus disclaims for himself any special aptitude for this, the most advanced stadium of instruction. He almost implies that it should be left to professed logicians. And yet many of his discourses are taken from it, and he is always sound on the theoretical issue that without such an unswerving rectitude of judgment no one can reach the highest level of progress, or so much as approximate to the ideal of the wise and good. But the dialectical certainty which these higher logical studies promote is only valuable as the necessary condition for moral certainty and infallibility. In thus separating the three stages of instruction, Epictetus must have had the needs of his pupils before his eyes. He wishes them to undergo from first to last a course of discipline (Askēsis), and, though the three stages are distinct, it is impossible to concentrate attention exclusively, first upon the will and desires, later upon the impulses and actions. Nor could the pupil become mature in these two lower stages without acquiring in a great degree that unerring certainty of judgment which it is the especial object of the third stage to secure. Doubtless the formal separation of three stages was expedient, not only for the pupil, but also for his instructor. But the discourses of the master preserved to us by Arrian are not so arranged; indeed, in the miscellaneous character of their contents and the choice of themes suggested by

[1] *Ib., Encheiridion*, 51.

trivial incidents or everyday occurrences, and in the absence of method and order they resemble the sermons of too many modern preachers. When, however, we come to take stock of the material so collected, it is obvious that Epictetus laid the greatest stress upon the first stage. This was the root of the whole matter; all subsequent improvement starts with this. The right attitude consists, first and foremost, in emancipation from evil passions. This is its negative side. But Epictetus insists repeatedly upon the positive side, the rational and permissible emotions, submission to the divine will, confidence as regards the future course of events, the peace of mind, the holy joy and gratitude which accompany the bringing of the will into harmony with reason. The second stage is intended to render the agent blameless and free from offence in all that he is impelled to do. It translates the inwardness of the reasonable will into particular resolves, which produce a multiplicity of external actions. In a hasty review we shall consider what Epictetus inculcates respecting duties (1) to self, (2) to God, (3) to one's neighbour, singling out special points for emphasis and comparison.

(1) The duties of personal perfection begin with cleanliness and proper care of the body. The body is the nearest object to a man, and in dealing with it he can show his faithfulness in little things. As far as possible, it must be preserved in its natural condition. Even in the totally uneducated (Epictetus uses this term to designate what a Christian teacher would call the unregenerate) some attention to the body is a hopeful sign, as implying something which the teacher can work upon. "I indeed would rather," says Epictetus, "that a young man, when

first moved to philosophy, should come to me with
his hair carefully trimmed, than with it dirty and
rough. For then he is seen to have a certain notion
of beauty and a love of what is becoming; and where
he supposes it to be, there also he strives that it
shall be. It is only necessary to show him what
beauty is and to say, 'Young man, you seek beauty
and you do well; you must know, then, that it springs
up in that part of you where you have the rational
faculty. Seek it there, where you have your impulses to strive for things and to avoid them, where
are your desires and aversions. For this is the
nobler part of yourself, but the poor body is by
nature only clay; why labour about it to no purpose ?' " [1] The whole discourse from which this is
taken has for its subject cleanliness or purity. We
see that the body is a little thing in his eyes, but the
preconception or intuition of beauty is something
which affords a starting-point for the teacher. He
has esteem and sympathy for the career of the
athlete, involving, as it must, endurance of hardship and strict discipline, and justifies the suicide
of the mutilated Olympian victor as the act, not of
an athlete or of a philosopher, but of a man.[2] But
he never forgets that the athlete holds a mistaken
view of life; all he does is for the sake of glory and
therefore from the wrong motive.[3] Next come
the duties of temperance, modesty, and chastity.
That a man should be temperate is taken for granted;
there is no need to urge men to nurture the body;
they must rather be warned against pampering
and surfeiting it. On one point, the use of wine,
Stoic opinion was divided. Some condemned, others
admitted, the use of wine beyond bare needs, and

[1] Arrian, IV, 11, 25.   [2] *Ib.*, I, 2, 26.   [3] *Ib.*, III, 12, 16.

those who maintained that even in intoxication the sage would preserve his reason must have condoned even a generous or undue indulgence. Epictetus holds the middle position. Sobriety with him is on the same footing as decency and modesty. That he should allow any drinking beyond natural necessity must be explained by the Stoic principle of accommodating or adapting one's self to established custom in social intercourse. Chastity is dealt with in the thirty-third section of the *Encheiridion*. The demands there made, if they do not in some points quite satisfy the Christian standard, are far in advance of the conventional code of the world either of his or of our own day. That the teacher should cherish a pure affection for a promising pupil capable of moral improvement was a survival, we may say, from old Greek habits and associations. In various passages it is recognised by Epictetus, but he does not call this zeal for education by the invidious name of love, nor does he regard it as associated with personal beauty in the pupil; and as to the purity of his regard there is absolutely no question. The retention of the old term love under these altered circumstances exposed the Stoics to the taunt that they loved men when at their ugliest, because destitute of moral beauty, and ceased to love them when by education they had attained to true beauty. It would be just as unfair to taunt the modern missionary with his enthusiastic zeal for the conversion of very unattractive heathen. The fruit of philosophy is the extirpation of the passion for sensual beauty and the cultivation of the love of moral beauty. Sexual love was, as Seneca defined it, *insana amicitia*, and Musonius courageously demands from men the same self-control as even

in his day men demanded from women. That
Epictetus himself was no stranger to the passion
may be inferred from a curious remark on the love
of philosophy: "If any one among you has been
in love with a charming girl, he knows that what I
say is true." [1] His language often reminds us of the
sermon on the mount.[2] The subject of the fourth
discourse of the second Book is an outspoken de-
nunciation of an adulterer who had the audacity
to present himself at a lecture. "How shall I consider you, man? As a neighbour, as a friend?
What kind of one? As a citizen? Wherein shall I
trust you? So if you were an utensil, so worthless,
that no one could use you, you would be pitched
out on to the dung heaps, and no man would pick
you up. But if, being a man, you are unable to
fill any place which befits a man, what is to be
done with you? For suppose that you cannot
hold the place of a friend, can you hold the place of a
slave? And who will trust you? Must not you
also submit to be thrown on a dung heap as a useless utensil?" With this scathing rebuke compare
St. Matthew, V, 13.[3]

The importance he attached to decency, personal
dignity, modesty, and propriety led him to discounte-
nance gossip and idle talk, and the novice is recommended to maintain a discreet silence in society,
unless he can turn the conversation to serious
themes.[4] A passive, almost quietistic demeanour
toward the external goods of life is inculcated, quite
distinct from any tendency to asceticism. He lays
down no such rules about dress as Musonius did, nor

---

[1] Arrian, III, 5, 19.
[2] *Cf.* Arrian, II, 18, 15, with St. Matthew, V, 28.
[3] *Cf.* also Arrian, III, 7, 21; II, 8, 13.   [4] *Encheiridion*, 33.

was he, like him, a vegetarian. Musonius was far
removed from Diogenes, and Epictetus still further.
At the same time Epictetus was too fond of denouncing as effeminate luxury whatever exceeds
simplicity. With the luxuries he rejects all the comforts of life, even a cushion, and it is odd that he
should recommend the simplest furniture on the
ground that anything beyond this might be a temptation, either to ourselves or to others, to steal. Nor
is this extreme simplicity altogether consistent with
passages in which servants, the use of wine, and the
enjoyment of objects of art are permitted. Besides, he is quite clear that asceticism in any form
is only a means to an end, a discipline to secure
moral freedom, relatively necessary, but not in itself
an essential phase of the moral life. To personal
example he attributes more influence than to all
doctrine. For this reason the ideal preacher or
missionary, whom he calls the Cynic, occupies an
exceptional position. His extreme asceticism is
not a pattern for general imitation, but is practised
as an extraordinary means for the improvement of
the masses, just as total abstinence is by some advocated to-day in the cause of social reform. Epictetus is quite convinced that we must not plume ourselves on moderation and abstinence, and that the
moral life is just as possible amid external splendour
as in poverty. Veracity is conditioned by loyalty,
openness, and candour, which were always Stoic
ideals. In one passage the Stoic convert is forbidden to take an oath, so far as he can avoid it.[1] The
ancient commentator, Simplicius, attributed this prohibition to religious grounds, because it dishon-
ours God to call Him to witness for trivial things.

[1] Arrian, *Encheiridion*, 33.

More probably the prohibition is founded on the high importance attached to veracity. If veracity is implicit, the oath is unnecessary, and we are reminded of the usage of the Quakers with its appeal to the Gospel precept: "Let your Yea be Yea and your Nay, Nay." It is a well-worn question of casuistry whether the truth must under all circumstances be spoken. The Stoics permitted the necessary lie, if it be for the good of our neighbours.

Epictetus insists strongly on the dignity of labour. Earn your own living, he says; be independent. No employment is unworthy of the sage; manual toil is as honourable as statesmanship. A life of unemployed leisure is as bad as a life of ambition and the greedy pursuit of office. Such a pronouncement is all the more refreshing because it runs counter to a rooted prejudice of the Greek mind. Manual toil in Homer is honourable, but, as the Greeks advanced in civilisation during historical times, they came to despise both industrial and agricultural labour. The occupations which had once been consigned to slaves were no longer regarded as fit for free men.[1] That this prejudice was shared by the heterodox Stoic Panætius is clear from Cicero's treatise *De Officiis*, and it is greatly to the credit of the humble slave of Hierapolis that he returned to the sounder views indorsed by the Semitic founder of his school. Economic independence, then, is incumbent on every one's honour. But there are difficulties and pitfalls even here. Wealth has its value in the class of things preferred. That being

---

[1] Even more remarkable is the trace which this prejudice has left in the Greek language. Thus the adjective Ponēros, which originally meant toilsome, laborious, changed its meaning to that of bad and evil, or even wicked in the modern sense.

so, the duty of adding to one's wealth is clear, provided no moral interest be sacrificed; and to squander
money is as wrong as to squander health. The
acquisition of riches cannot be justified by the motive of benevolence, by the prospect of being able to
help one's friend or one's country; for the merit of
doing one's duty is not enhanced by large possessions; [1] witness the widow's mite of the Gospel.
Set not your heart on riches is the precept of Epictetus. All exertion for external things is reprehensible, if the object sought is treated as an end
in itself instead of a means to the moral life, if it be
pursued for the sake of external success rather than
as an outlet for mental activity. As things are,
Epictetus recognises that the gain of wealth generally
means the loss of modesty, fidelity, and magnanimity.
His sentiments on the pursuit of worldly honours
and of wealth are frankly stated in a passage of the
Encheiridion as follows: "Let not these thoughts
afflict you. I shall live unhonoured and be nobody
and nowhere. For if want of honour is an evil,
you cannot be in evil through the fault of another,
any more than you can be involved in anything base.
Is it then your business to obtain the rank of a magis-
trate or to be received at a banquet? By no means.
How, then, can this be want of honour? And how
will you be nobody and nowhere, when you ought
to be somebody in those things only which are in
your power, in which, indeed, it is permitted to you
to be a man of the greatest worth? But your friends
will be without assistance! What do you mean by
being without assistance? They will not receive
money from you nor will you make them Roman
citizens. Who, then, told you that these are among

[1] *Encheiridion*, 24.

the things which are in our power and not in the power of others? And who can give to another what he has not himself? Acquire money then, your friends say, that we also may have something. If I can acquire money, and also keep myself modest and faithful and magnanimous, point out the way and I will acquire it. But if you ask me to lose the things which are good and my own, in order that you may gain the things which are not good, see how unfair and silly you are. Besides, which would you rather have, money or a faithful and modest friend? For this end, then, rather help me to be such a man, and do not ask me to do that by which I shall lose this character. But my country, you say, so far as it depends on me, will be without my help. I ask again, what help do you mean? It will not have porticoes or baths through you. And what does this mean? For it is not furnished with shoes by means of a smith nor with arms by means of a shoemaker. But it is enough if every man fully discharges the work that is his own; and if you provided it with another citizen, faithful and modest, would you not be useful to it? Yes. Then you, also, cannot be useless to it. What place, then, you say, shall I hold in the city? Whatever you can, if you maintain at the same time your fidelity and modesty. But if when you wish to be useful to the state you shall lose these qualities, what profit could you be to it if you were made shameless and faithless?" [1]

(2) Since all moral action may be summed up in the formula "to reverence God, imitate Him and obey Him," the term "duty to God" must be restricted to acts of worship and religious observance.

[1] *Encheiridion*, 24.

"As to piety toward the gods," says Epictetus, "you must know that this is the chief thing, to have right opinions about them, to think that they exist, and that they administer the All well and justly; and you must fix yourself in this principle, to obey them and to yield to them in everything which happens, and voluntarily to follow it as being accomplished by the wisest intelligence. For if you do so, you will never either blame the gods, nor will you accuse them of neglecting you. And it is not possible for this to be done in any other way than by withdrawing from the things which are not in our power, and by placing the good and the evil in those things only which *are* in our power. He who takes care to desire as he ought and to avoid as he ought, by so doing also takes care to be pious. But to make libations and to sacrifice, and to offer first fruits according to the custom of our fathers, purely and not meanly nor carelessly, nor scantily, nor above our ability, is a thing which belongs to all to do."[1]

It will presently be seen how closely the Stoic conception of true piety agrees in the main with the views of the opposite school as laid down by Epicurus,[2] subject, of course, to the fundamental divergence of opinion which must always exist between two schools, when one affirms and the other denies a moral purpose in the government of the universe. Epictetus insists before all things upon right convictions. He believes that some dogmas are necessary to religion. In the next place, the outcome of these views is submission to the divine will and the course of Providence. No one but the sage is capable of this; he alone knows the true value of things,

[1] *Encheiridion*, 31.　　　　[2] *Cf.* pp. 168, 172, 200, 289, 298.

and impiety in a greater or less degree is inevitable in those who have not this knowledge. When these great results are secured, the external manifestations of piety follow as a matter of course, in accordance with the use and ritual of our fathers, *i. e.*, of the particular society into which we are born, but it must always be with sincerity. Epictetus was no innovator. He accepted from the popular religion the whole of its cultus as well as divination. But cults and ritual are only valuable to him when they proceed from right convictions and inward piety. So far from recommending compliance as a concession to human weakness,[1] he held that none but the wise man could perform the external acts properly. Whatever the views held by earlier Stoics, it is not true of Epictetus that he did not share the beliefs of the multitude.[2] He continually attacks the godless Epicureans and the Sceptics of the Academy because, by their teaching, popular morality, patriotism and the love of truth were undermined. He could not make this a reproach against them, if he himself shared their views. On the contrary, like the fearless, fanatical dogmatist he was, he could only explain the stand-point of his opponents by their moral degeneracy. They had cast off and deadened shame, and therefore their philosophy was all frivolity and their teaching frigid subtleties. "Grateful, indeed, and modest are men who, if they do nothing else, are daily eating bread, and yet are shameless enough to say, We do not know if there is a Ceres or her daughter Proserpine or a Pluto."[3] Such is his in-

---

[1] Zeller, *Stoics, Epicureans, and Sceptics*, c, XIII.
[2] Zeller, *Ib.*; also Hirzel, *Untersuchungen*, II, p. 878, with especial reference to the attitude of Polybius the historian to the popular faith.
[3] Arrian, III, 20, 32.

dignant protest: could it have found expression if he
had not shared the beliefs of the multitude?

But how, it may be asked, is the polytheism
of the national faith to be reconciled with the many
pantheistic and even monotheistic utterances so common in Epictetus? It may be remarked that, though
he uses God in the singular and gods in the plural
indifferently, the singular predominates, and we
may conclude that the plural form implies a single
force, a single will, which in truth surrenders
polytheism. Moreover, Zeus alone is eternal. He
is the father of gods as well as men; the other deities
are transitory. He has created them and assigned
them their several spheres of operation. He uses
them as ministers and co-regents. They execute
His will and no more prejudice His omnipotence than
the angels of Judaism and Christianity. Zeus is
primitive substance which has produced all the
other divinities. They are the first creation at the
end of every cosmical epoch, and so Epictetus is
entitled to use the plural. Zeus is omnipotent;
there are no limits to His sovereignty. On this
point Epictetus often recalls the Old Testament, *e. g.*,
Psalm CIV, Isaiah, XLV. "When asked how a
man could be convinced that all his actions are done
in the sight of God, he answered, Do you not think
that all things are united in one? I do, was the reply.
Well, do you not think that things on earth have a
natural agreement and union with things in heaven?
I do. And how else so regularly as if by God's
command, when He bids the plants to flower, do
they flower? How is it that when He bids them to
send forth shoots, they shoot; when He bids them
to bear fruit, they bear fruit; when He bids the
fruit to ripen, it ripens; when again He bids them

drop their fruit, they drop it; when He bids them
shed their leaves, they shed their leaves; and when
He bids them fold themselves up and remain quiet
and at rest, they remain quiet and at rest?"[1]   The
tendency to a monotheistic conception becomes
clearer when the other attributes of God, omnipresence and omniscience, are considered. We have
seen that God is everywhere. Because He is everywhere no thought is hidden from Him.[2]   And yet
this spiritual being is not pronounced immaterial,
though His substance is the finest and the purest
ether. Physical purity, mental strength, and moral
goodness always go together for Epictetus, as for the
rest of his school. That pantheism should occasionally employ monotheistic expressions is not more surprising in Epictetus than in Cleanthes.

A further objection must be stated. Since external things are of secondary importance, is it not
inconsistent to pray for them? And, since the only
true good is in man's own power to procure, is not
prayer for it unnecessary? May it not be argued in
like manner that all acts of worship are at most symbolical? How else except as a symbol could sheaves
and cattle be offered to a spiritual being? Is not a
song of thankfulness in the heart and admiration
of His works sufficient worship? Seneca is very
outspoken[3] and declares all religious observances
futile. But the wise man will observe them in the
interests of civil law and order, and justify them as
symbolical expressions of a pious frame of mind.
Seneca also holds that the gods have left some
things in suspense to be prayed for. Prayers are
offered, not to compel the gods to help, but to remind

---

[1] Arrian, I, 14, 1 *sqq.*   [2] *Ib.*, I, 14, 1; II, 14, 11.
[3] *Epist.* 41, 1; *Nat. Quaest,* ii. 35, 1.

them of human circumstances. This reminder has subjective not objective value. Man is his own accuser, his own judge, his own intercessor and pardoner, *in foro conscientiæ*. But Epictetus, in upholding the popular faith, had the authority of his master, Musonius, who even recommended prayer for external goods. With this we may compare Marcus Aurelius: "An Athenian prayer, 'Rain, rain, dear Zeus, upon Athenian tilth and plains.' We should either not pray at all or else in this simple, noble sort." [1] Marcus Aurelius speaks of "sacrifice and prayer and oaths and all other observances by which we own the presence and the nearness of the gods." [2] True obedience to God, he holds, consists in obedience to His law. "Live with the gods. And he lives with the gods who ever presents to them his soul accepting their dispensations and busied about the will of God, even that particle of Zeus which Zeus gives to every man for his controller and governor—to wit, his mind and reason." [3] Like Seneca, he would have us pray chiefly for what is really good, for emancipation from evil passions, and the like. His own prayerfulness is attested by his words: "Solace your departure with the reflection: 'I am leaving a life in which my own associates, for whom I have so striven, prayed, and thought, themselves wish for my removal, their hope being that they will perchance gain something in freedom thereby.'" [4]

(3) It has already been said that social duties rest upon our relationships to others, either born with the individual or voluntarily entered upon by him. First come the family relationships. The day had long been past when they were open to

---

[1] Marcus Aurelius, V, 7.   [2] *Ib.*, VI, 44.
[3] *Ib.*, V, 27.   [4] *Ib.*, X, 36.

serious discussion. The founders of the school had, indeed, raised the question whether nature invariably intended mankind for monogamy and separate family life, or whether, in a higher state, community of wives and children was not reason's more perfect way. But the question even then was purely theoretical and had no practical consequences. By the later Stoics, at any rate, the monogamic family was accepted and upheld as the natural basis of existing society. Accordingly, marriage and the rearing of families were encouraged as in strict conformity with reason.[1] Epictetus allows a special dispensation in the case of his ideal missionary or Cynic, but he will remain unmarried solely in order that he may be unimpeded in his arduous task.[2] Besides insisting on the primary duty of fidelity in both husband and wife, the later Stoics were much interested in the position of women. Musonius did not wish men and women to have the same occupations; but he defended the right of women to education, and was even anxious that girls should be taught philosophy. The objections to this proposal he met with arguments much the same as those at present urged by the advocates of female education.[3] He was, of course, thinking primarily of moral education, and he refused to allow that, if his principles were consistently carried out, women would be taught athletics and men spinning. In all that concerns morality he firmly maintained the equality of the sexes, and his disciple, Epictetus, also seems to countenance the education of girls. Seneca dwells with appreciation on the heroic deeds of women,[4] and even in his keen criticism of the

[1] Arrian, III, 7, 26.　　　　　　　[2] *Ib.*, III, 22, 67.
[3] Stobæus, *Eclogæ* 235 *sqq.*, 244 *sqq.* (W.).　　[4] Ad Helviam, 19, 5.

women of his own time,[1] he is anxious to uphold an
ideal of that womanly excellence of which his mother,
Helvia, his wife, Paulina, and Marcia, the daughter
of Cremutius Cordus, were types.   The love of
parents for their offspring was an ordinance of
nature, and Epictetus sarcastically observes that the
parents of Epicurus would not have disowned him
even if they had foreseen the principles their son
would afterward advocate.   And again he argues
that if parental love had not been founded in nature,
Epicurus would not have taken such pains to dis-
suade men from marriage and family life.   Epictetus requires unlimited obedience of children in all
matters indifferent, irrespective of the character of
the parent.   Nothing short of a command to do
something which is immoral justifies the child in
disobeying.   His conception of these elementary
duties can be gathered from the following: "After
this, remember that you are a son.   What does this
character promise?   To consider that everything
which is the son's belongs to the father, to obey him
in all things, never to blame him to another nor to
say or do anything which does him injury, to yield
to him in all things and give way, co-operating with
him as far as you can.   After this, know that you
are a brother, also, and that to this character it is
due to make concessions; to be easily persuaded,
to speak good of your brother, never to claim in
opposition to him any of the things which are independent of the will, but readily to give them up
that you may have the larger share in what is dependent on the will.   For see what a thing it is, in place
of a lettuce, if it should so happen, or a seat, to gain
for yourself goodness of disposition.   How great is

[1] *E. g.*, Ad Helviam, 17, 4.

the advantage." [1] That these were not mere copy-book maxims, but that under favourable circumstances they bore excellent fruit, may be seen from the touching way in which the Stoic emperor gratefully reviews all that he conceives himself to have owed to his father, mother, and brother.[2]

As regards civic duties, the position of the Stoics was peculiar. They were at once conservative and radical. Patriotism, they maintained, and active participation in public life is a duty which has its foundation in human nature. But the duty is conditioned by the assumption that external circumstances conform to reason, which, as a matter of fact, they seldom do. Hence, whether they did or did not take part in civil affairs, they were open to the reproach of inconsistency. Seneca urges that when they draw back, it is not that they shrink from the trouble of political activity, but that they fear to lose their self-respect owing to the corruption of the times. No doubt the excuse was often abused, but it comes strangely from the minister of Nero, who cannot escape all responsibility for some of that tyrant's worst crimes. Plutarch, on the other hand, holds that the greater inconsistency is for the Stoic to engage in public affairs at all.[3] That the first founders of the school, Zeno, Cleanthes, and Chrysippus, should have taken no part in political life admits of easy explanation. They were foreign residents at Athens, and not Athenian citizens, and Seneca is entitled to claim for them that by their career as teachers they effected far greater good than they could have done by holding any public offices. But it is idle to deny that cosmopolitanism

---

[1] Arrian, II, 10, 7.   [2] Marcus Aurelius, I, 2, 3, 14, 16, 17.
[3] Plutarch, *De Stoicorum Repugnantiis*, c. 3.

is, in the long run, incompatible with a restricted patriotism. The idea of a man's discharging his human mission only as a member of some one nation or state, the idea which dominated Rome, and was the source at once of her strength and her weakness, was foreign to Stoicism. The condition of existing states, even of the Roman empire, was so far from his ideal that the Stoic could not serve in any of them with honest enthusiasm. Besides, his depreciation of external goods hindered him from bringing real interest to bear on the economic and progressive tasks of any community. Nevertheless, though inconsistently, the Stoics defended patriotism and the duty of altruistic effort, and enjoined on magistrates faithful and conscientious care for the common good. This duty is especially emphasised by Marcus Aurelius, whose example far outweighed his precepts, for he wore himself out in the toils and labours of his imperial office. Epictetus holds that faithful service in public office is a natural instinct, which man can no more resist than the instinct to love and care for his children. Man is, by nature, adapted and inclined for society and the formation of fellowships and work for the common good. He himself would like to die while performing some noble and beneficent service of public utility. He thus explains his conception of citizenship: "It is to have no selfish private interest, to deliberate about nothing as if he were detached from the rest, but to act as the hand or foot would do if they had reason and could obey the arrangements of nature, for they would have no desire, no impulse which had not reference to the whole." [1] This ideal temper made the Stoic a quiet and harmless citizen.

[1] Arrian, II, 10, 4.

War was universally condemned; it was always the result of blindness and infatuation. Musonius nearly lost his life by his courageous interposition in the last stage of the civil conflict between Vitellius and Vespasian, when he harangued the troops on both sides on the duty of concord, the blessings of peace, and the horror of war.[1] Epictetus did not go so far as this, but he lectured a procurator of Epirus for his partisanship, and for the bad example he set his inferiors, in very outspoken terms.[2] Another official he boldly confronts thus: " ' But,' said the official, 'I can throw into prison any one whom I please.' 'So you can do with a stone.' 'But I can beat with rods any one I please.' 'So you may an ass. This is not to govern men. Govern us as rational animals. Show us what is profitable to us and we will follow it. Show us what is unprofitable and we will turn away from it. Make us imitators of yourself, as Socrates did.' "[3] Seneca proclaims that the ruler's best safeguard is the love of his subjects.[4] As with magistrates, so with laws. The Stoic was irresistibly impelled to measure his reverence for existing laws by the degree to which they approximate to law universal.

The last and highest social duties are founded on the most universal relation, that of the individual man to his fellow-men. Every human being is a member of a rational system, an all-embracing commonwealth, the city of Zeus, the community of gods and men. It is to this, primarily, that he owes allegiance, and the isolated communities which pass for states are only imperfect and reduced copies of it. Hence, cosmopolitanism becomes philanthropy and

---

[1] Tacitus, *History*, III, 81.   [2] Arrian, III, 4, 5.
[3] *Ib.*, III, 7, 32.   [4] Seneca, *De Clementia*, I, 19, 6.

civic duties are merged in those of humanity. Such
a conception, besides abolishing the national distinction between Greek and barbarian, brings us face
to face with the institution of slavery, which has been
in every age the main obstacle to the recognition of a
common humanity. From the principles that the
wise alone are free and immoral persons slaves, and
that all external things are indifferent, it follows
directly that the institution is indefensible. There
can be no real difference between bond and free.
Epictetus clearly teaches that all men have God for
their father and are by nature brothers. To the
question: How can one endure such a person as
this slave? he replies: "Slave that you are yourself,
will you not bear with your own brother, who has
Zeus for his progenitor, and is like a son from the
same seeds and of the same descent from above?
But if you have been put in any such higher place,
will you immediately make yourself a tyrant? Will
you not remember who you are and whom you rule?
that they are kinsmen, that they are brethren by
nature, that they are the offspring of Zeus? 'But
I have purchased them and they have not purchased
me.' Do you see in what direction you are looking, that it is toward the earth, toward the pit, that
it is toward these wretched laws of dead men? But
toward the laws of the gods you are not looking." [1]
Slavery, then, is a law of the dead. It affects the
body alone; the mind of the slave is free.[2] No man
can make another either slave or free. "I have considered all these matters," says Epictetus, addressing
an imaginary master; "no man has power over me.
I have been made free by God; I know His commands; no man can now lead me as a slave. I have

[1] Arrian, I, 13, 5.   [2] Seneca, *De Beneficiis*, III, 20, 1.

a proper person to assert my freedom; I have
proper judges. Are you not the master of my body?
What, then, is that to me? Are you not the master
of my property? What, then, is that to me? Are
you not the master of my exile or of my chains?
Well, from all these things, and all the poor body
itself, I depart at your bidding, when you please.
Make trial of your power, and you will know how
far it reaches." [1] Again: "Zeus has set me free;
do you think that He intended His own son to be
enslaved? But you are master of my carcass; take
it. 'So, when you approach me, you have no regard to me?' No, but I have regard to myself;
and if you wish me to say that I have regard to you
also, I tell you that I have the same regard to you
that I have to my porringer." [2] Seneca often says
the slave is capable of virtue and worthy of the
friendship of the free.[3] He can bestow a benefit on
his master, for the merit of the service depends upon
the intention, not upon the external condition.[4] The
Roman gradation of ranks: knights, freedmen,
slaves, he maintains to be only empty names
sprung of ambition and wrong.[5] Any one can be
ennobled by overcoming what is low and common.[6]
In principle, then, the Stoics had surmounted slavery, but they did not press forward and work for
its complete abolition any more than the Christians
of the first century. When the end of the world was
deemed so close at hand, wide social changes seemed
to the Christians unnecessary, and there was force in
the Apostle's precept: "Wast thou called being a
bond-servant? care not for it; but if thou canst be-

[1] Arrian, IV, 7, 16.   [2] *Ib.*, I, 19, 9.
[3] Seneca, *De Ben.*, III, 18, 2; *Ep.*, 31, 11.
[4] *Ib.*, *De Ben.*, III, 28, 1.   [5] Seneca, *Ep.*, 31, 11.   [6] *De Ben.*, III, 28.

come free, use it," *i. e.*, slavery, "rather. For he that was called in the Lord, being a bond-servant, is the Lord's freedman; likewise, he that was called being free is Christ's bond-servant. Ye were bought with a price; become not bond-servants of men." [1] So, too, the Stoics were most anxious that the slave should attain to true inward freedom and escape the moral slavery to vice and evil passions. The amelioration of his external lot, being a thing indifferent, was of secondary importance. No doubt many slaves profited directly by the humanity of Stoic masters, but it was long before these humane principles, permeating society, had the indirect consequence of gradually raising the slave to the improved position of the serf. This great change, which was not completed at the break-up of the Roman empire, is ascribed by Lecky to Stoic rather than Christian influences.

But what are the duties which I owe to my fellowmen? First, there are the passive duties, not to requite evil with evil, patiently to suffer all wrong and insult, and repress all movements of hate, revenge, anger, and envy. "To suppose that we shall be easily despised by others," says Epictetus, "unless in every possible way we do injury to those who first show us hostility, is the mark of very ignoble and foolish men; for this implies that inability to do injury is the reason why we are thought contemptible, whereas, the really contemptible man is not he who cannot do injury but he who cannot do benefit." [2] The best revenge is to show ourselves blameless and, if possible, improve the evil-doer. "To take the insult coolly," says Seneca, "is in some

---

[1] I Cor., 7 : 21–23.
[2] Arrian, *Fragment* 70 (Schweighäuser).

sort to be revenged." [1] Marcus Aurelius, again, says: "Not to do likewise is the best revenge." [2] Epictetus does not strictly forbid the attempt to get legal satisfaction for our wrongs, though he discourages it by remarking that we ought to be thankful we were not worse treated, but escaped with our lives.[3] If we do go into court, we should be neither cowardly nor arrogant, neither descend to unworthy appeals nor irritate and challenge the judge unnecessarily.[4] But the same Stoics who thus demanded patience under wrong refused to allow compassion and pardon, and stoutly opposed any interference with the course of justice by remission of penalty. Critics profess to discover an inconsistency in this. But they fail to put themselves in the position of the Stoic; they overlook the doctrine of apathy. If once it be granted that no morbid emotion can ever be indulged by the sage, and that pity is morbid emotion, a form of grief or mental pain, it is hard to see why the sight of others' misfortunes should be an excuse for this particular form of vice. They were not hard-hearted, but they grounded the impulse to help and save, not upon pity, but upon the tie of a common humanity, the knowledge of the rights and duties in which all men share. The sage will be patient with the suffering, not because of their external woes, but because of their inward weakness and blindness.

As with pity, so with forgiveness. The sentimentalist exclaims: "How inhuman! Is not pardon the noblest prerogative of man?" and falls to quoting: "The quality of mercy is not strained," etc. But the Stoic also pardons in his own way. If he is wronged

[1] *De Constantia Sapientis*, 17, 11.
[2] Marcus Aurelius, VI, 6.   [3] Arrian, IV, 5, 9.   [4] *Ib.*, II, 2, 17.

or insulted, he does not take it ill, does not allow himself to give way to anger or resentment, but attributes
the act to human weakness and folly. He does not
consider that he is wronged or insulted, but thinks
the wicked man has done the greater harm to himself and has received his punishment in the loss of
self-esteem, which always accompanies sin.[1] He is
not concerned for his own personal honour, but only
for the improvement of the evildoer; and if the latter
repents and is willing to make friends, he is quite
ready to meet him. This tolerant attitude toward
human infirmity is abundantly illustrated by Marcus
Aurelius. He is always ready with excuses for others. "Cruel, is it not, to prevent men from pushing for what looks like their own advantage? Yet
in a sense you forbid them that when you resent
their going wrong. They are doubtless bent upon
their own objects and advantage. 'Not so,' you say,
'in reality.' Teach them so, then, and prove it,
instead of resenting it." [2] "When any one does you
a wrong, set yourself at once to consider what was
the point of view, good or bad, that led him wrong.
As soon as you perceive it you will be sorry for him,
not surprised or angry. For your own view of good
is either the same as his or something like in kind,
and you will make allowance. Or, supposing your
own view of good and bad has altered, you will find
charity for his mistake come easier." [3] "Whom-
soever you meet, say straightway to yourself: What
are the man's principles of good and bad ? For if he
holds such and such principles regarding pleasure
and pain and their respective causes, about fame
and shame, or life and death, I shall not be surprised
or shocked at his doing such and such things; I

[1] Marcus Aurelius, IX, 4.   [2] *Ib.*, VI, 27.   [3] *Ib.*, VII, 26.

shall remember that he cannot do otherwise." [1]
"When offended at a fault in some one else, divert
your thoughts to the reflection, What is the parallel
fault in me? Is it attachment to money? or pleasure?
or reputation? as the case may be. Dwelling on this,
anger forgets itself and makes way for the thought:
'He cannot help himself; what else can he do? If
it is not so, enable him, if you can, to help himself.'" [2]
In Epictetus, again, we find the following: "When
any person treats you ill or speaks ill of you, remember that he does this or says this because he thinks
that it is his duty. It is not possible, then, for him
to follow that which seems right to you but that
which seems right to himself. Accordingly, if he is
wrong in his opinion, he is the person who is hurt,
for he is the person who has been deceived; for if a
man shall suppose the true proposition to be false, it
is not the proposition which is hindered but the
man who has been deceived about it. If you proceed,
then, from these opinions you will be mild in temper
to him who reviles you; for say on each occasion:
It seemed so to him." [3]

On the question of punishment, again, the line
taken by the Stoic is intelligible and consistent. If
he is convinced that in the interests of public order
and of the wrong-doer himself punishment is necessary, he knows no forgiveness. He will not let the
offender off on account of weak pity. For to remit
the penalty under these circumstances would be to
pronounce the original infliction of the punishment
unjust. That violations of law must be punished
was always energetically maintained by the school.
They insisted, however, that the punishment should

---

[1] Marcus Aurelius, VIII, 14. [2] *Ib.*, X, 30.
[3] Arrian, *Encheiridion*, 42.

be dictated, not by anger, but by mature deliberation. It should aim at the reclamation of the offender, and, in order to this end, as well as to act as a sufficient deterrent, it should be both as mild, as speedy, and as certain as possible. The death penalty cuts off the absolutely bad as excrescences upon the body politic.[1] But, while the Stoic refusal to pardon or remit penalties can be fully justified against all weak sentimentality, it must be allowed that they did not take sufficient account of the possibility of error, either (a) as to the guilt or innocence of the accused or (b) as to the extent of his guilt. From Seneca's treatise on Clemency it can plainly be seen that they strove to find the correct mean between cruel harshness and strictness on the one hand, and weak indulgence on the other. Clemency, according to Seneca, is neither weak indulgence nor yet morbid pity. One might be tempted to object that this is a mere verbal quibble, and that he who makes clemency his principle acts in the same way as he who pardons, but from higher motives and with clearer insight. Seneca's conclusion is, briefly, that perfect justice is also the highest and most perfect love. In holding such a view as this, far from being harsh, he was well in advance of his own time—it may be, of ours.

[1] Seneca is here our chief authority, especially the treatises *De Ira* and *De Clementia*. "Bonis nocet qui malis parcit" (Fragment 114) is the key-note of his remarks. In meting out punishment, regard must be had to mildness, as far as possible (*De Ira*, I, 19; *De Clementia*, I, 2, 2; I, 5, 1), not to the satisfaction of rage or revenge (*De Ira*, I, 12; I, 6; I, 15). The mildest punishment is the most effective for reformation (*De Clementia*, I, 22). The death penalty should not be unduly deferred (*De Ben.*, II, 5, 1). Cicero, *Pro Murena*, cc. 29–31, §§, 60–66, does his best to ridicule the Stoics in general, and Cato in particular, for what he considers their impracticably rigid adherence to fixed principles on this matter.

To Epictetus the active duty of benevolence and readiness to help others is an essential part of morality, the highest manifestation of rational will. Marcus Aurelius expresses the same thought thus: "Does the eye demand a recompense for seeing, or the feet for walking? Just as this is the end for which they exist, and just as they find their reward in realising the law of their being, so, too, man is made for kindness, and whenever he does an act of kindness or otherwise helps forward the common good, he thereby fulfils the law of his being and comes by his own."[1] "Nature," says Seneca, "bids me be of use to men, no matter whether they are slave or free, freedmen or free-born. Wherever there is a human being there is room for benevolence."[2] Persistent kindness conquers the bad, and no one is so hard-hearted, so hostile to what he should value, that even to his own hurt he refuses to love good men.[3] We are required to love men genuinely, and from the heart.[4] "Make the most of a short life," says Seneca; "let it be peaceful both for yourself and others. See that you are beloved by all while you live and regretted when you die."[5] This help and service was interpreted to mean, not merely external aid, but the effort to teach, admonish, and reform others, a task beset with difficulties, calling for tact and even temper, and the gift of sweet reasonableness. That we must love the sinner and try earnestly to improve him is a favourite thought of the Stoic emperor. "It is man's special gift to love even those who fall into blunders; this takes effect the moment we realise

---

[1] Marcus Aurelius, IX, 42, s. f.   [2] Seneca, De Vita Beata, 24, 3.
[3] Ib., De Ben., VII, 31, 1.
[4] Marcus Aurelius, VII, 13; Seneca, De Ira, III, 28, 1 sq.
[5] De Ira, III, 43, 1.

that men are our brothers, that sin is of ignorance and unintentional, that in a little while we shall both be dead, that, above all, no injury is done us; our inner self is not made worse than it was before." [1] "Use your moral reason to move his; show him his error, admonish him." [2] "If you can, set the doer right." [3] "Men exist for one another. Teach them, then, or bear with them." [4] "Convert men, if you can; if you cannot, charity, remember, has been given you for this end. See! the gods, too, have charity for such, helping them to divers things, health, wealth, and reputation; so good are they. You, too, can do the same; who hinders you?" [5] "If a man is mistaken, reason with him kindly and point out his misconception. If you fail, blame yourself or no one." [6] "Reverence the gods, help men." [7]   In the face of this evidence it would be blind prejudice to deny that the Stoics preached philanthropy in its highest and noblest form.   But it would be unfair to ignore the fact that it was not the centre of their view of life, as it is in Christianity, or that it lacked the force, warmth, and influence which a deeper conviction of sin and the conception of self-sacrificing love lend to the teaching of the New Testament.   However willing to serve and help his fellows, the Stoic never forgets that vice is folly, and can hardly repress a smile at the human comedy, the follies, errors, and blunders of mankind.

From this imperfect sketch it appears that the later Stoics, and especially Epictetus, in their practical teaching adhered firmly to the principles laid down by Zeno.   The system of morality which they enforced by precept and example possessed consid-

---

[1] Marcus Aurelius, VII, 22.   [2] *Ib.*, V, 28.   [3] *Ib.*, VIII, 17.
[4] *Ib.*, VIII, 59.   [5] *Ib.*, IX, 11.   [6] *Ib.*, X, 4.   [7] *Ib.*, X, 30.

erable merits which no inquirer can afford to disregard. In this system happiness depends solely on the will, and the value of an act is estimated by the intention; vice or sin is misery and carries its own punishment with it; virtue consists, not in performing such and such actions, but rather in the right view of life, the attitude in shaping the whole of conduct in conformity with right reason or—which comes to the same thing—with God's will; nothing external can dishonour a man, and the true nobility of virtue is within the reach of the slave. These and other kindred doctrines can all be traced to the tendency of the system to regard morality as an affair of the inner life—in short, to the inwardness of Stoicism.

CHAPTER V

EPICURUS AND HEDONISM

Epicurus was an Athenian citizen and belonged to the deme Gargettus. Hence he is often called the Gargettian sage. The few simple facts and dates of his uneventful career as a teacher and writer are particularly well established. He was born in the year 341 B. C., in the lunar month Gamelion, the tenth day of which was kept in his honour. Probably it was three days earlier, on the seventh of the month, that he first saw the light. The Attic civil year began, theoretically, with the summer solstice, and Gamelion, the seventh month, would naturally fall after the winter solstice, in our January. Epicurus was born in Samos, whither his father, Neocles, had gone out from Athens to settle as a colonist. His father bore the same name as the father of Themistocles, a fact which led Menander to compose an epigram comparing the achievements of their respective sons. The son of one Neocles had freed his country from slavery; Epicurus, the son of the other, from the worse bondage of superstitious folly. Many philosophers and founders of religion have aimed at emancipation, deliverance—in a word, freedom. Seldom has the world seen one who went to the same lengths in this direction as Epicurus. In the extreme individualism of his ethical no less than of his physical doctrine, and his refusal to base the co-operation of his units on anything else but voluntary consent, he would seem to anticipate the principles professed by modern anarchists, when these latter pride themselves on their distinction from collectivist socialists. The family of Neocles was never well-to-do; his occupation was that of an elementary schoolmaster. The gossip of a later day affirmed that, when a boy, the son helped the father in his duties and prepared ink for the pupils. From the same perhaps untrustworthy source we learn that his mother, Chærestrata, performed certain dubious rites, half religious, half magical, intended to propitiate the deities and avert disease and misfortune by charms and incantations. At these rites, celebrated at the cottages of her neighbours, it was the boy's part to assist his mother by reading the incantations. If this story is true, the employment must have been singularly uncongenial to one who all his life long hated falsehood, deceit, and superstition. In 323 B. C. he proceeded to Athens to be enrolled as a citizen and to undergo that training in military duties which the constitution assigned to youths between the ages of eighteen and twenty. In this service he made the acquaintance of the poet Menander, who, born in the same year as himself, became his friend and admirer. The spirit of the Epicurean philosophy may be said to pervade the works of this great dramatist of the New Comedy. About this time Xenocrates was teaching in the Academy and Theophrastus in the Lyceum; Aristotle had retired to Chalcis, where in the next year he died.

But events marched apace. The death of Alexander was followed by the unfortunate Lamian war, and in 322 B. C. Perdiccas expelled the Athenian colonists from their holdings in Samos. Epicurus joined his father, now more than ever a broken

man, at Colophon. Of the next dozen years we
have little information, but we find him in 310 B. C.,
in his thirty-second year, at Mitylene, where he came
forward as a teacher of philosophy. Even as a
schoolboy he is said to have given proofs of an in-
quiring mind. When reading in Hesiod how all
things had their origin in Chaos, he puzzled the
master by asking, "Whence came Chaos?" In
after days he boasted that he had been self-taught.
His writings and conversation were enlivened with
scoffs, gibes, and sneers at all other schools of so-
called wisdom, a precedent of liberty which in the
later Epicureans ran to unbounded licence. "The
followers of Plato he used to call 'the flatterers of
Dionysius,' and Plato himself 'the man of gold,' and
Aristotle 'a profligate who, after squandering his
patrimony, joined the army and sold drugs.' Protagoras he called 'the porter' and 'the copyist of Democritus,' and said that 'he taught grammar in villages.'
Heraclitus he called 'the confusion-maker,' and
Democritus 'the babbler.'"[1] It is quite certain,
however, that he studied the system of Democritus
with unusual care, and there is no ground for rejecting the story that he was for some time a pupil
of the Democritean Nausiphanes of Teos, whom he
sarcastically styled a "mollusc," to express contempt
for his want of backbone. At Mitylene, Epicurus
gained over Hermarchus, afterward his successor,
and at Lampsacus, on the Hellespont, he made the
most enduring friendships of his life. Here he became acquainted with Idomeneus and Leonteus,
men of great influence in that town, who were his
patrons and lifelong correspondents and, with

[1] Usener, *Epicurea*, p. 363, l. 8. This invaluable work will be our
main source throughout the next two chapters.

Metrodorus and Polyænus, the ablest among his disciples.

Though his teaching in Asia had been eminently successful, he must have felt the attraction of the home of philosophy. Athens was still the centre of intellectual activity and social intercourse for the ancient world, as Paris for the modern world. Here was the most refined society, the greatest possibilities for the æsthetic enjoyment of life. Accordingly, about 306 B. C., Epicurus removed with his pupils to Athens, which he never afterward quitted except for short visits to Asia Minor. Of one such visit we have a charming memorial, unearthed, like so much besides of Epicurean literature, from beneath the ashes of Herculaneum. It is a letter written by the master to a little child, possibly the daughter of Metrodorus, of whom more hereafter. We may premise that Themista was the wife of Leonteus, of Lampsacus, and Matron obviously a domestic in charge of the child.

"We came to Lampsacus, Pythocles, Hermarchus, Ctesippus, and myself, and we are quite well. We found there Themista and our other friends, and they are quite well. I hope you are well, too, and your mamma, and that you obey her and papa and Matron in everything, as you used to do. For you know quite well, my pet, that I and all the others love you very much, because you are obedient to them in everything.[1]

Even Swinburne[2] admits the genius of the childless George Eliot for understanding the ways of children, and we may well believe that the bachelor Epicurus, like the bachelor Herbert Spencer, was a

---

[1] *Epicurea*, Fragment 176, p. 154, 11.
[2] In his *Note on Charlotte Brontë.*

welcome guest in a family where there were children.
For more than thirty years, then, Epicurus resided
continuously in Athens.   He founded a school by the
simple expedient of purchasing for eighty minæ a
house and garden in the quarter known as Melite,
where his friends and disciples might have easy access to him.   Hence his followers were often known
as the Garden Philosophers.   The little society was
united together by no other tie than that of a common
affection to their teacher.   Friends and admirers
quickly gathered round him, among them his three
brothers, who almost worshipped him.   Nor were
women excluded, and even slaves were numbered
among his pupils.   Though leading the life of a recluse and holding aloof from political parties, he
enjoyed intercourse with the best minds of the day.
These years were not spent idly.   Like Democritus,
Plato, and Aristotle before him, he was an inde-
fatigable and voluminous author.   He wrote some
three hundred separate treatises, being surpassed in
the wealth of his philosophic output by Chrysippus
alone among the ancients.   At the same time he
kept up a vigorous correspondence with friends at
a distance who shared his aims.   As we know from
Herculaneum, selections were published from the
letters of Epicurus, Metrodorus, Polyænus, Hermarchus, and their acquaintance.   His great work,
On Nature, in thirty-seven books or rolls, occupied
him for several years.   It had reached Book XV in
300-299 B. C., while Book XXVIII was finished in
296-5 B. C.   In the production of a quantity of
literature so prodigious, something had to be sacrificed.   Ancient critics complain sadly that the
qualities of elegance and lucid arrangement so conspicuous in his three great predecessors above men-

tioned were totally wanting in him. Yet even Cicero admits that, crude and commonplace as his ideas were, the meaning was always plain; and probably this was all their author cared for. He was too much in earnest to cultivate the graces of style, and he looked down with contempt upon the accomplishments of an ordinary Athenian education, in which high-flown rhetoric and hair-splitting logic played a leading part.[1]

The last years of Epicurus were clouded. His favourite disciple, Metrodorus, died in 277 B. C., at the age of fifty-three, and another able pupil, Polyænus, predeceased him. The former left a son and daughter, the latter a son, and Epicurus must have deemed himself in a special sense responsible for the education and future welfare of these orphans, to whom he was probably guardian. By his will his executors are charged [2] to provide for their maintenance in consultation with Hermarchus, and in due course to provide a dowry for the girl on her marriage. Epicurus had always been in delicate health. In his boyhood, if we may trust Suidas, he had to be lifted down from his chair, was bleareyed, and of so sensitive a skin that he could not bear any clothing heavier than a tunic. He was long subject to gout and dropsy, for many years he was unable to walk, and finally renal calculus carried him off in 270 B. C., in his seventy-second year. These painful disorders he endured with the utmost

---

[1] To judge by the scanty remains, the diction of Epicurus is not pure Attic, but already betrays signs of that fusion of Greek dialects, generally known by the name of Koinē, which began about the time of Alexander's conquests. In this respect Epicurus stands midway between Aristotle and Polybius. See P. Linde, *De Epicuri vocabulis ab optima Atthide alienis.*

[2] *Epicurea*, p. 166, 13.

fortitude. Scraps have come down to us from two letters written by him in his last illness, the one to his successor Hermarchus, the other to Idomeneus, of Lampsacus. The latter [1] runs as follows:

"On this last, yet blessed, day of my life, I write to you. Pains and tortures of body I have to the full, but there is set over against these the joy of my heart at the memory of our happy conversations in the past. Do you, if you would be worthy of your devotion to me and philosophy, take care of the children of Metrodorus."

To the members of his little society he seems to have been at all times extremely generous in contributions from his own means, though he scouted the notion of a common purse, as savouring too much of mistrust and suspicion between friends. It appears from his letters that the aged philosopher had accepted annual contributions sent for his support from his wealthy friends in Lampsacus and possibly from other quarters. Here we are reminded of the pecuniary help which Auguste Comte received from his friends and admirers. In the character of Epicurus the conspicuous traits are sympathy, generosity, and sweet reasonableness. No man was ever more vilely slandered or more cruelly misunderstood, but the severest critics of his teaching, Cicero, Seneca, Plutarch, in the most honourable way dissociate themselves entirely from the aspersions cast upon his personal character. "Of his unequalled consideration toward all there is ample testimony," says an ancient writer.[2] "I appeal to his native country, which honoured him with a statue, to the great number of his friends, who could be counted by whole cities, to the followers

---

[1] *Epicurea*, Fragment 138, p. 143, 16.   [2] *Ib.* p. 364, 1.

attracted and held fast by the siren-charms of his doctrines, to the long continuance and perpetuation of his school in strong contrast to the checkered fortunes of its rivals, to his gratitude to his parents, his generosity to his brothers, his gentleness to his slaves, as attested by his will and also by the fact that slaves were among his pupils—in fact, to his universal kindness to all men." No less positive is the evidence as to his frugality and abstemious mode of life. "Send me some cheese of Cythnos," he writes to a friend, "that I may be able to fare sumptuously when I like." [1] He was usually contented with mere bread and water. The school made experiments in frugal living. In a letter to Polyænus the master tells him that, while Metrodorus had only reduced his expenses to fourpence a day, he himself had contrived to subsist on less.[2] Whatever else he was, such a man was at all events no epicure. At the same time such abstemiousness, if practised universally, would not be without its dangers. It has often happened that to raise the standard of comfort and so to create wants is the first step in social advance. What satisfied Epicurus would fail to satisfy all men, or even the average man. He must be credited with a certain lack of imagination if he did not perceive this. Similarly with another characteristic trait, his quietism. The love of adventure, the thirst for honour, the cravings of ambition found no response in his breast; but neither would his own love of study, meditation, and retirement ever appeal to any but a small section of men, invalids, the elderly or the disillusioned. One detail serves to illustrate the practical turn of his

---

[1] *Epicurea*, Fragment 182, p. 156, 17.
[2] *Ib.*, Fragment 158, p. 149, 20.

mind. He foresaw that many would be curious to learn the main outlines of his system without possessing the leisure, inclination, or ability to master its details. Instead of repelling the advances of such honest folk, as Plato had done when he inscribed over the portals of the Academy "Let no one enter here who is ignorant of geometry," Epicurus is careful, even anxious, to cater for their peculiar needs. He brought out an epitome of his doctrines, itself a work of considerable length, known as the "larger" epitome. As scholars now recognise, this was the work which the poet Lucretius made the basis of his poem in six books and over seven thousand lines. But this was not enough. A shorter summary was prepared and possibly the extant epistles to Herodotus and Menœceus formed part of this. They may, however, be distinct compilations. Lastly, either the master himself or some authorities of the school picked out a selection of golden sentences or maxims,[1] articles of belief, which the members of the society were exhorted to commit to memory, to recite, and make the subject of meditation. The Epicurean literature is full of allusions to them. Not only are they preserved in the pages of Diogenes Laërtius, but they were actually discovered a few years ago inscribed on the walls of the market-place of Œnoanda, an obscure Pisidian town in the heart of Asia Minor, where they might best catch the eye alike of the rustic from the country and of the cultured traveller.

Thus, though the three hundred treatises of the master are either wholly lost or survive only in the buried treasures of Herculaneum, yet, as a result of these precautions, we are better informed upon most

---

[1] *Epicurea*, p. 71, *sqq.*

points of Epicurean doctrine than upon the system of any ancient philosopher with the sole exception of Plato and Plotinus. But in fact the subsequent history of the school is in itself a sufficient proof of its founder's talent for organisation. Elsewhere we find contending influences at work, perpetual change of view and shifting of opinion, particularly when a succession of teachers interpreted, enlarged, or violently combated the doctrines bequeathed to them. The Academy was not content to preserve the tenets of Plato unaltered, but passed by violent reactions from dogmatism to scepticism, and probabilism, and back to dogmatism again. In the Epicurean society there was nothing comparable to this. From first to last its members were united by a common reverence for their founder, and hardly a trace is to be discovered of any serious dissent. It is their constant boast that they frequently won adherents from the rival schools, but that no Epicurean had gone over to another school. To this rule there are only one or two exceptions, the most conspicuous being Timocrates, who seems, on personal grounds, to have had a feud with his brother Metrodorus. Numenius [1] compared the school of Epicurus to a republic free from party strife, having only one mind, one opinion, in which an innovation would have been regarded as an impiety. When Lucretius speaks of himself as repeating oracles more holy, and far more certain than those of the Pythian prophetess, he merely voices the convictions of the whole brotherhood. Their reverence for the writings of their master is the counterpart of the attitude of evangelical Protestants toward the Bible.

It is now time to inquire into the nature of that

[1] Eusebius, *Præp. Evangel.*, XIV, 5.

teaching which met with such an enthusiastic reception and was greeted almost like a revelation. Philosophy was defined by Epicurus as "a daily business of speech and thought to secure a happy life."[1] Here is struck the note of intense earnestness characteristic alike of Epicurus and his age. Philosophy is a practical concern; it deals with the health of the soul. It is a life and not merely a doctrine. It holds out the promise of well-being and happiness. This is the one thing needful. Literature, art, and the other embellishments of life are not indispensable. The wise man lives poems instead of making them. "It need not trouble any one," said Metrodorus,[2] "if he had never read a line of Homer and did not know whether Hector was a Trojan or a Greek." Accordingly, as we have seen, Epicurus regarded with indifference the ordinary routine education of the day in grammar, rhetoric, dialectic, and music, and for mere erudition he had a hearty contempt. The only study absolutely necessary for a philosopher was the study of nature, or what we now call natural science, and this must be cultivated, not for its own sake, but merely as the indispensable means to a happy life. Unless and until we have learned the natural causes of phenomena, we are at the mercy of superstition, fears, and terrors.

We must defer to a subsequent chapter the consideration of the steps by which Epicurus was led to the conclusion that the external world is a vast machine built up by the concourse of atoms in motion without an architect or plan. Suppose, however, this conclusion firmly established; what has our philosopher to tell us respecting human life and action? In what consists the happiness which is our

---

[1] *Epicurea*, Fragment 219, p. 169, 4.   [2] Fragm. 24, ed. Körte.

being's end and aim? This had, by the time of
Epicurus, become the chief question of philosophy,
and, strange as it may appear, the answer is no new
doctrine, but one which had often been proposed
and discussed in the ancient schools. He identifies
happiness, at least nominally, with pleasure, and he
means the pleasure of the agent. His is a system of
Egoistic Hedonism. Verbally, then, he is in agreement with Aristippus, the founder of the Cyrenaics,
with the Socrates of Plato's *Protagoras*, and with
Eudoxus, whose doctrine of pleasure is criticised by
Aristotle in the *Nicomachean Ethics*. The same
doctrine is discussed in more than one of Plato's
dialogues, sometimes apparently with approval, sometimes with disapproval. The historical Socrates
never, so far as we know, reached a final definition
of Good. He knew no good, he said, which was not
good for somebody or something. His teaching
would serve equally well as an introduction to Egoistic Hedonism, to Universal Hedonism, to Utili-
tarianism, or to Eudæmonism. The difficulty at
once occurs; if pleasure and good are identical, why
is it that some pleasures are approved as good and
others condemned as evil? Why, on this hypothesis,
should life ever present conflicting alternatives in
which we are called upon to choose between doing
what is good and doing what is pleasant? Every
hedonistic system must face this problem. Some
progress had been made by Plato in the *Protagoras*.
There his spokesman, Socrates, maintains that since
every one desires what is best for himself, and since
he further identifies good with pleasure, evil with
pain, he avoids pleasure when it is the source of still
greater pain, and only chooses pain when a greater
amount of pleasure results from it. In this Epicurus

heartily concurred.   He never recedes from the position that pleasure is always a good and pain always
an evil, but it does not follow that pleasure is always
to be chosen, pain to be shunned. For experience
shows that certain pleasures are attended by painful
consequences, certain pains by salutary results, and
it is necessary to measure or weigh these after-effects
one against the other before acting.   "No one beholding evil chooses it, but, being enticed by it as by
a bait, and believing it to contain more good than
evil, he is ensnared." [1]

We now get a clearer notion of the end of action,
which turns out to be the maximum of pleasure to the
agent after subtraction of whatever pain is involved
in securing the pleasure or directly attends upon it.
At this point Epicurus parts company with Aristippus, whose crude presentation of hedonistic doctrine
identified the end with the pleasure of the moment.
So soon as conditions and consequences are taken
into account, pleasure tends to become an ideal element capable of being realised in a series of actions,
or in the whole of life, but not to be exhausted at any
given point of the series.   More important, however,
for determining the exact significance of this conception is the incursion which Epicurus makes into the
psychology of desire.   Desire is prompted by want;
unsatisfied want is painful.   When we act in order
to gratify our desires, we are seeking to remove the
pain of want, but the cessation of the want brings a
cessation of mental trouble or unrest, and this must
carefully be distinguished from positive pleasure,
which is itself a mental disturbance.   Experience
shows a succession of mental disturbances, painful
wants, the effort to remove them, and the pleasurable

[1] Wotke, *Wiener Studien*, X, p. 192, sent. 16.

excitement which attends their removal. But all this shifting train has for its natural end and aim a state which is neither want nor desire nor the pleasurable excitement of satisfying want. All of them are fugitive states as contrasted with the resultant peace and serenity in which they end. The former are compared to an agitated sea, whether swept by storms or tempests or in gentle, equable motion, the latter to the profound calm, waveless and noiseless, of a sheltered haven. Beyond this neutral state of freedom from bodily pain and mental disturbance it is impossible to advance. We may seek new pleasures by gratifying new desires; we are only returning to the old round of painful want, desire, and pleasurable excitement of removing the want. There is only one way to escape from this round, and that is to be content to rest in the neutral state. After all, this is the maximum of pleasure of which we are capable; any deviation from it may vary our pleasure but cannot increase it. "The amount of pleasure is defined by the removal of all pain. Wherever there is pleasure, so long as it is present, there is neither bodily pain nor mental suffering, nor both." [1] The consideration of these elementary facts should regulate preference and aversion. Prudence demands the suppression of all unnecessary desires. Epicurus does not carry renunciation so far as the Buddhists, who hold that to live is to suffer, and explain the will to live as that instinctive love of life which, partly conscious, partly unconscious, is inherent in all living beings. They look for their rest in Nirvana. Certain things, says Epicurus, we must desire, because without them we cannot live, and life to Epicurus is worth living; and yet the repose which consists in

[1] *Epicurea*, p. 72, 1, golden maxim No. 3.

the cessation of desire is, after all, not altogether unlike the Nirvana of the Buddhists.

In this negative conception of happiness as freedom from pain, whether of body or mind, Epicurus
must have been influenced by the ethical teaching
of Democritus, who also made happiness in its
essential nature consist in the cheerfulness and well-
being, the right disposition, harmony, and unalterable peace of mind which enable a man to live a calm
and steadfast life. Democritus also exalted mental
above bodily pleasures and pains, and laid stress
upon ignorance, fear, folly, and superstition as causes
of those mental pains which tend most to disturb
life. With Epicurus the great obstacle to happiness
is neither pain nor poverty, nor the absence of the
ordinary good things of life; it is rather whatever
contributes to disturb our serenity and mental satisfaction, whatever causes fear, anxiety—in a word,
mental trouble. To be independent of circumstances is his ideal; that a man should find his true
good in himself. He is ready with practical suggestions for realising this independence. Groundless fear
must be removed by the study of nature, which shows
that the fear of death, the fear of the gods, belief in
Providence and in divine retribution are chimeras;
desire must be regulated by prudence and the virtues
cultivated as the indispensable means to a pleasant
life. Fatalism is not true any more than the doctrine
that all things happen by chance. The future is not
in our power; our actions alone are in our power to
make them what we please. The letter to Menœceus [1]
sets forth the ethical doctrine of Epicurus in a convenient summary as follows:

"Let no one be slow to seek wisdom when he is

[1] *Epicurea*, p. 59 *sqq*.

young nor weary in the search thereof when he is
grown old.   For no age is too early or too late for
the health of the soul.   And to say that the season
for philosophy has not yet come, or that it is passed
and gone, is like saying that the season for happiness
is not yet or that it is now no more.   Therefore, both
old and young ought to seek wisdom, that so a man
as age comes over him may be young in good things,
because of the grace of what has been, and while he
is young may likewise be old, because he has no fear
of the things which are to come.   So we must exercise ourselves in the things which bring happiness,
since, if that be present, we have everything and, if
that be absent, all our actions are directed toward
attaining it.

   "Those things which without ceasing I have declared unto thee, those do and exercise thyself therein,
holding them to be the elements of right life.   First,
believe that God is a being blessed and immortal,
according to the notion of a God commonly held
amongst men; and so believing, thou shalt not affirm of him aught that is contrary to immortality or
that agrees not with blessedness, but shalt believe
about him whatsoever may uphold both his blessedness and his immortality.   For verily there are
gods, and the knowledge of them is manifest; but
they are not such as the multitude believe, seeing
that men do not steadfastly maintain the notions
they form respecting them.   Not the man who
denies the gods worshipped by the multitude, but he
who affirms of the gods what the multitude believes
about them, is truly impious.   For the utterances of
the multitude about the gods are not true preconceptions but false assumptions, according to which
the greatest evils happen to the wicked and the

greatest blessings happen to the good from the hand of the gods, seeing that they are always favourable to their own good qualities and take pleasure in men like unto themselves, but reject as alien whatever is not of their kind.

"Accustom thyself to believe that death is nothing to us, for good and evil imply sentience and death is the privation of all sentience; therefore, a right understanding that death is nothing to us makes enjoyable the mortality of life, not by adding to life an illimitable time, but by taking away the yearning after immortality. For life has no terrors for him who has thoroughly apprehended that there are no terrors for him in ceasing to live. Foolish, therefore, is the man who says that he fears death, not because it will pain when it comes, but because it pains in the prospect. · Whatsoever causes no annoyance when it is present causes only a groundless pain in the expectation. Death, therefore, the most awful of evils, is nothing to us, seeing that when we are, death is not come, and when death is come, we are not. It is nothing, then, either to the living or the dead, for with the living it is not and the dead exist no longer. But in the world, at one time men shun death as the greatest of all evils and at another time choose it as a respite from the evils in life. The wise man does not deprecate life nor does he fear the cessation of life. The thought of life is no offence to him nor is the cessation of life regarded as an evil. And even as men choose of good, not merely and simply the larger portion, but the more pleasant, so the wise seek to enjoy the time which is most pleasant and not merely that which is longest. And he who admonishes the young to live well and the old to make a good end, speaks foolishly, not

merely because of the desirableness of life, but because
the same exercise at once teaches to live well and to
die well.   Much worse is he who says that it were
good not to be born, but when once one is born to
pass with all speed through the gates of Hades.   If he,
in truth, believes this, why does he not depart from
life ?   It were easy for him to do so if once he is
firmly convinced.   If he speaks only in mockery
his words are foolishness, for those who hear believe
him not.

"We must remember that the future is neither
wholly ours nor wholly not ours, so that neither
must we count upon it as quite certain to come nor
despair of it as quite certain not to come.

"We must also reflect that of desires some are
natural, some are groundless;   and that of the
natural, some are necessary as well as natural and
some are natural only.   And of the necessary desires,
some are necessary if we are to be happy, some if
the body is to be rid of uneasiness, some if we are
even to live.   He who has a clear and certain understanding of these things will direct every preference
and aversion toward securing health of body and
tranquillity of mind, seeing that this is the sum and
end of a blessed life.   For the end of all our actions
is to be free from pain and fear, and when once we
have attained this all the tempest of the soul is laid,
seeing that the living creature has no need to go in
search of something that is lacking nor to look for
anything else by which the good of the soul and of
the body will be fulfilled.   When we are pained
because of the absence of pleasure, then, and then
only, do we feel the need of pleasure;   but when we
feel no pain, then we no longer stand in need of
pleasure.   Wherefore we call pleasure the alpha and

omega of a blessed life. Pleasure is our first and kindred good. It is the starting-point of every choice and of every aversion, and to it we come back, inasmuch as we make feeling the rule by which to judge of every good thing.

"And since pleasure is our first and native good, for that reason we do not choose every pleasure whatsoever, but ofttimes pass over many pleasures when a greater annoyance ensues from them. And ofttimes we consider pains superior to pleasures when submission to the pains for a long time brings us as its consequence a greater pleasure. While, therefore, all pleasure because it is naturally akin to us is good, not all pleasure is choiceworthy, just as all pain is an evil but all pain is not to be shunned. It is, however, by measuring one against another, and by looking at the conveniences and inconveniences, that all these matters must be judged. Sometimes we treat the good as an evil and the evil, on the contrary, as a good. Again, we regard independence of outward things as a great good, not so as in all cases to use little, but so as to be contented with little if we have not much, being honestly persuaded that they have the sweetest enjoyment of luxury who stand least in need of it, and that whatever is natural is easily procured and only the vain and worthless hard to win. Plain fare is not more distasteful than a costly diet, when once the pain of want has been removed, while bread and water confer the highest possible pleasure when they are brought to hungry lips. To habituate one's self, therefore, to simple and inexpensive diet supplies all that is needful for health, and enables a man to meet the necessary requirements of life without shrinking, and it places us in a better condition when we approach

at intervals a costly fare and renders us fearless of
fortune.

"When we say, then, that pleasure is the end and
aim, we do not mean the pleasures of the prodigal
or the pleasures of sensuality, as we are understood
to do by some, through ignorance, prejudice, or wilful
misinterpretation. By pleasure we mean the absence of pain in the body and trouble in the soul.
It is not an unbroken succession of drinking feasts
and of revelry, not sexual love, not the enjoyment of
the fish and other delicacies of a luxurious table
which produce a pleasant·life; it is sober reasoning,
searching out the grounds of every choice and
avoidance, and banishing those beliefs through
which greatest tumults take possession of the soul.
Of all this the beginning and the greatest good is
prudence. Wherefore, prudence is a more precious
thing even than philosophy; from it spring all the
other virtues, for it teaches that we cannot lead a
life of pleasure which is not also a life of prudence,
honour, and justice; nor lead a life of prudence,
honour, and justice which is not also a life of pleasure.
For the virtues have grown into one with a pleasant
life, and a pleasant life is inseparable from them.

"Who, then, is superior, in thy judgment, to such a
man? He holds a holy belief concerning the gods,
and is altogether free from the fear of death. He
has diligently considered the end fixed by nature, and
understands how easily the limit of good things can
be procured and attained; that as for evils either
their duration or their poignancy is but slight.
Destiny, which some introduce as sovereign over all
things, he laughs to scorn, affirming that certain
things happen of necessity, others by chance, others
through our own agency. For he sees that necessity

destroys responsibility and that chance or fortune
is inconstant; whereas our own actions are free,
and it is to them that praise and blame naturally
attach. It were better, indeed, to accept the legends
of the gods than to bow beneath that yoke of destiny which the natural philosophers have imposed.
The one holds out some faint hope that we may
escape by honouring the gods, while the necessity of
the philosophers is deaf to all supplications. Nor
does such an one make chance a god, as the world
in general does (for in the acts of God nothing is
irregular), nor yet regard it as a vacillating cause,
for he believes that chance dispenses to men no good
or evil which can make life blessed though it furnishes means and occasions for great good and great
evil. He believes that the misfortune of the wise is
better than the prosperity of the fool. It is better,
in short, that what is well judged in action should not
owe its successful issue to the aid of chance.

"Exercise thyself in these and kindred precepts
day and night, both by thyself and with him who is
like unto thee; then never, either in waking or in
dream, wilt thou be disturbed but wilt live as a god
amongst men. For by living in the midst of immortal blessings man loses all semblance of mortality."

In this document scientific ethics, as the term is
now understood, is overlaid with a variety of other
topics. The practical exordium, the dogmatic in-
culcation of moral precepts, the almost apostolic
fervour and seriousness of tone find their nearest
counterpart in the writings of religious teachers.
We are reminded by turns of the Proverbs of Sol-
omon and of the Epistles of St. Paul. The rejection of the popular religion and the denial of
divine retribution are coupled with an emphatic

affirmation of the existence of blessed and immortal gods. The instinctive fear of death is declared to be groundless; and here the writer enlarges upon a theme, first started by the sophist Prodicus, that death is nothing to us. Incidentally, the value of life is vindicated and the folly of pessimism exposed. The limitation of desire is seen to involve habituation to an almost ascetic bodily discipline, in order that the wise man may become self-sufficing, that is, independent of external things. Lastly, the freedom of human action is stoutly maintained in opposition to the doctrine of natural necessity first promulgated by the earlier Atomists Leucippus and Democritus, but at the time of Epicurus developed with the utmost rigour and consistency by the Stoics.

On the main question there is no uncertainty. The pleasure of the agent is the foundation upon which Epicurus, like many after him, sought to construct a theory of morality which would explain scientifically the judgments of praise and blame passed by the ordinary man. All systems allow that there are self-regarding virtues and self-regarding duties, and when he has given his peculair interpretation of pleasure, Epicurus has no great difficulty with these. But the case is different when we come to the social virtues and the duties which a man owes to his neighbour. In a system which makes self-love the centre of all virtues, and in which all duties must be self-regarding, if we accept, as he did, as a psychological truth that by instinct and nature all are led to pursue their own pleasure and avoid their own pain, how can any conduct savouring of disinterestedness find rational justification? This was the great problem of the English and French moralists in that age of enlightenment, the eighteenth cen-

tury. As then, so two thousand years before in
Greece, extreme individualism was the order of
the day. The primary fact is individual man as he
is given by nature, and all that lies outside this,
all that he has been made by institutions like the
family and the state, all the relations that go beyond the individual are subsequent, secondary, de-
rivative, requiring to be explained from him and to
justify their validity to the reason. Take a concrete
instance. Whence came the rules of justice? What
makes actions just and how is my obedience to such
rules, enjoined by Epicurus, an indispensable means
to my own happiness? In short, how does disinterested conduct arise under a selfish system? The
answer given to this question was often repeated
later. It reappears in Hobbes and Rousseau. Before dealing with it, it is necessary to consider briefly
the Epicurean conception of the growth of human
civilisation from the earliest times.

Looking back at the past history of our planet,
Epicurus derives all organisms, first plants, then animals, from mother earth. The species with which we
are familiar are those which, being adapted to their
environment, prospered in the struggle for existence.
They were preceded by many uncouth creatures and
ill-contrived monsters, many races of living things,
which have since died out from lack of food or some
similar cause. Apart from the undeniable suggestion
of one feature in the doctrine of evolution, the account
of the origin of life is in its details wholly unscientific
and even repulsive. But with surer insight primitive
man is described as hardier than now: destitute of
clothing and habitation, he lived a roving life like the
beasts with whom he waged ceaseless warfare, haunt-
ing the woods and caves, insensible to hardship and

privation. The first step in advance was the discovery of fire, due to accident. Afterward man learned to build huts and clothe himself with skins. Then the progress of culture is traced with the beginnings of domestic life through the discovery and transmission of useful arts. As comforts multiplied, the robust strength of the state of nature was gradually impaired by new disabilities, particularly susceptibility to disease. Language was not the outcome of convention, but took its rise from the cries which, like the noises of animals, are the instinctive expression of the feelings and emotions. Experience is the mother of invention and of all the arts. They are all due to the intelligent improvement of what was offered or suggested to man by natural occasions. None of the blessings of civilisation are due to the adventitious aid of divine agency. Man raised himself from a state of primitive rudeness and barbarism and gradually widened the gulf which separated him from other animals. From the stage when men and women lived on the wild fruits of the wood and drank the running stream, when their greatest fear was of the claws and fangs of savage beasts, to the stage when they formed civic communities and obeyed laws and submitted to the ameliorating influences of wedlock and friendship, all has been the work of man, utilising his natural endowments and natural circumstances. Religion has been rather a hinderance than a help in the course of civilisation. Next to the use of money, the baleful dread of supernatural powers has been the most fruitful source of evil.

In this historical survey, where shall we find the origin of law and justice? Epicurus was fully convinced that in the present state of society "the just man enjoys the greatest peace of mind, the unjust is

full of the utmost disquietude";[1] and yet injustice is
not in itself an evil, and in the state of nature man
is predatory. The explanation tendered by Epicurus,
as by Hobbes and Hume, is that of a compact which,
once made, is ever afterward strictly observed. Yet
it is not easy to discover why men should carry out a
compact made in their natural, that is, predatory state.
Why should the wise man observe it if he find secret
injustice possible and convenient? Epicurus frankly
admits that the only conceivable motive which can
deter him is self-interest, the desire to avoid the painful anxieties that the perpetual dread of discovery
would entail. Even if the compact could be evaded,
prudential considerations forbid it, since the risk of
detection is enormous and the mere possibility of discovery is an ever-present evil sufficient to poison all
the goods of life. That such motives do not weigh
with criminals is irrelevant; we are dealing now with
the wise and prudent man. "Natural justice is a
contract of expediency, to prevent one man from
harming or being harmed by another."[2] "Those
animals which were incapable of making compacts
with one another, to the end that they might neither
inflict nor suffer harm, are without either justice or
injustice. Similarly those tribes which either could
not or would not form mutual covenants to the same
end are in the like case."[3] Justice, then, is artificial,
not natural. The view could not be more clearly
expressed. This is just the position taken up by
modern international law and just the attitude adopted by Christian nations; in historical times to those
outside the pale of civilisation, who are assumed

---

[1] *Epicurea*, p. 75, 3, golden maxim No. XVII.
[2] *Ib.*, p. 78, 8, golden maxim No. XXXI.
[3] *Ib.*, p. 78, 10, golden maxim No. XXXII.

to have no rights. So, too, Hume holds that we
should not, properly speaking, lie under any re-
straint of justice with regard to rational beings who
were so much weaker than ourselves that we had no
reason to fear their resentment. "There never was
an absolute justice," says one of the golden sentences, "but only a convention made in mutual intercourse, in whatever region, from time to time, providing against the infliction or suffering of harm." [1]
"Injustice is not in itself an evil, but only in its consequence, viz., the terror which is excited by apprehension that those appointed to punish such offences
will discover the injustice." [2] "It is impossible for
the man who secretly violates any article of the social
compact to feel confident that he will remain undis-
covered, even if he has already escaped ten thousand
times; for until his death he is never sure he will not
be detected." [3] It was easy for the Stoics to present
this in an unfavourable light as does Epictetus when
he says: "Not even does Epicurus himself declare
stealing to be bad, but he admits that detection is,
and because it is impossible to have security against
detection, for this reason he says, Do not steal." [4]
"Taken generally," to quote another Epicurean saying, "justice is the same for all, but in its application to particular cases of territory or the like, it
varies under different circumstances." [5] In other
words, justice is the foundation of all positive law,
but the positive law of one state will differ from that of
another. "Whatever in conventional law is attested
to be expedient in the needs arising out of mutual

[1] *Epicurea*, p. 78, 15, golden maxim No. XXXIII.
[2] *Ib.*, p. 79, 1, golden maxim No. XXXIV.
[3] *Ib.*, p. 79, 4, golden maxim No. XXXV.
[4] *Ib.*, p. 322, 6.
[5] *Ib.*, p. 79, 8, golden maxim No. XXXVI.

intercourse is by its nature just, whether the same for all or not, and in case any law is made and does not prove suitable to the expediency of mutual intercourse, then this is no longer just. And should the expediency which is expressed by the law vary and only for a time correspond with the notion of justice, nevertheless, for the time being, it was just, so long as we do not trouble ourselves about empty terms but look broadly at facts." [1] Thus a law judged to be inexpedient is no longer binding. The old sophistical quibble that no positive law can be unjust Epicurus, from his stand-point, can easily expose, and he is equally well able to meet the conservative dislike and dread of legislative innovation as something essentially immoral. "Where without any change in circumstances the conventional laws when judged by their consequences were seen not to correspond with the notion of justice, such laws were not really just; but wherever the laws have ceased to be expedient in consequence of a change in circumstances, in that case the laws were for the time being just, when they were expedient for the mutual intercourse of the citizens, and ceased subsequently to be just when they ceased to be expedient." [2] "He who best insured safety from external foes made into one nation all the folk capable of uniting together, and those incapable of such union he assuredly did not treat as aliens; if there were any whom he could not even on such terms incorporate, he excluded them from intercourse whenever this suited with his own interests." [3]

Thus civilisation is an advance upon the condition of primitive man; nor does Epicurus ever contem-

---

[1] *Epicurea*, p. 79, 12, golden maxim No. XXXVII.
[2] *Ib.*, p. 80, 6, golden maxim No. XXXVIII.
[3] *Ib.*, p. 80, 15, golden maxim No. XXXIX.

plate the possibility of undoing what has been done. Applying the standard of human good in his own conception of it as tranquil enjoyment, he pronounces government to be a benefit to the wise so far as it protects them from harm. But it does not therefore follow that they should themselves take part in political administration; they are only advised to do so in circumstances where it is necessary and so far as it is necessary for their own safety. Experience shows that as a rule the private citizen lives more calmly and safely than the public man. The burdens of office are a hinderance rather than an aid to the end of life. "The Epicureans," says Plutarch, "shun politics as the ruin and confusion of true happiness."[1] An unobtrusive life is the ideal. To strive at power without attaining one's own personal security is an act of folly certain to entail lasting discomfort. Moreover, as Philodemus remarks, "If any one were to inquire which influence is of all others the most hostile to friendship and the most productive of enmity, he would find it to be politics, because of the envy of one's rivals and the ambition natural in those so engaged and the discord recurring when opposite notions are proposed."[2] Restless spirits, however, who cannot find satisfaction in retirement are permitted to face the risks of public activity. To all forms of government the Epicureans were theoretically indifferent, but the impossibility of pleasing the multitude and the necessity of strong control inclined them to favour the monarchical principle. Under all circumstances they recommended unconditional obedience. The traditions of the old republican life of petty Greek states demanded from the citizen far more than this—active co-operation, personal sacrifice, enthusi-

[1] *Epicurea*, p. 327, 20.   [2] *Ib.*, p. 328, 4.

asm for the common cause. Judged by this standard, the Epicurean would seem to take an unfair
advantage of the state. He got all the protection it
afforded and shirked as much as he could of its
burdens. But, in reality, what he was prepared to
contribute would fully satisfy the demands of the
modern territorial state. To obey the laws, to pay
taxes, to assist by an occasional vote in the formation
of public opinion constitutes nowadays the whole of
civic duty for the vast majority of citizens. Under
existing conditions how can it be otherwise? For,
in order to integrate, as it were, these multitudinous
infinitesimals organisation is required; but division
of responsibility and specialisation of function cir-
cumscribe personal effort. Again, when the popular
cry has been adequately voiced by press or platform
and has taken effect through proportional representation or other constitutional means, the greatness
of the results secured and the very perfection of the
machinery for securing them leave less and less scope
to private initiative.

The consistent application of individualist principles might enjoin a severance, so far as is possible,
from the ties of the family no less than of the state,
and the picture of the wise man represents him as
shirking these responsibilities also. But such a
counsel of perfection has regard to special circumstances, and in all fairness the actual conduct of the
man should be allowed to correct the supposed tendency of his system. Now, by his kindness to his
brothers, his gratitude to his parents, and his tender
solicitude for his wards, Epicurus is proved to have
cherished warm family affection himself. Nor is it
reasonable to presume that the philosopher who
deprecated suicide, except in extreme cases, and set

the example by so cheerfully enduring severe physical pain, can ever seriously have intended race suicide. Political association, even if originally based upon a contract, has its present sanction in pains and penalties. It is at best a compromise, a *pis aller* of only relative and subsidiary value. Men submit to the compulsion and constraint which it entails for fear of finding something worse. The true form of association is that in which man surrenders nothing of his original freedom, and this Epicurus believed to be realised in friendship, upon which he set the highest value. The only duties that Epicurus recognises are those voluntarily accepted on reasonable grounds, not from natural instinct or compulsion of circumstances. "No one," says Epicurus, "loves another except for his own interest." [1] "Human nature alone does not give natural affection for nothing, nor can it love without advantage to itself." [2] "Of all things which wisdom provides for the happiness of a lifetime, by far the greatest is the acquisition of friendship." [3] The terms in which it is extolled recall the eulogies lavished upon the Christian grace of charity or love. It was the signal characteristic of the little society in the founder's lifetime, and it continued a prominent trait of the sect to the latest times. Upon its own principles no ethical system which starts with self-love can recognise disinterested conduct. Nor did Epicurus anticipate Hume's discovery and call in sympathy as a necessary supplement to self-interest. He is, therefore, obliged to maintain that friendship, like justice, is based solely upon mutual utility. The services rendered have the same selfish motive which prompts

---

[1] *Epicurea*, p. 324, 16; *cf.* Wotke, *Wiener Studien*, X, p. 193, sent. 23.
[2] *Epicurea*, p. 320, 12.   [3] *Ib.*, p. 77, 11.

the farmer to commit the seed to the soil in expectation of a future harvest. So alone the theory is consistent; friendship, like the cynic's gratitude, must
needs be a lively sense of favours yet to come. There
is, of course, a difficulty at the beginning. Some one
must make the start. "Neither those who are over-
ready nor those who are too slow to enter into
friendships are to be approved; one must even run
some risk in order to make friends." [1] "To do
good," says Epicurus, "is not only more noble, but
also more pleasant" (mark the predicate) "than to
receive good." [2] Benevolence would cease to be a
virtue if it ceased to be self-regarding. Yet it was
upon this unsound basis that devoted friendships
were based. When we are told that the wise man
will, upon occasion, even die for his friend, the suggestion of disinterested action, however inconsistent,
can hardly be dismissed. "The wise man suffers
no more pain when on the rack himself than when
his friend is upon it; but if any man suspects his
friend, his whole life will by his distrust be confounded and turned upside down." [3] And there are
other utterances to the same effect. "What we require is not so much to have our needs supplied by
our friends as to be assured that our needs will be
supplied by them." [4] "The wise man, when brought
into distress in company with others, shows himself
a comrade ready to give rather than to receive; so
great a treasure of self-reliance has he found." [5]

In the foregoing sketch the main questions of
ethics have come before us and the answers of

---

[1] Wotke, *Wiener Studien*, X, p. 193, sent. 28.
[2] *Epicurea*, p. 325, 10.
[3] Wotke, *l. c.*, p. 196, sentt. 56, 57.
[4] *Ib.*, *l. c.*, X, p. 193, sent. 34.   [5] *Ib.*, *l. c.*, X, p. 194, sent. 44.

Epicurus have been indicated in outline. Like his rivals the Stoics, he made his appeal to the world primarily as a moral teacher, an inquirer whose aim was to deal comprehensively and systematically with moral problems. To this inquiry the study of nature, which will occupy us in the next chapter, was subordinate. He had convinced himself that the main fruit of philosophy consisted in happiness of life and that philosophy was successful just in so far as this was promoted. This aspect of the system will become more apparent if we now consider the remarkable collection of its more important tenets, which has come down to us in the form of some forty isolated quotations from his voluminous writings. Whether Epicurus himself made this collection or whether it was formed by his disciples cannot now be precisely determined. At a very early time it obtained a wide circulation among his followers, who were ever afterward recommended to commit to memory this collection of golden maxims as well as other shorter or longer epitomes of the master's teaching. The importance attached to these authoritative pronouncements must be our excuse for reproducing the greater part of them, although it will be obvious that except the first, which lays the foundation for his views upon religion, and the twenty-second, twenty-third, and twenty-fourth, which deal with his theory of knowledge, they are of an ethical character and must therefore simply recapitulate the ethical theory which we have already attempted to expound. The following, then, are the main tenets or golden maxims of Epicurus: [1]

I. A blessed and eternal being has no trouble itself and brings no trouble upon any other being;

[1] The golden maxims are given in Usener, *Epicurea*, pp. 71 *sqq.*

hence it is exempt from movements of anger and favour, for every such movement implies weakness.

II. Death is nothing to us; for the body, when it has been resolved into its elements, has no feeling, and that which has no feeling is nothing to us.

III. The magnitude of pleasures is limited by the removal of all pain. Wherever there is pleasure, so long as it is present, there is no pain either of body or of mind or both.

IV. Continuous pain does not last long in the flesh, and pain, if extreme, is present a very short time, and even that degree of pain which barely outweighs pleasure in the flesh does not occur for many days together. Illnesses of long duration even permit of an excess of pleasure over pain in the flesh.

V. It is impossible to live a pleasant life without living wisely and well and justly, and it is impossible to live wisely and well and justly without living pleasantly. Whenever any one of these is lacking, when, for instance, the man does not live wisely, though he lives well and justly, it is impossible for him to live a pleasant life.

VI. As far as concerns protection from other men, any means of procuring this was a natural good.

VII. Some men sought to become famous and renowned, thinking that thus they would make themselves secure against their fellow-men. If, then, the life of such persons really was secure, they attained natural good; if, however, it was insecure, they have not attained the end which by nature's own promptings they originally sought.

VIII. No pleasure is in itself evil, but the things which produce certain pleasures entail annoyances many times greater than the pleasures themselves.

IX. If all pleasure had been capable of accumulation, if this had gone on not only in time, but all over the frame or, at any rate, the principal parts of man's nature, there would not have been any difference between one pleasure and another as, in fact, there now is.

X. If the objects which are productive of pleasures to profligate persons really freed them from fears of the mind—the fears, I mean, inspired by celestial and atmospheric phenomena, the fear of death, the fear of pain—if, further, they taught them to limit their desires, we should not have any reason to censure such persons, for they would then be filled with pleasure to overflowing on all sides and would be exempt from all pain, whether of body or mind, that is, from all evil.

XI. If we had never been molested by alarms at celestial and atmospheric phenomena, nor by the misgiving that death somehow affects us, nor by neglect of the proper limits of pains and desires, we should have had no need to study natural science.

XII. It would be impossible to banish fear on matters of the highest importance if a man did not know the nature of the whole universe but lived in dread of what the legends tell us. Hence, without the study of nature there was no enjoyment of unmixed pleasures.

XIII. There would be no advantage in providing security against our fellow-men so long as we were alarmed by occurrences over our heads or beneath the earth, or in general by whatever happens in the infinite void.

XIV. When tolerable security against our fellowmen is attained, then on a basis of power arises most genuine bliss, to wit, the security of a private life withdrawn from the multitude.

XV.   Nature's wealth has its bounds and is easy to procure, but the wealth of vain fancies recedes to an infinite distance.

XVI.   Fortune but slightly crosses the wise man's path; his greatest and highest interests are directed by reason throughout the course of life.

XVII.   The just man enjoys the greatest peace of mind, the unjust is full of the utmost disquietude.

XVIII.   Pleasure in the flesh admits no increase when once the pain of want has been removed; after that it only admits of variation.   The limit of pleasure in the mind is obtained by calculating the pleasures themselves and the contrary pains, which cause the mind the greatest alarms.

XIX.   Infinite time and finite time hold an equal amount of pleasure, if we measure the limits of that pleasure by reason.

XX.   The flesh assumes the limits of pleasure to be infinite, and only infinite time would satisfy it.   But the mind, grasping in thought what the end and limit of the flesh is, and banishing the terrors of futurity, procures a complete and perfect life and has no longer any need of infinite time.   Nevertheless, it does not shun pleasure, and even in the hour of death, when ushered out of existence by circumstances, the mind does not fail to enjoy the best life.

XXI.   He who understands the limits of life knows how easy it is to procure enough to remove the pain of want and make the whole of life complete and perfect.   Hence he has no longer any need of things which are not to be won save by conflict and struggle.

XXII. We must take into account as the end all
that really exists and all clear evidence of sense to
which we refer our opinions; for otherwise everything
will be full of uncertainty and confusion.

XXIII. If you fight against all your sensations
you will have no standard to which to refer, and thus
no means of judging even those sensations which you
pronounce false.

XXIV. If you reject absolutely any single sensation without stopping to discriminate between that
which is matter of opinion and awaits further confirmation and that which is already present, whether
in sensation or in feeling or in any mental apprehension, you will throw into confusion even the rest
of your sensations by your groundless belief, so as
to reject the truth altogether. If you hastily affirm
as true all that awaits confirmation in ideas based
on opinion, as well as that which does not, you will
not escape error, as you will be taking sides in every
question involving truth and error.

XXV. If you do not on every separate occasion
refer each of your actions to the chief end of nature,
but if instead of this in the act of choice or avoidance
you swerve aside to some other end, your acts will
not be consistent with your theories.

XXVI. Some desires lead to no pain when they
remain ungratified. All such desires are unnecessary,
and the longing is easily got rid of when the thing
desired is difficult to procure or when the desires
seem likely to produce harm.

XXVII. Of all the means which are procured
by wisdom to insure happiness throughout the whole
of life, by far the most important is the acquisition
of friends.

XXVIII. The same conviction, which inspires

confidence that nothing we have to fear is eternal or even of long duration, also enables us to see that even in our limited life nothing enhances our security so much as friendship.

XXIX. Of our desires, some are natural and necessary; others are natural, but not necessary; others, again, are neither natural nor necessary, but are due to groundless opinion.

XXX. Some natural desires, again, entail no pain when not gratified, though the objects are vehemently pursued. These desires also are due to groundless opinion, and when they are not got rid of, it is not because of their own nature, but because of the man's groundless opinion.

XL.[1] Those who could best insure the confidence that they would be safe from their neighbours, being thus in possession of the surest guarantee, passed the most agreeable life in each other's society, and their enjoyment of the fullest intimacy was such that, if one of them died before his time, the survivors did not lament his death as if it called for pity.

To the foregoing we may add a few ethical fragments of Diogenes of Œnoanda, which may or may not be actual words of Epicurus:[2]

"Nothing is so productive of cheerfulness as to abstain from meddling and not to engage in difficult undertakings, nor force yourself to do something beyond your power. For all this involves your nature in tumults."[3]

"The main part of happiness is the disposition which is under our own control. Service in the field is

---

[1] Numbers XXXI to XXXIX, which deal with justice, have already been quoted in this chapter, pp. 177 *sqq.*

[2] See *Diogenis Œnoandensis Fragmenta* (Ioh. William), p. xi.

[3] Diogenes of Œnoanda, Fragment LVI (William).

hard work, and others hold command. Public speaking abounds in heart-throbs and in anxiety whether you can carry conviction. Why, then, pursue an object like this, which is at the disposal of others?" [1]

"Not nature, which is the same in all, makes men noble or ignoble, but their actions and dispositions." [2]

"Wealth beyond the requirements of nature is no more benefit to men than water to a vessel which is full. Both alike must be supposed to overflow. We can look upon another's possessions without perturbation and can enjoy purer pleasure than they, for we are free from their arduous struggle." [3]

"Nature forces us to utter an exclamation when groaning under pain, but to indulge in lamentations because we cannot rejoice in the ranks of the healthy and prosperous is the result of groundless opinion." [4]

It is one thing to trace the outlines of an ethical system; it is quite another to comprehend its inner spirit. When a philosopher's works have not come down to us, it is some compensation if some of his memorable and characteristic utterances have been preserved, because they impressed themselves upon contemporaries and on posterity. Epicurus was a fearless and original thinker, contending at great odds against the sympathies and prejudices of the world. It is worth while to collect a few of his striking sayings in order, if possible, to get some idea of the workings of his mind.

"You must become a slave to philosophy if you would gain true freedom." [5]

"The most precious fruit of independence and plain living is freedom." [6]

---

[1] *Ib.*, Fragment LVII. [2] *Ib.*, Fragment LIX. [3] *Ib.*, Fragment LX.
[4] *Ib.*, Fragment LXI. [5] *Epicurea*, p. 160, 25.
[6] Wotke, *Wiener Studien*, X, p. 197, sent. 77.

"Let us completely drive out evil habits as if they were wicked men who have for long wrought us great harm." [1]

"Among the other ills which attend folly is this: it is always *beginning* to live." [2]

"We are born once; twice we cannot be born, and for everlasting we must be non-existent. But thou, who art not master of the morrow, puttest off the right time. Procrastination is the ruin of life for all; and, therefore, each of us is hurried and unprepared at death." [3]

"A foolish life is uncomfortable and restless; it is wholly engrossed with the future." [4]

"It is absurd to run to death from weariness of life when your style of life has forced you to run to death. What so absurd as to court death when you have made life restless through fear of death?" [5]

"Learn betimes to die or, if thou like it better, to pass over to the gods." [6]

"He who is least in need of the morrow will meet the morrow most pleasantly." [7]

"Vain is the discourse of that philosopher by which no human suffering is healed." [8]

"We must both study philosophy and manage our household affairs at the same time, and use the rest of our resources, and never cease to proclaim the maxims of true wisdom." [9]

"How fleeting a thing is all the good and evil of the multitude! But wisdom has naught to do with Fortune." [10]

---

[1] *Ib.*, p. 194, sent. 46.
[2] *Epicurea*, p. 308, 19; *cf.* Wotke, *l. c.*, p. 196, sent. 60.
[3] *Ib.*, p. 162, 4.
[4] *Ib.*, p. 307, 19.   [5] *Ib.*, p. 309, 26.   [6] *Ib.*, p. 162, 18.   [7] *Ib.*, p. 307, 9.
[8] *Ib.*, 169, 14.   [9] Wotke, *Wiener Studien*, X, p. 194, sent. 41.
[10] *Epicurea*, p. 307, 3.

"The repose of most men is a lethargy and their activity a madness." [1]

"Though he is being tortured on the rack, the wise man is still happy." [2]

"If the wise man is being burned, if he is being tortured—nay, within the very bull of Phalaris, he will say: 'How delightful this is! How little care I for it!'" [3]

Many critics before and after the time of Cicero concur with Cicero himself in treating this famous utterance as unjustifiable exaggeration or even as mere sentimental rhodomontade. But a French scholar [4] has recently called attention to a remarkable fact. Modern psychology seems to show that, given the right set of conditions, Epicurus was, after all, right. Even now we know very little of the extent to which the mind, under the obsession of certain ideas, can ignore or even be unconscious of what goes on in the body.

"It is the wise man alone who will feel gratitude to his friends, but to them equally whether they are present or absent." [5]

"If you live by nature, you will never be poor; if by opinion, you will never be rich." [6]

"Great wealth is but poverty when matched with the law of nature." [7]

"If any one thinks his own not to be most ample, he may become lord of the whole world and will yet be wretched." [8]

"With many the acquisition of riches is not an end to their miseries but only a change." [9]

[1] Wotke, *Wiener Studien*, X, p. 192, sent. 11.

[2] *Epicurea*, p. 338, 1.   [3] *Ib.*, p. 338, 4 *sqq.*

[4] V. Brochard, in *L'année philosophique* for 1903.   The article is entitled *La Morale d'Epicure*.   See especially pp. 8-12.

[5] *Epicurea*, p. 335, 1.   [6] *Ib.*, p. 161, 19.   [7] *Ib.*, p. 303, 24.

[8] *Ib.*, p. 302, 29.   [9] *Ib.*, p. 304, 23; *cf. ib.*, 304, 19.

"The perturbation of the soul is not removed nor any considerable joy produced by the possession either of the greatest wealth or of honour and reputation with the multitude or by anything else due to indeterminate causes." [1]

"Happiness and blessedness do not consort with extent of wealth or weight of responsibilities or public office or power, but with painlessness, with mildness of feeling, and that disposition of soul which defines what is according to nature." [2]

"Trust me, your words (professions of philosophy) will sound grander in a common bed and a rough coverlet; they will not be merely spoken then, they will be proved true." [3]

"The knowledge of sin is the beginning of salvation." [4]

"The first duty of salvation is to preserve our vigour and to guard against the defiling of our life in consequence of maddening desires." [5]

"It is an evil thing to live in necessity, but there is no necessity to live in necessity." [6]

"Let us not accuse the flesh as the cause of great evils, neither let us attribute our distresses to outward things. Let us rather seek the causes of this distress within our souls, and let us cut off every vain craving and hope for things which are fleeting, and let us become wholly masters of ourselves. For a man is unhappy either from fear or from unlimited and vain desires, but if a man bridle these he may secure for himself the blessing of reason. In so far as thou art in distress, thou art in distress because

[1] Wotke, *Wiener Studien*, X, p. 198, sent. 81.
[2] Usener, *Epicurea*, p. 325, 30.
[3] *Epicurea*, p. 162, 25.   [4] *Ib.*, p. 318, 12.
[5] Wotke, *Wiener Studien*, p. 198, sent. 80.
[6] *Epicurea*, p. 306, 7; also Wotke, *Wiener Studien*, p. 191, sent. 9.

thou hast forgotten Nature, for thou layest upon thyself fears and desires which have no limits. And it were better for thee to have no fears and to lie upon a bed of straw, than to have a golden couch and lavish table, yet to be troubled in mind." [1]

"Give thanks to Nature, the blessed, because she hath made necessary things easy to procure, while things hard to be obtained are not necessary." [2]

"By the love of true philosophy every troublous and painful desire is destroyed." [3]

"If you wish to make Pythocles happy, add not to his riches, but take away from his desires." [4]

"No one of the foolish is content with what he has, but rather he is distressed on account of what he has not. Just as those who are fever-stricken are always athirst, owing to the severity of their disease, and desire things of the most opposite kinds, so those who are sick in soul are always in need of everything, and through their excessive craving they fall headlong into manifold desires." [5]

"Nothing is enough for him to whom enough is too little." [6]

"Cheerful poverty is an honourable thing." [7]

"Having bread and water, I revel in the pleasure of the body, and I loathe the pleasures of costly living, not on their own account, but because of the inconveniences which follow them." [8]

"We strive after independence, not that in all cases we may use that which is cheap and plain, but that we may have no anxiety as to such matters." [9]

"We must select some good man and keep him

[1] *Epicurea*, p. 291, 9; 305, 33; 161, 29; 163, 4.
[2] *Ib.*, p. 300, 26.   [3] *Ib.*, p. 296, 12.   [4] *Ib.*, p. 143, 3.
[5] *Ib.*, p. 300, 12.   [6] Wotke, *Wiener Studien*, p. 197, sent. 68.
[7] *Epicurea*, p. 303, 8.   [8] *Ib.*, p. 156, 4.   [9] *Ib.*, p. 345, 30.

ever before our eyes, that so we may live as if he were beholding us, and may do everything as if in his sight." [1]

"Do everything as if Epicurus saw you." [2]

"Reverence for the wise man is a great good for the reverer." [3]

"The wise man will not punish his slaves, but will take pity on them, and will show consideration to any that are zealous." [4]

"Turn not away from the prayer of thine enemy when he is in distress, yet take heed to thyself, for he is no better than a dog." [5]

"Nobility is best brought out in wisdom and friendship, whereof the one, wisdom, is an immortal; the other, friendship, a mortal good." [6]

"We ought to look round for people to eat and drink with before we look for something to eat and drink; feeding without a friend is the life of a lion or a wolf." [7]

"Sweet is the memory of the friend who is dead." [8]

Upon politics and the pursuit of fame Epicurus is very plain-spoken.

"I never wished to please the people; for that which I know, the people does not approve; and what the people approves, that I know not." [9]

"Man is not by nature adapted for living in civic communities and in civilisation." [10]

"The wise man will be fond of living in the country." [11]

---

[1] *Epicurea*, p. 163, 18. Compare the similar precept of Epictetus given above, Chapter IV, p. 115.   [2] *Ib.*, p. 163, 26.

[3] Wotke, *Wiener Studien*, X, p. 193, sent. 32.

[4] *Epicurea*, p. 335, 14.   [5] *Ib.*, p. 164, 21.

[6] Wotke, *l. c.*, p. 197, sent. 78.   [7] *Epicurea*, p. 324, 25.

[8] *Ib.*, p. 164, 6.   [9] *Ib.*, p. 157, 26.   [10] *Ib.*, p. 327, 9.

[11] *Ib,*, p. 331, 5.

"The wise man will take just so much thought for fame as to avoid being despised." [1]

"I have said this not to many persons, but to thee, for we are a large enough theatre one to the other." [2]

"Amid so many blessings, it has done us no harm that our glorious Greece not only does not know us, but has hardly heard of us." [3]

"Epicurus spurns under his feet the achievements of Themistocles and Miltiades, and makes them cheap. . . . The Epicureans name statesmen only to ridicule them and to destroy their fame, saying that Epaminondas had some merit in him, but it was small or 'wee'—such is the word they use—while they nickname him 'Iron Bowels,' and ask what possessed him to go marching through the middle of the Peloponnesus, and why he did not sit at home with a woollen cap on his head." [4]

But Epicurus was no harder on the great Athenians than Plato had been before him in the *Gorgias*. The following extracts are controversial and directed against the Stoics:

"Epicurus makes a jest of our distinctions between 'what is honourable' and 'what is base,' and says we are taken up with words and utter mere empty sounds. He says that he does not understand what 'honourable conduct' means, if it be not a thing accompanied by pleasure, unless, perchance, it mean what is praised by the popular breath. The praise of men, Epicurus says, is sought after for the sake of pleasure." [5]

"Ask Epicurus, and he will say that moderate pain is a greater evil than the utmost disgrace." [6]

---

[1] *Epicurea*, p. 331, 12.   [2] *Ib.*, p. 63, 7.   [3] *Ib.*, p. 58, 13.
[4] *Ib,,* p. 329, 13 *sqq.*, 16 *sqq.*
[5] *Ib.*, p. 340, 32 *sqq.*; 123, 4 *sqq.*   [6] *Ib.*, p. 326, 14.

"Courage is a thing enslaved to fashions, and to the blame of men, and shaped by foreign opinion and notions; you practise courage, and you encounter hardships and dangers, not because you have no fear of them, but because you are still more afraid of those other things." [1]

Here again we are reminded of Plato, who in the *Phædo* disparages civic or popular courage (that is, the virtue of the ordinary citizen as distinct from that of the philosopher) on precisely the same grounds, that it is inspired by fear. But there is this difference, that Plato, who upheld the absolute value of true courage, as of the other virtues, would cultivate and develop even its imperfect and inadequate manifestations; while Epicurus, who denied the absolute value of virtue, and made it simply a means to pleasure, is free to reject it whenever it does not conduce to that end.

This chapter may fitly close with a few more gleanings from the sayings of Epicurus:

"There is no need to spoil the present by longing for what is not; rather reflect that even what you have was beyond your expectations."

"Envy no one; the good do not merit it, while as for the wicked, the more they prosper, the more harm they do to themselves."

"It is vain to ask the gods for what we can procure for ourselves."

"Confront every desire with this question: What shall I gain by gratifying this desire and what shall I lose by suppressing it?"

"The man of tranquil mind causes no annoyance either to himself or to others." [2]

---

[1] *Epicurea*, p. 317, lines 4 *sqq.* of *Notes.*
[2] Wotke, *Wiener Studien*, X, pp. 194 *sqq.*, sentt. 35, 53, 65, 71, 79.

It is worth while to make an effort to discover the real Epicurus, to understand what manner of man he was. Our best materials are his own writings. The letter to Menœceus has already been translated; that to Herodotus will occupy us in the next chapter, perhaps to the weariness and impatience of the reader. These letters together with other fragmentary records certainly convey the impression of a strong personality. We see that Epicurus had a logical mind, was a great systematiser, belonged, in short, to the class of daring and self-confident innovators. Like others of this class, he felt that he had a mission, and under great difficulties, in face of much opposition, laboured with unremitting industry to accomplish a self-imposed task. It may not be amiss to compare him with other such men. If amid great differences points of resemblance are disclosed, these may enable us to fill in the outlines of our mental picture and to form a better judgment of Epicurus himself. For this purpose we select two eminent modern philosophers, Jeremy Bentham and Herbert Spencer, men who far surpassed the Athenian sage in the greatness of their aims and achievements, but yet may be said, in a sense, to have continued his work and to have sustained, in later ages and under altered conditions, the same cause.

Bentham lived the life of a recluse as much as Epicurus. The great influence he exercised was due solely to his writings. We are told that his constitution was weakly in childhood, but strengthened with advancing years so as to allow him to get through an incredible amount of sedentary labour, while he retained to the last the fresh and cheerful temperament of a boy. This might be said almost word for word of Epicurus.

Bentham was able to gather around him a group of congenial friends and pupils; so did Epicurus. Though not a morose visionary, he thought general society a waste of time, disliked poetry as misrepresentation, but gave good dinners, delighted in country sights, and in making others happy. We have seen that each one of these traits is reproduced in our accounts of Epicurus. When Rush, at that time the American minister in England, visited Bentham at the Hermitage, he tells us that he was received with the simplicity of a philosopher amid shrubberies and flowers, green and large shaded walks. So, we may well believe, were visitors received by Epicurus in his gardens. Rush further records that Bentham had the benevolence of manner suited to the philanthropy of his mind. The visitor to Epicurus would, we may be sure, have said the same. Bentham's conversation revealed a typically logical as opposed to a historical mind, a contempt for the past, and a wish to be clear of all association with it. The same trait is suggested by what we learn of Epicurus, who evidently believed he was inaugurating a new era in which the search for happiness might at last be prosecuted with success.

Turning now to Spencer, one of the most striking features of his character was the small weight he attached to authority or, to be more exact, his utter disregard of it. Professed apologists admit this.[1] The prominence of the same trait in Epicurus is unmistakable. As we have seen, he avowed that he was self-taught, and did not scruple to assail the most eminent of his predecessors with merciless ridicule. As Spencer grew up to manhood, his constitutional proneness to set authority at defiance became, we are

[1] *Life*, by Duncan, c. XXIX, p. 489.

told, less an instinctive impulse and more a matter
of principle.   In his thinking, as well as in his acting,
he set authority at naught.   That with Epicurus also
contempt for authority was a matter of principle is
very obvious.   "All my life long," writes Spencer, "I
have been a thinker and not a reader, being able to
say with Hobbes that 'if I had read as much as other
men I should have known as little.'" [1]   Epicurus
would have indorsed this sentiment, as Heraclitus
had done before him.   But Spencer's disregard of
authority was, we are told, a disregard of personal
authority only, and was accompanied by a whole-
hearted fealty to principles.   So too emphatically
with Epicurus.   Spencer's father wrote of him: "It
appears to me that the laws of nature are to him what
revealed religion is to us, and that any wilful infrac-
tion of those laws is to him as much a sin as to us is
disbelief in what is revealed." [2]   His biographer insists that though Spencer did not accept the dogmas
of any creed, he was, in the truest sense, religious.
"To pay homage to royal persons, while showing
little respect for the principles that underlie human
society, drew from him the reproof: 'It is so disloyal.'
To bend the knee and utter praise to a Divine person,
while ignoring the principles of religion and morality,
met with a similar condemnation: 'It is so irre-
ligious.'" [3]   This may help us better to understand
the position of Epicurus on the subject of religion.
With all his outspoken condemnation of the prevailing
polytheism, he claimed for himself and his followers
the possession of the only true and genuine piety.
Indeed, the approximation is yet closer than at first
appears.   No one can read his own fragmentary
utterances, much less the splendid poem of Lucretius,

[1] Duncan, p. 490.   [2] *Ib.*, p. 491.   [3] *Ib.*, p. 490.

without perceiving a deep undertone of religious fervour. It was impious, they held, to acquiesce in the popular faith, but it is not in the reverence due to the shadowy deities of the intermundia that their religious spirit finds its true manifestation. The laws of nature, *fœdera naturæ*, excite, especially in the Roman poet, a higher emotion, a more reverent awe.

The comparison holds good of less pleasing traits. Spencer, his biographer admits, had an abundant share of self-confidence. "The possible failure of any of his many inventions was seldom taken into account. His doctrines were from the outset deemed secure against attack, notwithstanding repeated experiences of having to modify or enlarge or restrict his previous expositions. On Spencer, accustomed to think and act for himself, 'the other side' did not obtrude." [1] It is hardly necessary to point out that all this is eminently true of Epicurus, whose confidence in himself again and again becomes arrogance, while his dogmatism was not "occasional" but a permanent habit. Had this not been the case, he would never have rejected the natural necessity of Democritus with such scorn, would never have excogitated the declination of the atom, to say nothing of other less serious errors. Galton writes of Spencer: "He loved to dogmatise from *a priori* axioms"—how true this is of Epicurus—"and to criticise, and I soon found that the way to get the best from him was to be patient and not to oppose." [2] The subservience of the Epicurean brotherhood to the master was proverbial in antiquity; the man who expected his disciples to get his doctrines by heart and memorise the epitomes he prepared for their use must have had more than Spencer's share of dogmatism. But the

[1] Duncan, p. 492.   [2] *Ib.*, p. 501.

two resembled each other in more important matters, in the passion for systematisation, the determination to deduce, so far as possible, all the consequences of one wide-reaching principle; again, in freedom from worldly ambition and in whole-hearted devotion to their task.   Spencer often spoke, we are told, as if he had a mission, a message to deliver to mankind.   We have noticed the same trait in Epicurus and it is a clue to much of his conduct.

No one can be better aware than the present writer that the foregoing coincidences are useful only by way of illustration and must be taken *cum grano salis*. Historical parallels, however interesting, are apt to be purely fanciful.   At the best they have little independent value, just because so much depends upon the point of view from which the comparison is made.

CHAPTER VI

THE ATOMIC THEORY

Science has been defined as ordered knowledge of phenomena and the relations between them. There can be no doubt that the beginnings of modern science go back to the Greeks; in certain departments, such as geometry, astronomy, and medicine, the affiliation and transmission of ideas is particularly well attested. We must not, however, overlook the great difference between the position of the Greeks and that of the modern inquirer. The latter has at his command instruments and appliances of wonderful accuracy and precision for making observations and experiments. The ancients had no microscope, no telescope, no scientific apparatus of any sort save the carpenter's rule and a pair of compasses. In our days every new theory can be directly tested by comparison with the store of facts already accumulated through the ages. With the Greeks this was not so. So scanty was their knowledge that they seldom had at hand any means of checking a new theory beyond the phenomena which it was invented to explain. Under such circumstances, it was inevitable that conjecture and discussion should usurp the part now played by observation and experiment. In science then, as in metaphysics now, each thinker had his own system, starting anew with first principles and reaching conclusions which had no more validity than the premisses. The reader must be careful, then, not to confuse ancient atomism with the modern atomic theory, which from the time of Dalton has found its place in the text-books of chemistry. The modern conception of atoms and molecules serves to explain certain definite and detailed facts of chemistry and physics. The theory is the best working hypothesis which the science of Dalton's time could excogitate for explaining them, and until the discovery of Röntgen rays and the radio-active properties of certain substances it held the field. What modifications it will undergo in the physics of the future no man of science will be bold enough to predict. The modern atomic theory, then, was suggested by and meant to explain certain indisputable definite facts of chemical combination and gaseous volume. But these facts were unknown to the ancient Atomists. They put forward their theory at a time when men's minds were busy, not with the laws of combination of seventy or eighty known elements, but with more fundamental and far-reaching problems. They were in quest of some permanent and primary element which by its transformations would account for the variety of nature. Controversy raged over the question, more ontological than physical, whether one such primary element should be assumed or more than one or an infinite number. Some thought they had discovered it in water, some in air, some in fire. It might seem that no progress could be made on these lines, yet gradually there emerged the conception of primary matter with three properties. It must be (1) indestructible or quantitatively constant, (2) immutable or qualitatively constant, and (3) impenetrable. Empedocles assumed four elements, earth, water, air, and fire; Anaxagoras, an infinity of qualita-

tively unlike particles. Leucippus, the earliest of the
Atomists, postulated an infinite number of primary
particles, homogeneous and indivisible, but quantitatively different, that is, differing only in shape and
size. Already Empedocles had derived the endless
difference in things known to sense from the varying
combination and separation of his four elements;
Leucippus now resolved the qualitative differences
of things into quantitative differences, that is, into
varieties of position, order, and arrangement of combining atoms, and the different sizes and shapes of
the atoms themselves.

Of any scientific theory we are entitled to ask:
Is it fruitful? Does it point out the way for further
inquiry? Does it explain one set of phenomena
in terms of something simpler? The atomic theory possessed these merits in a high degree. Tried
by every test, from the stand-point of modern science it evinces its superiority to all its rivals. And
yet it was never popular; we may even say it was
unpopular and discredited in antiquity. In this respect it shared the fate of that other great discovery of the Greeks, the heliocentric hypothesis
in astronomy. Both alike were uncongenial Greek
prejudices and made their appearance long before
the world at large was prepared to appreciate them;
for the path of progress is not always a straight
line, but often more nearly resembles a spiral.
Whatever the cause, the mechanical explanation of
nature was abandoned by Plato and Aristotle, the
acutest intellects of the time, in favour of a teleological
system. It was no slight feat to have reduced the
world of physical change to modes of matter in
motion. But to their main hypothesis the Atomists
attached certain corollaries not so well calculated to

command universal assent. Body, they held, is the sole reality; nothing incorporeal exists. Motion, again, was taken to be the sole form of energy. And here we may be permitted to remark that the history of modern physical theories as to the constitution of the sensible world is little more than an account of the way in which energy has gradually taken its place alongside of matter as an equally real thing and has tended more and more to replace it altogether. But to the early Atomists in the infancy of science matter and energy were still undistinguished under the single conception of body; body was the form in which both were imagined. The existence of body is attested by the senses, but motion, in the view of Leucippus and his great follower Democritus, was inconceivable apart from empty space or void, to which they also attributed existence. Here, again, we may note that the meaning of the term existence is enlarged, for the mode of existence of space is not the same as that of body. Moreover, the existence of empty space or vacuum is not directly attested by the senses, but reached by reasoning. It is instructive to compare the procedure of those acute reasoners the Eleatics, who undoubtedly influenced all the physical theories subsequent to them. They argued thus: Motion is impossible without a vacuum; there is no vacuum; *ergo*, there is no motion. Accordingly, the Eleatic Parmenides regarded the phenomenal world of change and motion as mere illusive appearance. In his view there is no other ultimate reality but the one immutable Being. Leucippus and Democritus may be supposed to argue from the same premiss thus: Motion is impossible without a vacuum; there is undoubtedly motion, for the senses attest it; *ergo*, there is vacuum, or empty space. But this is a conclusion of reason, precisely as the Eleatic one immutable Being is a conclusion of reason. The senses no more tell us directly of the one than of the other. Thus, on the possibility of motion and the existence of void, Eleatics and Atomists are diametrically opposed; but in spite of this the atom of Democritus inherits most of the characteristics which the Eleatics claimed for their one immutable Being.

This system Epicurus found ready to his hand, and with this he was satisfied. Only modifications in detail were required to adapt it to his purpose. The writings of Leucippus and Democritus, with the exception of a few fragments, have perished. Almost all our knowledge in detail of their speculations is derived from the form given to them by Epicurus and by his follower, the Roman Lucretius, in his celebrated poem, *On the Nature of Things*. That marvellous work has made a deep and lasting impression on the modern world, particularly on men of science. They have vied with one another in extolling the poet's firm grasp of scientific principles, his clear conception of law in the physical universe, his sympathetic and penetrating observation, his unrivalled power of bringing together scattered facts and embracing them in one comprehensive view, his bold use of the scientific imagination, his insight into multitudinous hidden processes and motions on too small a scale to be seen, which yet in every way conform to the processes and motions on a larger scale attested by our senses. It was natural, therefore, that Lucretius himself or, at any rate, his master, Epicurus, should be proclaimed as the one true scientific thinker of antiquity. But it is not properly to them that such praise belongs. The system unfolded in the poem did not originate with the poet or with his master. So far as we can judge, they added very little of real worth; some of their alterations were for the worse, and in one particular they came very near to imperilling the very foundations of the system. The credit to which Epicurus is justly entitled is that of having made a wise selection. Among conflicting theories he chose to stand by the mechanical conception of the physical universe, when it had fallen into disfavour, and unhesitatingly rejected the fashionable teleology. His doing so testifies to his acute intellect and critical insight, but still more to the honesty, fearlessness, and independence with which he invariably followed his convictions. He also popularised the system he adopted and lent it a new lease of life. So much will be readily admitted, but an impartial estimate of his services cannot go beyond this. He made no discoveries in science himself, nor did any Epicurean after him. He rather discouraged the prosecution of physical inquiries of any sort beyond a certain point. His attitude to natural science as a whole deserves careful consideration. He takes it up because, if we are to be happy, we must be released from mental trouble, above all from groundless fears, more particularly the terrors of superstition, the fear of the gods, and the dread of death. Without this strong impelling motive Epicurus would never have engaged in the study of nature at all. His sole aim is to convince himself that these terrors are unreal and imaginary, and if, incidentally, he discovers a great deal about the constitution of the world and man's place in nature, it is because he cannot otherwise banish these terrors from the mind. Scientific investigation is permissible only so far as it

conduces to this end by laying down the true place
of man in the system of things. Beyond this there
is no need to go. The laboratories, museums, ob-
servatories, and other appliances of modern times
for research and discovery, would thus be condemned in anticipation as superfluous. Knowledge
in itself and for its own sake he regarded as of little worth. And this was no mere passing phase;
it expressed the man's fundamental and settled conviction.

Reference has already been made to certain icono-
clastic tendencies of Epicurus. We have seen that
he disparaged the education which he, like other
Greeks, had received at school. Literature fared no
better. The whole poetic art he abhorred as "the
deadly bait of fiction." In this sweeping condemnation he agrees with one phase of Plato's many-
sided development, represented in the tenth book of
the *Republic*. In banishing the poets both philosophers were actuated by the same narrow fanatical
spirit which led the Puritans to shut up the theatres
in the interests of morality. The rejection of mathematical studies is, at first sight, harder to explain.
The fact, however, is certain. Before he became an
Epicurean, Polyænus had made great progress in
mathematics; after his conversion we are told that
he gave them up and unlearned the science. The
reason alleged is that in the view of Epicurus, geometry, astronomy, and kindred sciences rested on false
premisses, and could not, therefore, lead to true results. His concern was with the real world, in which
he could nowhere find points, lines, and surfaces, as
defined by the geometer. Again, he could not
understand why infinities should not all be equal;
he invariably treated them as if they were equal.

And why were line and surface bound to be continuous? Why could they not be reduced to successions or series of discrete, discontinuous magnitudes? The same objection to the foundations of geometry had already been made by the sophist Protagoras, who in his work on mathematics attacked the hypotheses of the science because they contradicted our sensible impressions. Thus Protagoras held that there was no such thing in nature as a straight line or a perfect circle, and denied that the tangent to a sphere touched it only at a single point. If this objection were valid, the whole of geometry would be a pretended science, which has nothing in real existence for its subject-matter. The same line of attack was afterward developed by the Sceptics, as we learn from Sextus Empiricus. It must be carefully distinguished from the reasons for which the antagonistic schools of Cynics and Cyrenaics for once united in rejecting the mathematical sciences. The ground of complaint of these Socratics was the inutility of the study. None of its students were made morally better by their proficiency. As Aristippus urged, caricaturing, if not echoing, the methods of Socrates: "Every common mechanic has something to say in his craft about good and evil, useful and useless, but these practical considerations never enter into the purview of the mathematician." Whether Epicurus was also moved by these considerations of practical utility, we are nowhere informed. Zeno of Sidon, a later Epicurean, attacked Euclid on different grounds, arguing that the proofs were insufficient and the definitions unsuitable, if not unintelligible; whereupon the Stoic Posidonius took up the challenge and wrote in defence of mathematics. In a similar spirit at a later time the Stoic Cleomedes, in a work still extant, defended the current astronomy against Epicurean assaults.

Epicurus, however, has had his modern champions and we will state their case, which is far stronger for astronomy than for geometry. According to them, the rejection of the current astronomy, instead of a reproach, is a crown of glory to our philosopher. They call attention to the fact that the science which he condemned was not the astronomy of to-day, which rests upon exact observation and theories universally accepted, apart from a handful of earth-flatteners, but something very different. In his time such observations of planetary movements as had been made were few and imperfect, and astronomy was a mass of conflicting theories, a field in which speculation, sometimes of the wildest sort, ran riot. Toward all such speculations he adopted an attitude of cautious reserve. He did not refuse to entertain any of the discordant explanations of celestial phenomena then in vogue, but upon examining and comparing them he found no grounds for preferring one to the other. Certain assumptions granted, they were all more or less probable, they all lacked convincing evidence, and Epicurus was determined to believe nothing of which he was not absolutely certain. Experiment being impossible, he was content to take up an attitude of suspense, excluding no possibility, but waiting for further evidence. This modest attitude, it is maintained, is more becoming to the true man of science than over-hasty speculation, which jumps to conclusions. Supposing this apology admitted for the rejection of astronomy, what have we to say about the foundations of geometry? Here, too, some sort of a case may be made out; for the controversy over Euclid, his definitions, his common notions, his postulates, and the whole basis of his science, we are reminded, is still raging, and we may believe, if we choose, that Epicurus, more far-sighted than his contemporaries, discerned the weak places in the structure. But a simpler explanation is far more probable. In the miscellaneous works collected under the name of Aristotle, there is a short tract on "Indivisible Lines," a model of terse and closely reasoned argument. The writer sets forth first the grounds on which such in-divisible units of length are assumed by one set of disputants, then he proceeds to retail the arguments by which another set meet them and attempt to refute them. Now the connection between mathe-matics and the general theory of the natural world which the ancients called physics was very close. The indivisible atom was the basis of all Epicurean physics. It seems highly probable, then, that Epi-curus himself would incline to the assumption of an indivisible unit of length, a sort of materialised point. If this surmise be correct, he found himself at vari-ance with what we may call the orthodox school of geometers. Their fundamental notions of line and point he could not accept, and, as they were involved in the whole of geometry, he would feel bound to condemn the science as false. As will hereafter be seen, there is some evidence that he did not alto-gether accept the continuity of motion, but rather re-solved it into a series of progressions, each taking place in an instant of time over an indivisible unit of space. His denial of continuous corporeal magni-tude would of itself suffice to bring him into collision with the mathematicians; and this hostility would be strengthened if he also inclined to regard space, time, and motion as in the ultimate analysis not continuous, but discontinuous as made up of discrete minima.

But, be this as it may, it is high time to inquire what scientific principles, if any, our philosopher admitted. He was certainly no sceptic. He did not hold that every statement is uncertain, because as much can be said against it as for it, and, as a necessary consequence, that all science is founded on nothing better than probability. On what general principles, then, did he conceive himself entitled to assert or believe anything? This inquiry, preliminary to his physics, he himself entitled Canonic, because it dealt with the canon or rule of evidence. First, every statement must relate to what is given, to facts or phenomena. Epicurus is not concerned with the grounds on which from one proposition we infer another, the subject of Aristotle's Analytic, but with the far more fundamental question: On what ultimate grounds is a statement of fact based? All phenomena are either immediately certain or not, and it is possible to pass from the one region where there is immediate certainty to the other region, which is not thus immediately certain; in other words, from the known to the unknown. Such a process is analogous to the modern induction. For deductive logic, the theory of the syllogism and definition, Epicurus had the utmost contempt. On the other hand, the few general and preliminary remarks of which his Canonic consists contain the germs of a thoroughgoing inductive logic. The Epicurean theory of the universe is built upon this foundation. The existence of the phenomenal universe is everywhere assumed. Things exist outside us. We know them only through sense, which alone gives a conviction of reality. This conviction of reality attaches not only to the external objects which are perceived, but with equal strength to the internal states or feelings, especially the feelings of pleasure and pain of which we are conscious.

All true belief and assertion, then, must be founded upon our sensations and feelings. What we immediately perceive and feel, that is true.

"We must take into account," he says, "what really exists, and all clear evidence, to which we refer our opinions, for otherwise all will be full of uncertainty and confusion." "If you fight against all your sensations, you will have no standard to which to refer and thus no means of judging even those sensations which you pronounce false." "If you reject absolutely any single sensation without stopping to discriminate between that which is matter of opinion and awaits further confirmation and that which is already present, whether in sensation or in feeling or in any mental apprehension, you will throw into confusion even the rest of your sensations by your groundless belief, so as to reject the test of truth altogether. If you hastily affirm as true all that awaits confirmation in ideas based on opinion, as well as that which does not, you will not escape error, as you will be taking sides in every question involving truth and error."[1]   Or, as Lucretius more graphically expresses it: "You will find that from the senses first has proceeded the knowledge of the true and that the senses cannot be refuted. For that which of itself is to be capable of refuting things false by true things must from the nature of the case be proved to have the higher certainty. Well, then, what must fairly be accounted of higher certainty than sense? Shall reason founded on false sense be able to contradict the senses, seeing that reason is wholly founded upon them? And if they are not true, then all reason as well is rendered false. Or shall the ears be able to take the eyes to

[1] Golden maxims, XXII-XXIV.

task or the touch the ears? Any one sense cannot confute any other. No, nor can any sense take itself to task, since equal credit must be assigned to it at all times. What, therefore, has at any time appeared true to each sense is true." [1]

It is only through sense that we come into contact with reality; hence all our sensations are witnesses to reality. The senses cannot be deceived. There can be no such thing, properly speaking, as sense-illusion or hallucination. The mistake lies in the misinterpretation of our sensations. What we suppose that we perceive is too often our own mental presupposition, our own over-hasty inference from what we actually do perceive. When we see an oar which is half immersed in water appear bent, the image or film which reaches the eye is really bent, but the judgment of the mind that the oar itself is bent is no part of the perception, it is a gratuitous addition to it. The mind confuses two quite distinct processes or movements, the perception which is infallible, and the conscious or unconscious inference from it, which is after all mere presupposition or opinion, a groundless belief. The region of certainty, then, confined as it is to the direct presentation of sense, is even so by no means as extensive as we might at first suppose. Sensations themselves must be scrutinised, and the element which the mind itself has added must be removed before we get back to the original data, the perceptions which put us in touch with reality.

Turning now to the other and vaster region of the unknown, which is not accessible to direct observation because sensation is strictly limited to here and now, we observe that some part of it may hereafter

[1] *De Rerum Natura*, IV, 478-499.

come within our ken and be directly observed. This Epicurus denotes as "that which awaits confirmation." Cognition is an interrogative process. We put the question and wait until experience and reality, under favourable circumstances, supply the answer. But our knowledge, confined within these limits, would be very inadequate. By what we have above called an inchoate induction Epicurus regulates the steps by which we anticipate all experience with certainty. His fundamental assumption is the uniformity of experience: that whatever occurs in the sphere beyond knowledge must follow the same laws of operation as what is known to occur within the range of our experience. It is right, then, to affirm about the unknown (1) what is confirmed and witnessed to by the known, or at least (2) what is not directly witnessed against by the known. Thus the criterion, the supreme test of validity, is future experience, experience repeated or, at all events, not contradicted. The second half of this canon is by no means so sound as the first. It is capable of wide application, and must allow many doubtful explanations to pass for matters of belief. What is the ground on which Epicurus believes that there is an infinity of worlds, that the blessed and immortal gods inhabit the intermundia, that films from external objects enter the sense-organs and the mind, thus causing sensation and thought—propositions for which there is not a tittle of positive evidence? His reply is: "Nothing that we know by direct observation contradicts any one of these assertions." And so Epicurus gives them, we may say, the benefit of the doubt.

Another caution is needed. If reasoning is to be anything better than mere quibbling, special attention to language is necessary. Every term that is used must call up a clear and distinct conception or idea, which again must be based upon one clear and distinct perception. To general terms, as we shall hereafter see, correspond not single images, but the resultant of an accumulated series of images, the individual peculiarities of which are blunted and fused in a single pictorial type, much in the same way as when the photographs of different individuals are superposed on each other in order to form a composite photograph. But every perception in the series must be clear and distinct, in order that the resultant may have these qualities. In this way we obtain what Epicurus called "preconceptions," which take their place beside perceptions and feelings. They are the nearest approach which his system allowed to general notions. When a general term like " man " is used, it calls up to the mind the preconception of man, the generic type in which the images of particular men are fused and blended. With this explanation and qualification we may even be permitted to substitute "general notion" for "preconception," always remembering that it is an inexact equivalent. It remains to explain what precisely Epicurus understood by reasoning in which general terms are used, and what part it plays for him in the acquisition of knowledge. Sense gives us the raw material of knowledge in trustworthy perceptions and internal feelings, but he never denied that we also attain knowledge by the exercise of reason. Indeed, all the more important propositions in the general theory to be hereafter unfolded are attained by its aid. Reason or reasoning is to him a mental operation, which deals, not with particular things, but with generic types or notions. If our knowledge did not go beyond sensation it would consist in isolated, particular facts.   In that case it would be difficult, if not impossible, to make the inductive leap from the known to the unknown.   Reasoning, then, is the application, in a region where direct observation fails us, of preconceptions or general notions derived from sense, ·their validity being guaranteed by repeated and uncontradicted experience.   But future experience is the sole criterion by which all our reasoned conclusions must be tested.   The great doctrine of atoms and void stands or falls by it.   The claims of reason and sense are thus adjusted.   Instead of subordinating sense to reason, Epicurus is bound by the rules he lays down to subordinate reason to sense. Conflict between them is really impossible, for, reason being derived from sensation, all its conclusions are controlled, checked, and verified at every turn by sensation.   Both, then, share in the making of knowledge.   We see with the eye; we see also with the mind.   The latter is no doubt the means to the knowledge of phenomena beyond the reach of sense. Only quantitative, not qualitative, difference, however, must be assumed between the two.   The atoms which we mentally perceive we might conceivably actually perceive, if our senses were differently constituted.   They are in no way different from sensible solids, except in minuteness, total absence of void, and consequent indivisibility.   They are thus of a totally different order of reality from those objects which Plato believed the mind to cognise.   Plato's ideas, as incorporeal, were for Epicurus non-existent.

We have now to give in outline, so far as we can in the words of Epicurus himself, his theory of the sensible world.   Where it would conduce to clearness, we can supplement the master's teaching as laid down in the letter to Herodotus from the poem of Lucretius. The proposition from which we start is by no means peculiar to the ancient Atomists but had long been widely accepted. It amounts to an assertion of the indestructibility of primary matter. This implies that, when a particular thing comes into being, the imperishable elements of things, whatever they be, unite to form a new combination, and when this combination is dissolved and the elements, themselves imperishable, which have been temporarily united, again separate, the particular thing is destroyed. Empedocles and Anaxagoras indorsed the theory in this form as fully as the Atomists. Nor did Heraclitus surrender the principle when in his doctrine of the perpetual flux of the sensible world he took the obvious step from being and not-being to the next category of becoming. What the proposition excludes is capricious, arbitrary, random agency; what it is feeling after and trying to express is orderly sequence—in short, law in nature.

"To begin with," says Epicurus, "nothing comes into being out of what is non-existent. For in that case anything would have arisen out of anything, standing in no need of its proper germs. And if that which disappears were destroyed and became non-existent, everything would have perished, there being nothing into which things could have been dissolved. Moreover, the sum total of things was always such as it is now and such it will ever remain. For there is nothing into which it can change. For outside the sum of things there is nothing which could enter into it and bring about the change."[1] The terse summary

---

[1] Letter to Herodotus, § 38, *Epicurea*, p. 5, l. 13 *sqq.* The letter to Herodotus is given by Diogenes Laërtius, Book X, §§ 35–83, and is reprinted in Usener, *Epicurea*, pp. 3–32. I follow throughout the order of the text.

of Lucretius, *Ex nihilo nihil, in nihilum nil posse reverti*, has passed into a proverb.

Epicurus goes on to state succinctly what is the kernel of his whole doctrine. Not only do atoms and void exist, but atoms and void are all that exists. "The whole of being, then, consists of bodies and space. The existence of bodies is everywhere attested by sense, and it is upon sensation that reason must rely when it attempts to infer the unknown from the known. If there were no space, which we call also room, void, and intangible existence, bodies would have nothing in which to be and through which to move, as they are plainly seen to move. Beyond bodies and space there is nothing which by mental apprehension or on its analogy we can conceive to exist. Here we are speaking of wholes or separate things as distinct from their essential and accidental qualities. Of bodies, some are composite, others the elements of which these composite bodies are made. These elements are indivisible and unchangeable; and necessarily so, if things are not all to be destroyed and pass into non-existence, but are to be strong enough to endure when the composite bodies are broken up, because they possess a solid nature, and are incapable of being anywhere or anyhow dissolved. It follows that the first beginnings must be indivisible, corporeal entities."[1]

The word here translated "indivisible" is identical with the word for "atom." Etymologically, "atom" means simply "indivisible thing," a thing which cannot be cut in two. "Body," the reader must observe, is not unambiguous in Epicurus and Lucretius.

Giussani's proposals for the transposition of certain sections seem unconvincing and are certainly confusing.

[1] Letter to Herodotus, § 39, *Epicurea*, p. 6, 5 *sqq.*

Properly speaking, atoms alone are bodies, for they alone of existent things have no admixture of void in them; but the term is extended to denote the composite things in which along with body proper, *i. e.*, the atoms, there are also found interstices of void. All the things which we perceive by the senses belong to this class of composite bodies. To express atoms themselves, Lucretius uses a variety of terms, such as "elements," "first bodies," "first beginnings of things," sometimes even "seeds," or singly, "bodies," where the context renders the term unambiguous. What Epicurus means by essential and accidental qualities is well illustrated by Lucretius. "For whatever things are named, you will either find to be properties linked to these two things," viz., to bodies and void, "or you will see to be accidents of these things. That is a property," *i. e.*, an essential quality, "which can in no case be disjoined and separated without utter destruction accompanying the severance, such as the weight of a stone, the heat of fire, the fluidity of water. Slavery, on the other hand, poverty and riches, liberty, war, concord, and all other things which may come and go while the nature of the thing remains unharmed, these we are wont, as it is right we should, to call accidents." [1] The subject will recur again in Epicurus.[2]

He now gives his reasons for believing the sum of things to be infinite. "The sum of things is infinite. For what is finite has an extremity, and the extremity of anything is discerned only by comparison with something else. Now the sum of things is not discerned by comparison with anything else; hence, since it has no extremity it has no limit, and since it has no limit it is unlimited or infinite. Moreover,

[1] Lucretius, I, 449 *sqq.*

the sum of things is infinite both by reason of the multitude of atoms and the extent of void. For, if void were infinite and bodies finite, the bodies would not have stayed anywhere, but would have been dispersed in their course through the infinite void, because they would not have met with anything which by coming into collision with them might support or check them. Again, if void were finite, the infinity of bodies would not have had anywhere to be." [1]

Epicurus now describes his atoms, their shapes, and their incessant motion. "The atoms, which have no void in them, out of which composite bodies arise and into which they are dissolved vary indefinitely in their shapes, for so many varieties of things as we see could never have arisen out of the recurrence of a definite number of the same shapes. The atoms of each shape are absolutely infinite, but the variety of shapes, though indefinitely great, is not absolutely infinite. The atoms are everlastingly in motion. Some of them rebound to a considerable distance from each other; other atoms merely oscillate when they have got entangled or are enclosed by a mass of other atoms shaped for entangling. This is because each atom is separated from the rest by void, which is incapable of offering any resistance to the rebound; while it is the solidity of the atom which makes it rebound after a collision, however short the distance to which it rebounds when it finds itself imprisoned in a mass of entangling atoms. Of all this there is no beginning, owing to the eternity of both atoms and void." [2]

The subject of the shapes of atoms is treated very fully by Lucretius. He begins thus: "Now mark,

---

[1] § 41, *Epicurea*, 7, 6 *sqq.*   [2] §§ 42–44 *Epicurea*, 7, 17 *sqq.*

and next in order apprehend of what kind and how
widely differing in their forms are the beginnings
of all things," *i. e.*, the atoms, "how varied by manifold diversities of shape; not that a scanty number
are possessed of a like form" (*i. e.*, instead of being
few, the atoms of a like shape are infinite in number,
as Lucretius subsequently proves; nevertheless all
the atoms are not cast in a single mould; they have
various shapes and sizes), "but because as a rule
they do not all resemble one the other. And no
wonder; for since there is so great a store of them
that, as I have shown, there is no end or sum, they
must sure enough not one and all be marked by
an equal bulk and like shape, one with another."[1]
By way of illustration he appeals to the fact that
the subtle fire of lightning passes through openings
through which earthly fire cannot pass. Hence he
infers that lightning is composed of finer atoms.
Light is transmitted through horn, which is imper-
vious to rain. The atoms of light, then, must be
finer than those of rain. Wine runs easily, oil slowly
through a strainer: *ergo*, the atoms of oil are larger
and more hooked than those of wine. Honey and
milk are pleasant to the taste, wormwood and the like,
nauseous; the former consist of smooth, the latter of
jagged atoms, which tear a way into the body. And,
generally, whatever affects the sense pleasantly or
unpleasantly must be formed of atoms more or less
smooth or rough, respectively. Again, some things
with a bitter flavour have atoms not hooked but
slightly prominent; those of fire and cold are jagged,
but in different ways, as shown by touch. Those of
stones, metals, and the like are hooked and branch-
ing, those of fluids smooth and round; those of

[1] II, 333 *sqq.*

smoke, mist, and flame, sharp but not tangled; while in sea-water round and rough atoms are mingled with round and smooth ones.

What Epicurus says about the motion of his atoms is not very clear. We may supplement it from Lucretius, whose account is as follows: "Sure enough no rest is given to first bodies throughout the unfathomable void, but driven on rather in ceaseless and varied motion they partly, after they have pressed together, rebound leaving great spaces between, while in part they are so dashed away after the stroke as to leave but small spaces between. And all which form a denser aggregation when brought together, and which rebound leaving trifling spaces between, held fast by their own close-tangled shapes these form enduring bases of stone and unyielding bodies of iron and the rest of their class, few in number, which travel onward along the great void. All the others spring far off and rebound far, leaving great spaces between; these furnish us with thin air and bright sunlight. And many more travel along the great void, which have been thrown off from the unions of things or, though admitted to such unions, have yet in no case been able likewise to assimilate their motions." [1]

The drift seems to be that we can imagine three conditions in which atoms find themselves: (1) free atoms, moving singly in space before and after collision; (2) atoms, once free, which after collision are entangled or interlaced, owing to difference of shape, with other atoms. When a shell of such entangled atoms has been formed, it may enclose (3) imprisoned atoms, only partially free, colliding with each other, but only rebounding to short distances because

[1] II, 95 sqq.

they cannot escape from the network of the entangled
mass or shell within which they are confined. The
difference between (2) and (3) can be illustrated
from the physical constitution of sensible bodies, all
of which, as seen above, are composite, having interstices of void between their constituent atoms.
In gases—the atmosphere is the most familiar case—
and probably also in liquids, the cohesion of the
parts is imperfect, and the system formed by the
constituent atoms requires, if it is to maintain even
this imperfect cohesion, to be enclosed within definite
bounds. Otherwise their constituent atoms, so imperfectly do they cohere, always tend to disperse
and become once more free. The only bounds
which we can imagine in the case of the air are the
"flaming walls" of our world. For liquids these
bounds are the sides of the vessel containing them.
The case is different with the great majority of composite bodies commonly denoted as solid, metals,
stones, etc., the component atoms of which have
become so closely entangled that they are not easily
separated. The degree of cohesion, then, depends
upon the closeness of the entanglement, and this in
the last resort upon the shape of the atoms. There
is one point on which more information would have
been welcome. When, in consequence of collision,
atoms have become entangled or interlaced, what is
the exact nature of their motion? All the atoms,
we are told, are everlastingly in motion; but there are
no details to show how precisely the motion of two
or more entangled atoms—such, for instance, as
these ⋊⋉ —differs from the motion of a single free
or unimprisoned atom. In the densest substance
known, so long as they are composite bodies there
are interstices of void. Even the atoms in a piece of

steel are everlastingly in motion, throbbing, palpi-
tating, oscillating so far as the interstices of void
allow. The narrower the interstices and the shorter
the path which the atom describes, since its velocity
is uniform, the more often must it retrace it. In the
case of composite bodies, the motion of translation
is evident to the senses. When a cannon ball is shot
into the air every one of its atoms executes the
trajectory motion. But when it has fallen to the
ground its atoms are still moving with uniform
velocity, throbbing and oscillating as before over the
tiny interstices of void within the cannon ball, but
then their motions are wholly internal, latent (*motus
intestini*, *clandestini*). Nor can we suppose that
these internal motions cease during its flight through
the air. Here a simile may help us. A swarm of
bees moves from tree to tree. Seen from a distance,
their motion is a simple one, a motion of translation,
immeasurably slower but still of the same nature as
the flight of a cannon ball. A nearer view discloses
each separate bee executing motions in all manner
of directions, upward, downward, to right, to left,
backward, forward. This it continues to do during
the flight precisely as it had done when the swarm
as a whole was at rest, but in such a way that each
bee in the entire swarm makes the transit from the
one tree to the other. The direction of the motion
is altered, not the motion itself. As the flight of the
single bee in the swarm to the flight of the whole
swarm, so is the invisible motion of a single atom in
a composite body to the visible motion of the whole
body.

Or take the example of Lucretius, the particles
of dust seen in a sunbeam through a hole in a
shutter. "Observe whenever the rays are let in and

pour the sunlight through the dark chambers of
houses: you will see many minute bodies in many
ways through the apparent void mingle in the midst
of the light of the rays, and as in never-ending conflict skirmish and give battle, combating in troops
and never halting, driven about in frequent meetings
and partings; so that you may guess from this what
it is for first beginnings of things to be ever tossing
about in the great void. So far as it goes, a small
thing may give an illustration of great things and put
you on the track of knowledge. And for this reason, too, it is meet that you should give greater heed
to those bodies which are seen to tumble about in
the sun's rays, because such tumblings imply that
motions also of matter latent and unseen are at the
bottom. For you will observe many things there
impelled by unseen blows to change their course, and
driven back to return the way they came, now this
way, now that way, in all directions round. All, you
are to know, derive this restlessness from the first
beginnings," [1] *i. e.*, the atoms. "For the atoms move
first of themselves; next, those bodies which form a
small aggregate and come nearest, so to say, to the
powers of the atoms, are impelled and set in movement by the unseen strokes of those atoms, and they,
next in turn, stir up bodies which are a little larger.
Thus motion mounts up from the atoms, and step
by step issues forth to our senses, so that those bodies
also move, which we can discern in the sunlight,
though it is not clearly seen by what blows they so
act." [2] So complicated, then, is the process by which
the motion of single, free atoms ascends by various
shifting stages, hard to discriminate, and gives rise
to the motion of atoms in groups, larger or smaller,

[1] II, 114 *sqq.*   [2] II, 133 *sqq.*

more or less closely associated, from mobile air to the toughest flint or steel.

After thus dealing with the motion of the atoms, Epicurus in the letter to Herodotus next passes abruptly to the infinite worlds whose formation is due to this motion. "There is an infinite number of worlds, some like this world, others unlike it. For the atoms, being infinite in number, as has just been proved, are borne ever further in their course. For the atoms out of which a world might arise or by which a world might be formed have not all been expended upon one world or a finite number of worlds, whether like or unlike this one. Hence there will be nothing to hinder an infinity of worlds."[1]

What he means by a "world" he explains elsewhere. "A world is a circumscribed portion of the universe which contains stars and earth and all other visible things."[2] He adds that it is cut off from the infinite and the circumscribing limit in which it ends, its outside boundary, may revolve or be at rest, and may be rounded, triangular, or of any other shape. In our world, so Epicurus thinks, the central earth plays the most important part, being vastly greater in size and mass than the sun and stars which surround it. This fundamental error arose from his refusal to treat astronomy as a serious or exact science, to which reference has already been made. The result is curious. If we neglect the miniature sun and flickering stars which the eye of sense perceives surrounding the earth in this our world, the boundless universe which Epicurus descries with his mental vision approximates to a far greater degree than we might at first sight suppose to the universe as it is

[1] § 45, *Epicurea*, 9, 4 *sqq.*
[2] Letter to Pythocles, *Epicurea*, p. 37, 7.

conceived by the modern astronomer. To the latter
the universe is resolved into countless suns, each with
its attendant planetary system, and the nebulæ out
of which such solar systems are believed to have developed. For him the many suns and planetary systems are dotted here and there throughout space, as
were the "worlds" of Epicurus. And yet of the
"solar"[1] as distinct from the "sidereal" system
the account given by Epicurus is flagrantly inadequate, and even puerile, not merely when judged from
a modern stand-point, but even when compared with
the current notions of the astronomers of his day.

The next division of the subject is concerned with
the manner in which we are affected by external objects, and we begin with a remarkable hypothesis,
that from the exterior surfaces of all composite bodies
there is a perpetual emission of particles of matter or
what we may call "films." "There are outlines, or
films which are of the same shape as the solid bodies,
but their fineness far exceeds that of any objects that
we see. For it is not impossible that there should be
found in the surrounding air emanations of this kind,
materials adapted for expressing the hollowness and
smoothness of surfaces, and effluxes preserving the
same relative position and sequence which they had
in the solid objects. To these films we give the name
of 'images' or 'idols.'"[2]

This doctrine of emission or efflux can be traced
back to Empedocles and Democritus. To the first
inquirers at the threshold of psychology the problem of sense-perception was mainly physiological or
rather frankly physical. The act of perception was

---

[1] Or, if the expression be preferred, the "planetary" system: that
made up of our sun and its attendant planets.
[2] § 46, *Epicurea*, p. 9, 12 *sqq.*

assimilated to the commonest cases of action and
reaction between external things, as when a stone
strikes the water or a seal is impressed on wax.
Bodies so acting and reacting were observed to be in
contact, and this fitted the senses of touch and taste.
But colours, sounds, and smells are perceived at a
distance. The problem was: How is this action at a
distance to be explained? Not much help could be
obtained from the very crude notion of attraction
expressed in the proverb "Like to like," although it
plays a large part both in the theory of knowledge
and the theory of vision set forth by Empedocles.
Both he and Democritus were driven to assume that,
as in the case of touch, there must somehow be contact even to allow of like acting upon like. Under
the stress of such necessities of thought they took
refuge in the theory of emanations. Vision was the
sense chiefly studied. Moreover, there was the concrete fact that an image of the object seen may be
observed in the pupil of the eye. Certain other
experimental facts, the losses of substance caused by
evaporation and corrosion, the way in which even
hard stones imperceptibly crumble and wear away
beneath the tread, may have contributed, as well as
the evidence of that perpetual change in the physical
universe which so powerfully impressed Heraclitus.
By whatever steps it was reached, this astounding
assumption was made the basis of the Atomists'
theory, not only of perception, but also of thought.
For when once it is granted that emanations are
given off by objects, it is comparatively easy to make
the further assumption that some of these emanations
are too fine to act upon the sense-organs, but not too
fine to affect the equally material soul or mind. For
the term "film" which we have used might equally

well be substituted "efflux," "husk," "filament," "layer," or even "membrane." We know that Democritus called them Deikela, a term which, like "idols," suggests likeness. The outside layer or film, as Epicurus is at pains to explain, may resemble the solid body from which it has parted in the mutual relation and inter-connection of its various parts, that is to say, in the two dimensions which a surface has in common with a solid. The all-important distinction between them is in the third dimension of depth. The film lacks depth. In stereoscopic slides this impression of depth is successfully imitated, and Epicurus, probably following Democritus, supposes a constant succession of films from the same object to be the means by which the impression of solidity is, in fact, conveyed to the eye.

It is obvious that the theory raises more difficulties than it solves. What becomes of all the films? Again, all solid bodies must be perpetually suffering loss. How is this loss made good? As to the last point, either we are referred to the enormous quantity of free atoms everywhere travelling in the void, which by their accession may be supposed to make these losses good, or we are reminded that all composite wholes are frail and perishable, and do as a fact, in the course of time, suffer diminution before they are finally dissolved. The modern reader hardly needs to be reminded how utterly inadequate to its special purpose this assumption was, and how enormous the work that had to be done by the sciences of anatomy, physiology, and optics before the conditions under which an object is seen could be understood. The Greeks knew nothing of the retina or the refractive properties of the crystalline lens, and had no idea of the eye as an optical instrument, of the nature of light or of the nerves. The knowledge we have, imperfect as it is, on these subjects has been acquired after painful efforts and strenuous researches carried on for generations. It would have been impossible without the microscope, and the continuance of those endeavours to systematise and extend knowledge for its own sake, which Epicurus discouraged on principle. Why should men busy themselves with minute investigations of the structure of the eye and the laws of reflection, so long as there were infinite atoms, enough and to spare, to bring a specimen of every visible object to the eye of every observer? Besides, an ingenious corollary provides an easy explanation of erroneous perceptions, hallucinations, and dreams. Not only may films from real objects become distorted and blunted, but films from different objects, or even casual atoms, may meet in the air, blend, and enter the eye, causing the vision of objects which never were on land or sea, both in our waking hours and in dreams. Such aggregates or complexes of atoms, taking on the delusive appearance of real objects, were technically designated Systaseis.

Epicurus goes on: "So long as nothing comes in the way to offer resistance, motion through the void accomplishes any imaginable distance in an indefinitely short time. For resistance encountered is the equivalent of slowness, its absence the equivalent of speed. Not that, if we consider the times perceptible by reason alone, the moving body arrives at more than one place simultaneously (for this, too, is inconceivable), nor that when in time perceptible to sense it arrives from any point you please of the infinite, it will not be starting from the point to which we conceive it to have made its journey. For, if it stopped there on its arrival, this would be equivalent to its meeting with resistance, even if up to that point we allow the speed of its journey to imply the absence of resistance."[1]

The reader will note that Epicurus is talking about films, and the enormous velocity with which they must travel in order to reach us, as in his view they appear to do, instantaneously. This, however, in no way detracts from the importance of these almost parenthetical remarks about motion; not the motion of atoms, which is at all times uniform, but the motion of systems of atoms. What is here said applies to all such systems, whether the union is loose and easily broken, as is the case with an invisible film, more close as with the air and other gases, closer still as in water and other fluids, or comparatively permanent and durable as in earth and the various composite bodies which we call solid. In all cases alike the system moves slowly if resistance is encountered, either externally from the medium, air or water, or internally—and this is far more important—from the jostling, collision, and backward rebound of the single atoms composing the system. Such internal resistance tends to impede the system. So, also, would the pause of rest, if the system reached a point, stopped, and then went on. But this, he explains, the film does not do unless it encounters resistance.

He continues: "This is an elementary fact which in itself is worth bearing in mind. In the next place, the exceeding fineness of the images is contradicted by none of the facts under our observation. Hence, also, their velocities are enormous, since they always find a void passage to fit them. Besides, owing to their infinitesimal fineness, they meet with no resistance or very little, though many structures, even if

[1] §§ 46, 47, *l. c.*, 10, 3 *sqq.*

they be of infinitesimal fineness, do at once encounter resistance."[1]

The sun's heat is the example given by Lucretius. He says: "First of all we may very often observe that things which are light and made up of minute atoms are swift. Of this kind are the light of the sun and its heat."[2] But, swift as they are, both light and heat are often obstructed. So Lucretius in another passage: "But that heat which the sun emits and that bright light pass not through empty void; and therefore they are forced to travel more slowly, until they cleave through the waves, so to speak, of air. Nor do the several minute atoms of heat pass on one by one, but closely entangled and massed together; whereby at one and the same time they are pulled back by one another and are impeded from without, so that they are forced to travel more slowly."[3] Here resistance, both from without and within, would seem to be very clearly indicated.

But to return to Epicurus. "The production of the images is as quick as thought. For particles are continually streaming off from the surface of bodies, though no diminution of the bodies is perceptible because other particles take their place. And those given off for a long time retain the position and arrangement which their atoms had when they formed part of the solid bodies, although occasionally they are thrown into confusion. Sometimes such films are formed very rapidly in the air, because they need not have any solid content, and there are other modes of their formation. For there is nothing in all this which is contradicted by sensation, if we look at the clear evidence of sense in order, in some degree, to learn what vehicles will transfer to our-

[1] § 47, *l. c.*, 10, 13 *sqq.*   [2] IV, 183 *sqq.*   [3] II, 150 *sqq.*

selves the mutual inter-connection of external objects."[1]

"We must also consider that it is by the entrance
of something coming from external objects that we
see their shapes and think of them.   For external
things would not have stamped on us their own nature of colour and form through the medium of the
air which is between them and us, or by means of
rays of light or currents of any sort going from us
to them, so well as by the entrance into our eyes or
minds of certain films coming from the things."[2]

Here two theories of vision are criticised.   Democritus, though it was from him that Epicurus borrowed his doctrine of films, appears to have combined
with it the view that the air is the medium by which
visual impressions reach the eye.   Possibly Gomperz
is right in supposing that Democritus conceived the
films or husks themselves entering the eye to account
for vision of near objects only, and introduced air
as the medium for visual impressions of objects at a
greater distance.   One remark of his has come down
to us to the effect that, if it were not for the intervening air, we should clearly descry even minute objects
at a great distance, such as an ant crawling along
the sky.   At any rate, he supposed, so we are told
by Theophrastus, that the air received impressions
from the objects of sight and transferred them to our
organs of vision, such impressions being literally
stamped on the air, like the mark of a signet on wax.
It was owing to this transference that they were often
blurred and indistinct when they reached us.

The second theory rejected, that of Plato in the
Timæus, is commonly held to have originated with
Empedocles, who certainly compared the structure

---

[1] § 48, *Epicurea*, 11, 48 *sqq.*   [2] § 49, *l. c.*, p. 11, 14–20.

of the eye to a lantern. The gist of his comparison
is that as the fire within the lantern, screened from
the winds by transparent sides of horn, talc, or linen,
nevertheless "leaps forth and casts a gleam through
the surrounding darkness," so visual rays of the nature of fire dart out or shine forth from the pupil of
the eye.[1] Plato's account of vision is more complicated; it involves the co-operation of three "fires,"
(1) that which streams forth from the eye (the visual
current), (2) the fire of daylight in the air, and (3) the
fire which is the colour of the object seen. Vision
takes place when these three coalesce.[2] Both Empedocles and Plato held that like is known by like.
"We see fire," says the former, "by the fire that is
in us."[3] Epicurus sticks to the film as a simple and
sufficient expedient and will have no medium like
air. His films travel along interstices of void through
the air, and he will not hear of rays emitted from the
eye to meet the films.

Our text continues: "These films or outlines are
of the same colour and shape as the external things
themselves, in spite of the difference in size; they
move with rapid motion and this again explains why
they present the appearance of the single continuous
object and retain, when they impinge upon the sense,
the mutual inter-connection which they had in the
object, such impact being due to the oscillation of the
atoms in the interior of the solid object from which
they come. And whatever presentation we derive by
direct contact, whether with the mind or with the
sense-organs, be it shape that is presented or properties, this shape as presented is the shape of the solid
thing, and it is produced by a frequent repetition of

---

[1] Empedocles, Fragment 84, Diels.[2]   [2] Plato, *Timæus*, 45B–46A.
[3] Empedocles, Fragment 109, Diels.[2]

the image or by the trace of itself which it leaves
behind it." [1]

In sensation an image strikes upon the sense-organ.
In every act of preconception or of memory an image
strikes the mind.   A series of repeated images or the
traces which they leave behind them in us produce
a presentation of the shape or properties of the external object from which they came.   And if the
presentation be obtained in this way by direct contact, whether on the senses or the mind, it corresponds
exactly in shape and properties with the external
object.   If these conditions are fulfilled, the shape as
presented to us in sensation and memory or in preconception is the real shape of the object, the properties so presented are the very properties which the
external object has.   Epicurus is here passing from
the subject of films in general to the veracity of the
reports of the senses.   A theory of mediate perception must answer the question: How do I know that
what I receive through the medium is an exact copy
of the object?

He continues: "Falsehood and error always depend upon the intrusion of opinion when a fact awaits
confirmation or the absence of contradiction, which
fact is afterwards frequently not confirmed or even
contradicted.   For the presentations which are received, e. g., in a picture, or arise in dreams, or from
any other form of apprehension by the mind or by
the other criteria of truth would never have resembled what we call the real and true things, had it
not been for the impact upon us of certain actual
things of the kind.   Error would not have occurred
if we had not experienced some other movement in
ourselves, conjoined with, but distinct from, the per-

[1] §§ 49, 50, *Epicurea*, p. 11, 20 *sqq.*

ception of what is presented. And from this movement, if it be not confirmed or be contradicted, falsehood results; while, if it be confirmed or not contradicted, truth results. And to this view we must adhere if we are not to repudiate the criteria founded on the clear evidence of sense, nor again to throw all things into confusion by supporting falsehood as if it were truth." [1]

The foregoing account is now applied to hearing and smelling. "Again, hearing takes place when a current passes from the object, whether person or thing, which emits voice or sound or noise, or produces the sensation of hearing in any way whatever. This current is broken up into homogeneous particles which at the same time preserve a certain mutual connection and a distinctive unity extending to the object which emitted them and thus cause the perception of it or, if not, merely indicate the presence of the external object. For without the transmission from the object of a certain inter-connection of the parts, no such sensation would have arisen. Therefore we must not suppose that the air itself is moulded into shape by the voice emitted or by similar sounds; for it is very far from being the case that the air is acted upon in this way. The blow which is struck in us when we utter a sound causes such a displacement of the particles as serves to produce a current resembling breath,[2] and this displacement gives rise

---

[1] §§ 50, 52, *l. c.*, p. 12, 10 *sqq.*

[2] The Greek word Pneuma means both breath and wind. Here the current or stream of voice-atoms is most probably compared to breath itself issuing from the lips. It is, however, just possible that it is compared to wind, for the same word Pneuma, when it denotes a constituent of that mixed substance, the soul, is translated by Lucretius *ventus*, and must therefore denote wind, especially as air, strangely distinguished from wind, is another constituent of the soul.

to the sensation of hearing. Again, we must believe that the sense of smelling, like that of hearing, would produce no sensation were there not particles conveyed from the object which are of the proper size for exciting the organ of smelling, some of one sort, some of another, some exciting it confusedly and strangely, others quietly and agreeably." [1]

The ordinary view made air the medium by which sound, conceived as a shock or blow of one thing upon another, was conveyed to the ear. Thus Empedocles held that particles of air were given off by the sonant body. Hearing, according to him, is caused by the impact of the air-wave against the cartilage or bony flesh which is suspended within the ear, oscillating as it is struck like a gong. As the organ of vision contains a lantern, so the organ of hearing contains a bell or gong, which the sound from without causes to ring. But the Atomists, to whom the air was not, as it was to Empedocles, a form of primary matter, but simply one of the composite bodies, were debarred from regarding the emanation from the sonant body as consisting of air. What is given off, *i. e.*, sound, considered as a physical thing, is a stream of atoms. At the same time Democritus would not altogether abandon the common belief that air is the medium by which we hear. His view, then, is a kind of compromise. The emanation, *i. e.*, the stream of atoms, from the resonant body sets in motion the air which lies before it. In this stream of atoms from the body and in the air which is moved by it like atoms come together according to the similarity of their shapes and sizes. The sensation of hearing occurs when the atoms of air, rolled along by and with the atoms of vocal sound, reach the

[1] §§ 52, 53, *l. c.*, p. 13, 10 *sqq.*

orifice of the ear. It will be seen that Epicurus is resolved to be perfectly consistent and excludes the agency of the air altogether, either as medium or emanation. The medium is the void, the particles of sound conveyed are atoms of that which is sonant. On this view we hear exactly as we smell, except that atoms of sound enter the ear, atoms of scent the nostril.

Atoms, then, streams of atoms emitted from the surface of composite bodies, are the causes of our perceptions of external things. The things perceived have colour, sound, and odour. Is this so with the atoms? Epicurus proceeds: "We must hold that the atoms possess none of the qualities belonging to things which come under our observation except shape, weight, and size, and the properties necessarily conjoined with shape. For every quality changes, but the atoms do not change, since, when the composite bodies are dissolved, there must needs be a permanent something, solid and indissoluble, left behind, which makes changes possible: not changes into the non-existent nor out of the non-existent, but through differences of arrangement and sometimes through additions and subtractions of the atoms. Hence these somethings capable of being differently arranged must be indestructible, exempt from change, but possessed each of its own distinctive mass and configuration. This must be assumed. For in the case of changes of configuration within our experience, the figure is supposed to be inherent when other qualities are stripped off, but the qualities are not supposed, like the shape, which is left behind, to inhere in the subject of change, but to vanish altogether from the whole body. Thus, then, what is left behind is sufficient to account for the differences in composite bodies, since something must necessarily be left instead of everything being annihilated." [1]

The atom is unchangeable *ex hypothesi*, and this may be secured provided that the qualities which the atom possesses are themselves unchangeable. So long as the shape remains unaltered through all the motions, collisions, and entanglements which befall the atom, since there is no void within it, there will be no alteration in size and, since weight depends upon size or mass, there will be no alteration in weight. In this way size and weight may be regarded as properties necessarily conjoined with shape. Neither of them would be affected by different arrangement or position of the atoms, on which ultimately depend the qualities which composite bodies have and atoms have not. Take colour. In a composite body or aggregate of atoms differently placed and arranged and, it may be, themselves different in shape and size, the colour which we perceive as belonging to this aggregate, and which by the canon of Epicurus really does belong to it, is a consequence of these same atomic positions, arrangements, shapes, and motions, and a change in them may change the colour of the thing or composite body without that thing necessarily ceasing to be what it was. The question may be asked: To which division of qualities does colour belong? Is it a property, a *coniunctum?* Or is it an accident, an *eventum?* It seems safest to reply that generic colour, colour of some sort or other, is a property of all visible things, so long as they are visible; but particular colour is an accident or *eventum* of a particular visible thing, which often changes like the hues of a sunset cloud

[1] §§ 54, 55, *l. c.,* p. 14, 14 *sqq.*

or in a peacock's tail, owing to the difference of atomic motions produced by light or some other external influence; lastly, that when a body ceases to be visible it has no colour. The qualities which are not inherent are accidental qualities, *eventa*, such as whiteness, triangularity, which a thing may gain or lose without ceasing to be what it is. Figure or shape in general, however, is not such an *eventum*, but an essential property, or *coniunctum*, of all material things whether visible or not. We regard shape as something which a material thing must have as long as it exists at all. We recognise that the shape changes, but we still think of the thing as being the same under an altered shape, as in the growth of animals and plants or when the same block of wax is moulded into different shapes. In other words, so long as a material thing persists it must have some shape or other.

Again, "we should not suppose that the atoms have any and every size lest we be contradicted by facts; but alternations of size must be admitted, for this addition renders the facts of feeling and sensation easier of explanation. But to attribute any and every magnitude to the atoms does not help to explain the difference of quality in things; moreover, in that case atoms large enough to be seen ought to have reached us, which is never observed to occur; nor can we conceive how its occurrence should be possible." [1] This is another correction of Democritus, who imposed no limitations on the size of atoms, arguing that, for all we know, they might be as large as you please somewhere in an infinite universe. "We must not suppose that there is an infinity of particles in any finite body. Hence, not

[1] §§ 55, 56, *l. c.*, p. 15, 12 *sqq.*

only must we reject as impossible subdivision *ad infinitum* into smaller and smaller parts, lest nothing
be left strong enough to form new aggregates and the
things that exist be necessarily pulverised and annihilated, but in dealing with finite things we must also
reject as impossible the progression *ad infinitum* by
less and less increments." [1]

The notion of such a progression is theg round-
work of the famous puzzle of Achilles and the tortoise, propounded by the Eleatic Zeno.   Achilles, who
runs ten times as fast as the tortoise, gives the latter
a start of a metre.   When Achilles has run one metre
the tortoise is one decimetre in advance;   when
Achilles has got as far as this he finds the tortoise a
millimetre in advance, and so on *ad infinitum;* whence
Zeno wished it to be inferred that Achilles will never
overtake the tortoise.   Epicurus simply denies the
possibility of continuing *ad infinitum* such a progression, formed by a series of increments, each term
in the series being a definite fraction of the preceding
term, precisely as he denies the possibility of continuing *ad infinitum* the process of subdivision of a finite
body, *e. g.*, by taking half, then the half of this half, or
one-quarter, next the half of this quarter, or one-
eighth, and so on.   The latter series of fractional
divisions is the complement of the former, that of
fractional increments.   The impossibility in the one
case and in the other is bound up with Epicurus's
assumption that in the last resort not only body,
i. e., matter, but the dimensions of body, which are
conceived as traversed in motion, are discrete.   To
the atom, the indivisible minimum of body, corresponds an indivisible minimum of a dimension, of spatial dimensions, length, breadth, and depth, at any

[1] § 56, *l. c.*, p. 16, 1–8.

rate when the space is filled and occupied with body, under which conditions alone we have the clear evidence of sense and intellect for progression from point to point upon it. "For, when once we have said that an infinite number of particles, of whatever size, are contained in anything, it is not possible to conceive how this should be. How, in the first place, could the magnitude which they form be any longer finite ? For clearly our infinite number of particles must have some definite size, and then, of whatever size they were, the aggregate they made would be infinite. And in the next place, since what is finite has an extremity which is distinguishable, even if it is not by itself observable, it is not possible to avoid thinking of another such extremity next to this. Nor can we help thinking that in this way, by proceeding forward from one to the next in order, by such a progression we can arrive in thought at infinity." [1]

Atoms of any and every size are here disproved on other grounds than the foregoing. The polemical reference is to Anaxagoras, who maintained an infinite number of infinitesimal "seeds," in his own words, "infinite, both in number and in smallness, for the small, too, was infinite." [2] Moreover, they are all present, Anaxagoras held, in every finite thing. The possibility of a minimum he denied, being on this point at issue with Leucippus and Democritus, the Atomist predecessors of Epicurus. Let us give the very words of Anaxagoras: "Nor is there a least of what is small, but there is always a smaller; for it is impossible that what is should cease to be by being divided." [3] And, since the portions of the great

[1] § 57, *l. c.*, p. 16, 8 *sqq.*   [2] Fragment 1, Diels[2].

[3] *Ib.*, 3, Diels[2].

and of the small are equal in amount, for this reason, too, all things will be in everything. Nor is it possible for them to be apart, but all things have a portion of everything. And in all things many things are contained and an equal number both in the greater and in the smaller of the things that have separate existence." [1]

Epicurus takes the doctrine to imply that the number of atoms in each thing is infinite, and he objects that, however small in size the individual atoms, an infinite number of them could produce a body not finite but infinite. His second objection is that, if the atoms be of finite size and an infinite number of them be contained in a single thing, the progression from the extremity of the first to the extremity of the next, and so on to that of the last, would be a never-ending progress, which he has before declared to be impossible. The word translated here "extremity" and in Lucretius "cacumen" will best be understood if we take an angular point or projection or extreme edge on any sensible body of finite size, *e. g.*, the "point" of a sharpened lead-pencil or the corner of a cube. If each atom has a certain shape it must be conceived on the analogy of finite bodies to project some part of this shape which the mental vision can distinguish. But what, it may be asked, of spherical atoms? As it is impossible to see the whole of a finite sphere with the bodily eye or to present to the eye of the mind the whole of a spherical atom at once, the part which we do see will be bounded. The outside or edge in the part we do see is in this case the extremity projecting into view. This applies to the visualised pictorial image as well as to actual perception.

[1] Fragment 6, Diels[2].

Before we go further into the thorny subject of discrete minima of area or surface, of length and other dimensions, whether of body or space, the modern student of philosophy will do well to remember where he stands at present. He is familiar with two doctrines of space,[1] the Kantian and Berkeleian. The former is not free from contradictions; it involves the idea of infinite divisibility in the space-world of our experience. The Berkeleian denies this infinite divisibility. We experience only an aggregate of *minima divisibilia;* no line is infinitely divisible. Zeno's problem of motion from one point to another, the moving body having to pass through an infinite number of points in the interval, does not exist for Berkeley any more than for Epicurus; the movement is through a discrete number of units of length. But Berkeley allowed for all manner of substituting in our construction of the world. One experience can stand for and symbolise another. Hence by substituting for the least part of the line perceived or *minimum divisibile,* its magnified representation as seen under a microscope, we treat that as the same line, and this we can divide, and this process can be repeated in thought indefinitely. The mathematician generalises our experience and gives us a conceptualised mathematical space which is infinitely divisible and without limits in extent. Berkeley's procedure furnishes an illustration and a clue to that of Epicurus. Over and over again we find the latter stating that the mental vision must be substituted for actual perception with the eye; that where direct observation is impossible we must visualise in thought. His conclusions, as we shall see, are very similar to

---

[1] *Cf.* G. S. Fullerton, *A System of Metaphysics,* cc. X–XII, where the two doctrines are expounded and compared.

Berkeley's, but we must not overlook one great difference between them. Berkeley's doctrine is phenomenological, that of Epicurus is ontological. For him the discrete minima have absolute existence.

Epicurus continues: "We must consider the minimum perceptible by sense as not corresponding to the extended which is capable of being traversed, nor again as utterly unlike it, but as having something in common with the extended things capable of being traversed, though it is without distinction of parts. But when, from the resemblance of what they have in common, we think we shall distinguish something in the minimum, one part on one side and another part on the other side, another minimum equal to the first must catch our eye. In fact, we see these minima one after the other, beginning with the first, and not as occupying the same space; nor do we see them touch each other with their parts, but we see that they afford a means of measuring magnitudes by force of their individuality: there are more of them if the magnitude measured is greater, fewer of them if the magnitude measured is less."[1] The magnitude measured by visible minima would naturally be area or surface. It appears, then, that Epicurus conceives a finite surface as reducible in the last resort to an assemblage of discretes which he terms sensible minima, and declares to be units of measurement. Now compare the mathematical conception of a finite surface. The geometer's surface contains an infinite number of lines, each line continuous but infinitely divisible, each division of a line being a point. Epicurus, on the contrary, holds that the finite area or surface consists of a finite

[1] § 58, *Epicurea*, p. 17, 1–11.

number of discontinuous units of area, minima which are discontinuous and discrete.

Hitherto we have been dealing with sensible things, with sensible minima, whether of surface or mass. Thus in the diagram the smaller square may be regarded as presenting four minima, the larger square nine.

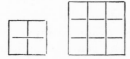

Epicurus now proceeds to apply his conclusions to the atom. "We must think that the minimum in the atom behaves conformably to this analogy. It is only in minuteness that it differs from the minimum seen by sense, but it follows the same analogy. We have already declared on the analogy of things within our experience that the atom has magnitude, and herein we have merely reproduced something small on a larger scale. And, further, the least and simplest of lengths must be regarded as boundary-points, furnishing from themselves as units the means of measuring lengths, whether greater or less, the mental vision being employed, since direct observation is impossible. For the community which subsists between them," i. e., boundary-points of length, "and the things without extension or incapable of being traversed," i. e., the minimal parts of area or surface, "is sufficient to justify the conclusion so far as this goes." [1] That is, as the visible minima measure area or surface, so the boundary-points or discrete minima of length measure lengths. This passage clearly shows that Epicurus regarded a line or length as made up

[1] § 58, *l. c.*, p. 17, 11 *sqq.*

of certain minima of length, his substitute for the geometrical point. Geometers denied that a line could be conceived as made up of, or could be resolved into, a series of points. But in their conception and definition of a point they differed widely from Epicurus. The geometers assumed infinite divisibility; there was a point wherever the line could be divided. Epicurus introduces us to discrete minima of length which bound finite perceptible lengths precisely as the geometer's points bound his lines. The validity of the geometrical point had been already questioned by others; even Plato, it is said, proposed to substitute the expressions "beginning of a line" or "indivisible line" for point.[1]

This by the way. Epicurus now returns to the minima of the atom. "But it is not possible that these minima of the atom should group themselves together through the possession of motion"[2]; in other words, these minima cannot first exist apart and then, in virtue of possessing the attribute of motion, unite together to form the atom. Our pressing business now is with the atom conceived on the analogy of finite bodies as occupying space and therefore extended, and, being extended (or, as Epicurus prefers to say, "capable of being traversed"), as having parts. We must not by one whit modify the conception of the atom as indestructible, immutable, impenetrable matter. It has parts, but it has no interstices of void; therefore no destroying agency can get between these parts and sever them. Hence we must recognise that, though the conception of atoms accounts for all composite bodies, analysis is not exhausted when these composite bodies have

[1] Aristotle, *Metaphysica*, A, 9, 992, a, 19–23.
[2] § 59, p. 18, 1, 2.

been reduced to atoms. There is a minimum smaller than the atom, but no such minimum separately exists. The atom is the least thing which can exist "in solid singleness," the limit of separate, individual existence. It would therefore be an error to suppose that minima of the atom exist at first apart and then combine to form atoms as atoms combine to form composite things. The minima of the atom are inseparable from each other and from the atom to all eternity.

In the following passage Lucretius reproduces his master's doctrine on this point: "Then again, since there is ever an extremity, a bounding point [to bodies which appear to us to be a least, there ought in the same way to be a bounding point the least conceivable] [1] to that atom which already is beyond what our senses can perceive: that point sure enough is without parts and consists of a least nature and never has existed apart by itself, and will not be able in future so to exist, since it is in itself part of that other; and so a first and single part and then other and other similar parts in succession fill up in close serried mass the nature of the atom; and since these cannot exist by themselves, they must cleave to that from which they cannot in any way be torn. Atoms, therefore, are of solid singleness, massed together and cohering closely by means of least parts, not compounded out of a union of those parts, but rather strong in everlasting singleness. From them nature allows nothing to be torn, nothing further to be worn away, reserving them as seeds for

---

[1] A couple of lines must have dropped out between 599 and 600 of our present text of Lucretius. Munro fills the gap with the words enclosed in square brackets, and thus renders the argument and general sense perfectly clear.

things. Again, unless there shall be a least, the very smallest bodies will consist of infinite parts, inasmuch as the half of the half will always have a half and nothing will set bounds to the division. Therefore, between the sum of things and the least of things, what difference will there be? There will be no distinction at all; for how absolutely infinite soever the whole sum is, yet the things which are smallest will equally consist of infinite parts. Now, since on this head true reason protests and denies that the mind can believe it, you must yield and admit that there exist such things as are possessed of no parts and are of a least nature. And since these exist, those atoms also you must admit to be solid and everlasting." [1] If you reject infinite subdivision you must admit the existence of minima (though not necessarily their separate existence). "Once more, if Nature, creatress of things, had been wont to compel all things to be broken up into least parts, then, too, she would be unable to reproduce anything out of those parts, because those things which are enriched with no parts cannot have the properties which begetting matter ought to have—I mean the various entanglements, weights, blows, clashings, motions by means of which things severally go on." [2] In other words, why, it may be objected, should we stop short at atoms? Why should not the minimum replace the atom as the ultimate unit? The answer is that, because the minimum is supposed to have no parts, it is impossible to conceive it to behave as the atom does. It cannot become entangled, collide, fall, or move in the same way as does the atom which is possessed of parts.

Hitherto the incessant motion of atoms has been

[1] I, 599 *sqq.*   [2] I, 628 *sqq.*

postulated and two of its species, (1) vibration or oscillation of the imprisoned atom and (2) rebound to a greater distance of the unimprisoned atom, have been mentioned, both species implying previous collision. There is another kind of atomic motion. Atoms have weight and, like all heavy bodies perceived by sense, tend to fall downward, i. e., to move in a certain empirically determined direction. In the summary of Epicurean doctrine which we have chosen as our principal authority this downward tendency of the atom is not explicitly stated, though a passage with which we shall shortly deal clearly distinguishes motion due to weight from motion due to collision, and the paragraph next to be cited is unintelligible, except on the assumption that Epicurus held the doctrine in question. As a necessary introduction we will cite the account given by Lucretius: "Since they travel about through void, the atoms must all move on either by their own weight or haply by the stroke of another. For when during motion they have, as often happens, met and clashed, the result is a sudden rebounding in an opposite direction; and no wonder, since they are most hard and of weight proportioned to their solidity and nothing behind gets in their way." [1] All atoms and all bodies compounded of atoms have a downward tendency. But, as this direction is liable to alteration in consequence of collision, we must add, "unless some force acting upon them, some blow, compel them to move laterally or even vertically upward." As sense-perception is the foundation of knowledge, especial care is needed here, for fire and vapour are seen to rise, not fall. As Lucretius says: "Now methinks is the place herein to prove this point

[1] II, 83 sqq.

also that no bodily thing can by its own power be
borne upward and travel upward; that the bodies
of flames may not in this matter lead you into error.
For they are begotten with an upward tendency and
in the same direction receive increase; and goodly
crops and trees grow upward, though their weights,
so far as in them is, all tend downward. And when
fires leap to the roofs of houses and with swift flame
lick up rafters and beams, we are not to suppose
that they do so spontaneously without a force pushing
them up. See you not, too, with what force the liquid
of water spits out logs and beams? The more deeply
we have pushed them sheer down and have pressed
them in, many of us together with all our might and
much painful effort, with the greater avidity it vomits
them up and casts them forth so that they rise and
start out more than half their length. And yet methinks we doubt not that these, so far as in them is,
are all borne downward through the empty void. In
the same way flames also ought to be able, when
squeezed out, to mount upward through the air, although their weights, so far as in them is, strive to
draw them down." [1] Meteors, lightnings, the sun's
light and heat are also adduced to illustrate the
universal tendency of bodies to fall.

To return to Epicurus: "In that which is infinite
we must not say that there is an up and down in the
sense of an uppermost or a nethermost point. Still,
a line may be drawn vertically upward and stretch
to infinity from the point, wherever it is, where we
stand, and we must not say that this distinction of up
and down will never be found in it. Nor, again, must
we say that, in respect of any point we think of, that
which is beneath it and extends to infinity is at once

[1] II, 184 *sqq.*

above and beneath as regards that same point. For this is inconceivable. Hence we can assume one motion in an upward direction, and only one, which we extend in thought to infinity, and one motion in a downward direction, and only one, even if ten thousand times over it happens that that which moves to the regions above our heads encounters the feet of those above us, or that which moves downward from us encounters the heads of those beneath us. For the motion in the two cases is conceived as extending to infinity in opposite directions throughout."[1]

The author is attempting to meet the objection that in infinite space there is no up and down, which he grants, if up and down are used in an absolute sense as implying a highest and a lowest point in infinite space. But he goes on to defend the use of the terms in a relative sense, and to deny that the same direction can be at once both up and down in reference to the same point of space. If it be granted that a line starting from a given point in a given direction may be produced both ways to infinity, then, he contends, if we call motion along this line in one direction up, we may also call motion along this line in the opposite direction down. A falling body which moves in the direction from our head to our feet and straight on in the same direction to infinity has for us a downward motion, and whatever moves in the contrary direction from our feet to our heads and straight on in the same direction to infinity has for us an upward motion. From the infinity of worlds it may be inferred that there are some worlds vertically over our heads and others beneath our feet; in the last sentence but one we

[1] § 60, *l. c.*, p. 18, 3–14.

seem to find a reference to the inhabitants of such worlds. A point on the vertical line may be "down" from their stand-point, though it is "up" from ours, or *vice versa*.

"When they are travelling through the void and meet with no resistance, the atoms move with equal velocity. Nor will heavy atoms travel more quickly than small, light ones so long as they meet with no obstruction, nor small atoms travel more quickly than great ones so long as they find a passage suitable for their size and provided they also do not meet with any obstruction. Nor will their upward or lateral motion, which is due to collisions, nor, again, their downward motion, due to weight, increase or lessen their velocity. As long as their motion lasts, whether it be vertical or not, their velocity will be quick as thought until they meet with some obstruction, whether due to external collision or their own weight, which overcomes the force of a previous impact. Moreover, of the atoms in composite bodies, one will not travel faster than another, since all have equal velocity; and this whether we consider the motion of the atoms in an aggregate in one direction during sensible and continuous time or their motions in different directions in times so short as to be apprehended only by the reason. But they frequently collide and are thrust back and forth before finally the continuity of their motion is appreciable by sense. For the assumption that beyond the range of direct observation even the minute times conceivable by reason will present continuity of motion is a gratuitous addition, which is not true in the case before us. Our canon is that direct observation by sense and direct apprehension by the mind are alone invariably true." [1]

[1] §§ 61, 62, *l. c.*, p. 18, 15 *sqq.*

The atomic theory of Democritus, for whom the polemical allusions are intended, undergoes in this passage considerable modifications. We have no precise information what the earlier Atomists conceived the original motion of atoms to be. There is little or no ground for attributing to them the belief of Epicurus that every atom has inherent in it a downward tendency which we may, if we like, call gravity. Their cosmogony starts with a confused motion of colliding atoms which by the force of impact move vertically, laterally, and in all directions. At the same time it appears from Aristotle's criticisms that Democritus did really suppose that if two atoms, one larger and heavier, the other smaller and lighter, moved in the same direction, the former would overtake the latter. Aristotle suggested that Democritus had omitted to take into account the resistance of the air, and that in perfectly empty space a large body and a small body would move with equal velocity. The opinion of Aristotle is indorsed by Epicurus, so firmly, indeed, that when he comes to the crux of his whole system he has to adopt a novel expedient to bring about collisions between atoms travelling with uniform velocity in the same direction. But of this more hereafter. In the present passage he simply affirms the uniform velocity of all atoms under all conditions and at all times, on the ground that they move in empty space which offers no obstruction. Such an affirmation bears an external resemblance to the doctrine of the conservation of energy. But Epicurus seems unconscious of the many assumptions which his statement involves. His atoms are absolutely hard and therefore inelastic. According to him the direction of motion changes after impact, but there is no loss of energy, and friction is ignored.

His own concern is first with Democritus, whom apparently he charges with confounding motion in a medium such as air with motion in a void, and next with the interesting and different problem, to which we have already referred, of the motions of atoms in which looser or closer association form composite bodies.   If we may expand the terse obscurity of the summary, the point he makes seems to be this.   In motion of translation the whole composite body in finite time passes from point A to point B in a straight line.   We are tempted, therefore, by the perversity of over-hasty presuppositions, and all those tendencies which we may call groundless opinion, inference, or belief, to argue that, if this finite time be subdivided into atoms of time distinctly conceivable by the mind but too short to be apprehended by sense, the uniform motion of translation will be maintained through each of them, not only for the composite moving body as a whole, but for each of its component atoms.   This he brands as a mistake.   We have clear and distinct apprehensions by the mind which are trustworthy, because in them the mind seizes and grasps objective images.   When we picture the actual course of a single atom in a composite body moving with motion of translation, we see clearly and distinctly that it does not describe a free course, but is in perpetual oscillation backward and forward on account of collision with the other atoms associated with it in the composite body, and we may suppose him to add— this is the gist of the argument, though nowhere expressed—that in this perpetual oscillation backward and forward each atom of the composite body moves with uniform velocity "quick as thought," as if it were moving singly and freely through space, although the movement of translation of the whole composite body, as attested by sense, is so immeasurably slower than the motion of the atom.

Lucretius describes the motion of the unimpeded atom as many times surpassing in velocity the sun's light and heat, which, he remarks, travel not through void but through intervening air. He corrects the error as he conceives it of Democritus thus: "But if haply any one believes that heavier bodies, as they are carried more quickly sheer through space, can fall from above on the lighter and so beget blows able to produce begetting motions, he goes most widely astray from true reason. For whenever bodies fall through water and thin air they must quicken their descents in proportion to their weights, because the body of water and subtle nature of air cannot retard everything in equal degree, but more readily give way, overpowered by the heavier; on the other hand, empty void cannot offer resistance to anything in any direction at any time, but must, as its nature craves, continually give way; and for this reason all things," i. e., all atoms, "must be moved and borne along with equal velocity though of unequal weights through the unresisting void." [1]

But motion due to weight and motion due to collision are not, so Epicurus thinks, the whole account of the matter. It is unfortunate that we have not his own statement but are forced again to borrow from Lucretius who is, however, well supported by independent authorities. We must also remember that, if Epicurus comes off badly, he is setting out on an adventure which the more prudent Democritus declined. The question why things should be as they are does not concern an empiricist. It is enough for him to find out how they are. Aristotle expressly

[1] II, 225 *sqq.*

testifies that Leucippus and Democritus declined to give any cause of motion. They said it was original, eternal, and without beginning, since each movement presupposes a preceding movement, and to seek for the beginning of an endless process is absurd. According to them a vortex motion of atoms preceded the very beginning of our world as it now exists. But beyond this they do not go back. Epicurus seems to have argued that vertical motion in the determinate direction which we call downward is prior to the motion resulting from collision, impact, and pressure, though why this should be so it is hard to see, and that atoms moving with equal velocity in the same direction would never collide. Feeling bound to offer some explanation, since both the tendency to fall downward and the collision seemed guaranteed by sense, he modified his premises in an arbitrary manner by the gratuitous assumption of an atomic declination from the perpendicular to a minimum extent. Sense tells us that heavy bodies fall downward to the earth, but sense never can assure us that they do not diverge from the perpendicular, provided the divergence is too small for sense to discern. Here, again, he avails himself of that convenient loose second clause of the canon with its fatal flaw: "Nothing in our experience contradicts such an assumption." Certainly not, when the assumption is expressly removed from the region of trustworthy observation. The all important evidence of sense does not, because it cannot contradict an imperceptible swerving. Over this assumption opponents made merry, while apologists almost as unkind would persuade us that our philosopher actually introduced spontaneity into nature out of sheer aversion for the natural necessity of Democritus.

According to M. Guyau, the power of atoms to decline from their path in whatever direction it is does not disappear after they have combined in matter, but still remains, endowing bodies with a power of spontaneous motion to a quite imperceptible degree. M. Guyau holds that such a blind latent force of spontaneity, working imperceptibly in the things around us, issues in those events which are ascribed to chance or accident. Instead of attributing atomic declination to so unworthy a motive we should rather regard it as a desperate device to which Epicurus thought himself driven, if, in Plutarch's words, stars and animals and chance and human action were to be saved from destruction. Here the same three causes can be distinguished as in the letter to Menœceus. The atoms by natural necessity have formed our world in which stars and animals are included; some things again are due to chance, while true spontaneity, as distinct from both of these, is to be found in human action alone. Atomic declination should be regarded, then, as coming under the first rather than the second or third of these heads. It is, Lucretius conceives, doubtless following Epicurus, a necessary postulate for the third, since the motions which are initiated by our will are in the last analysis movements of soul atoms. Epicurus was no determinist where human action is concerned, because, as it seemed to him and has seemed to many others since, the testimony of consciousness contradicts the determinist position. The problem, then, was how to reconcile free-will or spontaneous initiative with mechanical necessity in the natural world. The solution which he tendered must be judged on its merits. It is perhaps not more successful than any other. But great as is the departure from the true doctrine of mechanical necessity which Democritus consistently maintained, this is a very different thing from calling in spontaneity as a principle in nature.

But it is time to let Lucretius expound his master's doctrine in his own words: "When atoms are borne downward sheer through void by their own weights at quite uncertain times and uncertain spots they push themselves a little from their course; you just and only just can call it a change of inclination. If they were not used to swerve they would all fall down like drops of rain, through the deep void, and no clashing would have been begotten nor blow produced among the atoms; thus nature never would have produced aught." [1]

Here, then, we learn the truth. Go back as far as we may in the history of the universe, there is no rain of atoms downward. Epicurus, like Democritus, supposed atoms moving in all directions, the inherent force of pseudo-gravity with which Epicurus, in obedience to experience, endowed his atoms, being everywhere counteracted by the effects of collision. The actual universe shows on a large scale what we see of motes in a sunbeam, viz., a dance of particles in all directions. The ceaseless rain of eternal atoms racing through infinite space in the same downward direction, the conception which called forth the enthusiasm of Fleeming Jenkin, belongs to an unreal or imaginary universe in which free atoms never collide because they never decline. Such a conception Epicurus relegated to the limbo of false opinion, unreality, and error for the sufficient reason that our world, and infinite other worlds, actually exist, *i. e.*, have come into being, which could never have hap-

[1] II, 216 *sqq.*

pened on the hypothesis rejected. After refuting the
opinion attributed to Democritus, that heavier atoms
fall more quickly and overtake lighter ones, Lucretius
proceeds: "Therefore heavier things will never be
able to fall from above on lighter nor of themselves
to beget blows sufficient to produce the varied motions by which nature carries on things. Wherefore,
again and again I say bodies must swerve a little; and
yet not more than the least possible, lest we be found
to be imagining oblique motions, and this the reality
should refute. For this we see to be plain and evident that weights, so far as in them is, cannot travel
obliquely when they fall from above, *at least so far as
you can perceive;* but that nothing swerves in any
case from the straight course, who is there that can
perceive?" [1] The qualifying clauses should be carefully noted.

Lucretius goes on to adduce the evidence of consciousness for our own power of spontaneous initiative. "Again, if all motion is ever linked together
and a new motion ever springs from another in a
fixed order and atoms do not by swerving make some
commencement of motion to break through the de-
crees of fate, that cause follow not cause from everlasting, whence have all living creatures here on
earth, whence, I ask, has been wrested from the fates
the power by which we go forward whither the will
leads each, by which likewise we change the direction
of our motions neither at a fixed time nor fixed place,
but when and where the mind itself has prompted?
For beyond a doubt in these things his own will
makes for each a beginning and from this beginning
motions are welled [2] through the limbs. See you not,
too, when the barriers are thrown open at a given

[1] II, 240 *sqq.*   [2] *Per membra rigantur.*

moment, that yet the eager powers of the horses cannot start forward so instantaneously as the mind
itself desires? The whole store of matter through
the whole body must be sought out in order that,
stirred up through all the frame, it may follow with
undivided effort the bent of the mind, so that you
see the beginning of motion is born from the heart,
and the action first commences in the will of the
mind and next is transmitted through the whole body
and frame. Quite different is the case when we move
on propelled by a stroke inflicted by the strong might
and strong compulsion of another; for then it is
quite clear that all the matter of the whole body
moves and is hurried on against our inclination until
the will has reined it in throughout the limbs. Do
you see, then, in this case that, though an outward
force often pushes men on and compels them frequently to advance against their will, and to be
hurried headlong on, there yet is something in our
breast sufficient to struggle against and resist it?
And when, too, this something chooses, the store of
matter is compelled sometimes to change its course
through the limbs and frame, and after it has been
forced forward, is reined in and settles back into its
place. Wherefore in atoms, too, you must admit
the same, admit that besides blows and weights there
is another cause of motions, from which this power
of free action has been begotten in us, since we see
that nothing can come from nothing. For weight
forbids that all things be done by blows through, as
it were, an outward force; but that the mind itself
does not feel an internal necessity in all its actions,
and is not, as it were, overmastered and compelled
to bear and put up with this, is caused by a minute
swerving of atoms at no fixed part of space and no

fixed time." [1] The cogency of this reasoning depends upon the Epicurean theory of the atomic constitution of the soul.

Epicurus now treats of the soul. "Next, with constant reference to our perceptions and feelings (for so we shall have the surest grounds for belief), we must understand generally that the soul is a corporeal thing, composed of fine particles, dispersed all over the frame, most nearly resembling wind with an admixture of heat, in some respects like wind, in others like heat, but in part even superior to both of them in the fineness of its particles, and on that account in closer sympathy with the rest of the frame. And this is shown by all the mental faculties and sensations, by the ease of mental motion and by thoughts, and by that the loss of which causes death. And we must keep in mind that soul has the greatest share in causing sensation. Still, it would not have had sensation had it not been confined within the rest of the frame. But the rest of the frame, though it provides this indispensable condition for the soul, and has itself, too, shared in a like property, yet does not possess all the attributes of soul. Hence on the departure of the soul it loses sensation." [2] This means that atoms of soul can neither have sensation themselves nor cause the body to have sensation unless they are confined in the body. When so confined, they not only have sensation, but communicate it to the body, which becomes sentient. But other properties of the soul, e. g., the power to think, are not in this way communicated to the body, confinement in which is the indispensable condition that the soul should have sensation and thought. "For the body had not this power in itself, but something else when

[1] II, 251 *sqq.*   [2] §§ 63, 64, *Epicurea*, p. 19, 15 *sqq.*

conjoined thereto procured it for the body, which
other thing through the faculty brought to perfection
in it in virtue of motion at once acquired for itself a
quality of sentience, and in virtue of the neighbour-
hood and close sympathy between them, as I said,
imparted it to the body also. Hence, so long as the
soul is in the body, it never loses sentience through
the loss of some other part. The frame may be
loosened either wholly or in part and portions of the
soul may thereby be lost. Yet in spite of this the
soul, if it manages to survive, will continue to have
sentience. But the rest of the frame, whether the
whole of it survives or only a part, will no longer
have sensation when once that has departed which,
however small in amount, attunes the multitudinous
atoms to harmony and life. Moreover, when the
whole frame is broken up the soul is scattered, and
has no longer the same powers as before, nor does it
move, and hence it does not possess sentience. For
we cannot conceive the sentient subject as otherwise
than in this composite whole and moving with these
movements; nor can we conceive it when the body
which encloses and surrounds it is not the same as
that in which the soul is now located and in which
it performs these movements. There is a further
point to observe; I mean, what the incorporeal is
when the term is applied to a thing in itself incorporeal. It is impossible to conceive anything that is
incorporeal in itself except empty space, which cannot itself either act or be acted upon, but simply
allows body to move through it. Hence those who
call soul incorporeal talk foolishly. For if it were
so it could neither act nor be acted upon. But, as
it is, both these properties manifestly belong to
soul. Thus, then, if we refer all these arguments

concerning soul to the standard of our feelings and perceptions, and if we remember the propositions stated at the outset, we shall see that the subject has been adequately comprehended in outline and thus be able to verify with certainty the details." [1]

This account is for the most part quite plain and easy to follow. Special stress is laid on the mutual relation and inter-connection between the soul and the body, such that neither can exist without the other. We also learn that soul is a corporeal thing, a very fine substance, and a composite substance, wind and heat being mentioned as two elements in the compound. The words "the frame may be loosened either wholly or in part and portions of the soul may thereby be lost" most probably refer to the effects of a deadly blow causing a swoon, so that for some time life is apparently extinct though recovery is occasionally possible even then. If this is so the following parallel from Lucretius serves to interpret them: "Again, a blow more severe than its nature can endure prostrates at once any living thing and goes on to stun all the senses of body and mind. For the positions of the atoms are broken up and the vital motions entirely stopped until the matter, disordered by the shock through the whole frame, unties from the body the vital fastenings of the soul and scatters it abroad, and forces it out through all the pores. For what more can we suppose the infliction of a blow can do than shake from their place and break up the union of the several elements? Often, too, when the blow is inflicted with less violence the remaining vital motions are wont to prevail, ay, prevail and still the huge disorders caused by the blow and recall each part into its proper channels, and shake

[1] §§ 64–68, *l. c.*, p. 20, 13 *sqq.*

off the motion of death now reigning, as it were, paramount in the body and kindle afresh the almost lost senses. For in what other way should the thing be able to gather together its power of mind and come back to life from the very threshold of death, rather than speed on to the goal to which it had almost run and so pass away?"[1]

In the third book of his poem Lucretius deals with the soul and goes over much the same ground as Epicurus, but with far greater fulness of detail, and the additional statements he makes are confirmed by casual references from other authorities, even where they at first sight conflict with the bare summary given by his master. His account of the nature and composition of the soul starts with a refutation of the doctrine of harmony, so well known from its examination in Plato's *Phædo*. This doctrine, which reduces the soul from an actual part of the man, co-ordinate with the body, to a mere relation or harmony between the various parts of the body, had been revived by Dicæarchus and Aristoxenus, pupils of Aristotle. Lucretius passes on next to distinguish in the single substance of the soul two parts which he calls *animus* and *anima*. The former he describes as the superior or ruling part and as localised in the breast, the latter as diffused through the whole body. "Now I assert that the mind and the soul are kept together in close union, and make up a single nature, but that the directing principle which we call mind and understanding is the head, so to speak, and reigns paramount in the whole body. It has a fixed seat in the middle region of the breast; here throb fear and apprehension, about these spots dwell soothing joys; therefore here is the understanding or mind. All the

[1] II, 944 *sqq.*

rest of the soul disseminated through the whole body obeys and moves at the will and inclination of the mind." [1] Again: "And since we perceive that vital sense is in the whole body, and we see that it is all endowed with life, if on a sudden any force with swift blow shall have cut it in twain so as quite to dissever the two halves, the power of the soul will without doubt at the same time be cleft and cut asunder and dashed in twain together with the body." [2] A soldier's arm or foot or head, he goes on to say, cut off in the heat of battle will show for a time remains of sense and motion, and a serpent chopped in pieces may be seen to writhe and wriggle on the ground. These facts, which the poet adduces to prove that the soul is divisible and therefore mortal serve equally well to prove the diffusion of vital sense and therefore the presence of soul atoms through the whole frame.

Lucretius exaggerated the distinction between the two parts (1) *animus* or *mens*, and (2) *anima* by the choice of his Latin terms for them. Our Greek authorities speak of the former only as the ruling part of the soul and the latter as soul in general. It may be a consciousness of this exaggeration that leads the poet subsequently to say that he will in future ignore the difference between them and treat the *animus* and the *anima* as one single substance. [3] There is, indeed, merely a difference of function between them, and this may be traced back to the fact that in the breast soul atoms are closely huddled together and thus give rise to atomic motions more complicated than is the case when they are dispersed through the limbs and the periphery of the body, and are comparatively rare. These atoms are in

[1] III, 136 *sqq.*   [2] III, 634 *sqq.*   [3] III, 421.

all cases exceedingly minute, smooth, and spherical. But in the composite substance which they unite to form can be distinguished not only atoms of wind and of heat, but also atoms of air and of a fourth nameless substance in which all sensation begins. In the summary given by Epicurus above, the third and fourth classes of constituent atoms, the atoms of air and of the nameless substance are passed over, but that he recognised them is a well-attested fact. It causes some surprise that any distinction at all should be made between wind and air, especially when we learn from Lucretius that "wind is produced when the air has been stirred and set in motion." [1] But air, according to Epicurus, is not, so to speak, a simple body, but is composed of atoms which, though always fine and smooth, are yet of different kinds, some of them fiery, some moist, together with atoms of various things which have been evaporated or pulverised. In fact, the atmosphere is a medley of atoms of all sorts of things, provided these things have been volatilised. The poet tells us that "the air is changed over its whole body every hour in countless ways. For whatever ebbs from things is all borne away always into the great sea of air; and unless it in return were to give back bodies to things and to recruit them as they ebb, all things ere now would have been dissolved and changed into air," [2] i. e., they would have entered into that medley of which the atmosphere is constituted. It has been suggested [3] that the exact difference between air and wind is one of temperature, and that in air there is a predominance of atoms such as constitute a medium or calm temperature in the wind which blows a predominance of atoms slightly larger and less smooth, such as

[1] VI, 685.   [2] V, 275 *sqq.*   [3] Giussani, *Studi Lucreziani*, p. 184.

constitute a cold temperature. As to the fourth substance which Lucretius calls the "soul of the soul,"
the idea of some scholars that it was confined to the
breast is preposterous and absurd, for, if sensation
starts with it, it must be present in every part of the
frame which has sensation and therefore it must be
a constituent of every part of the soul. Moreover,
the doxographers inform us that in the opinion of
Epicurus sensation took place in the various sense-
organs, the eye, the ear, the tongue, the nostrils and
was not, as some other schools held, localised in or
transferred to a central organ, heart or brain.
Lucretius thus describes the part which this fourth
nameless substance takes in the initiation and transmission of sensation. "Thus some fourth nature, too,
must be added to these: it is altogether without
name; than it nothing exists more nimble or more
fine, or of smaller or smoother elements: it first
transmits the sense-giving motions through the frame;
for it is first stirred, made up as it is of small particles;
next the heat and the unseen force of the wind receive the motions, then the air; then all things are set
in action, the blood is stirred, every part of the flesh
is filled with sensation; last of all the feeling is
transmitted to the bones and marrow, whether it be
one of pleasure or an opposite excitement.[1]

Epicurus next explains the nature and mode of
existence which be ascribes to his two classes of
qualities, the permanent properties, *coniuncta* and
the variable accidents, *eventa*. "Shapes and colours,
magnitude and weights, and, in short, all those qualities which are predicated of body are properties, either
of all bodies or of visible bodies, and can be known
as belonging to body by sense-perception. All these

[1] III, 241 *sqq.*

properties must not be supposed to exist independently by themselves (for this is inconceivable), nor
again to be non-existent nor to be some other incorporeal essences present in body besides, nor yet to be
parts of body. We must consider a whole body in
general to derive its permanent nature from them,
though it is not, as it were, formed by grouping them
together in the same way as when from the particles
themselves a larger aggregate is made up, whether
these particles be primary," *i. e.*, the least perceptible which have the property in question, "or any
parts whatsoever less than the particular whole. All
these qualities, I repeat, merely give to body its own
permanent nature. They all have their own characteristic modes of being perceived along with the
whole body in which they inhere and never as separated from it; and it is in virtue of this complex
conception of body that they have received the appellation of properties." [1]

"Again, qualities often attach to bodies without
being permanent concomitants. They are not to be
classed among invisible entities nor are they incorporeal. Hence, using the term "accidents" in its
commonest sense, we say plainly that "accidents"
have not the nature of the whole thing to which they
belong, and to which, conceiving it as a whole, we
give the name of body, nor that of the permanent
properties without which body cannot be thought of.
And in virtue of certain peculiar modes of cognition
into which the complex body always enters each of
them can be called an accident. But the object,
whatever it is, in which the accident is said to inhere,
does not derive its permanent nature from the accidents which accompany it. There is no need to

[1] §§ 68, 69, *Epicurea*, p. 22, 13 *sqq*.

banish from reality this clear evidence that the accident has not the nature of the whole to which it
belongs, nor of the permanent properties which accompany the whole. Nor must we suppose the
accident to have permanent existence (for this is as
inconceivable in the case of accidents as in that of the
permanent properties). They are what they appear
to be. They must all be regarded as accidents of
body, not as permanent concomitants nor as having
the rank of independent existence. They are seen to
be exactly as sensation itself makes known their individuality." [1]

The question what we mean when we say that an
attribute exists is bound up with another question,
what exactly is meant by saying that a thing has an
attribute or quality, the question of the import of
predication. On both points ancient and modern
thinkers have been much divided. In some of his
dialogues Plato implies that there are "ideas," as he
calls them, of qualities, that qualities like beauty are
self-existent realities or essences, and that a particular
thing is beautiful because it partakes in self-existent
beauty, which therefore is immanent in it. This
Platonic view is the first which Epicurus rejects.
Again, in disclaiming the absolute non-existence of
properties he probably refers to Democritus, who
asserted that colour, sound, and odour did not in
reality belong to the external objects which we perceive as coloured, sonant, and odorous. The view
that qualities are "other incorporeal existences
present in body" is that of Aristotle, the view that
qualities are material parts of objects that of the
Stoics.

Now as to time. "There is another thing which

[1] §§ 70, 71, *l. c.*, p. 23, 13 *sqq.*

we must consider carefully. We must not investigate time as we do the other accidents which we investigate in a subject, viz., by referring them to the generic types present to our minds, but we must simply attend to the intuitive action itself in virtue of which we speak of 'a long time' or 'a short time' in the common acceptation of the term. We need not adopt any fresh terms as preferable, but should employ the usual expressions about it. Nor need we predicate anything else of time, as if this something else contained the same essence as is contained in the proper meaning of the word time (for this is also done by some)." [1] Time had been defined as "number of motion" or "measure of motion." Epicurus does not think this makes the idea conveyed by the word time any clearer. "We must chiefly attend to that to which we attach this peculiar character of time and whereby we measure it. No further proof is required; we have only to reflect that we attach time to days and nights and their parts, and likewise to feelings of pleasure and pain and to neutral states, to states of movement and states of rest, and consider that time itself is a peculiar accident of all these, and so it is in virtue of this accident that we apply the name 'time.' " [2]

Unlike empty space, which has real and separate existence, time, as above explained, is merely an accident, and, further, that to which it attaches, that of which it is an accident, is not anything real or corporeal but is itself an accident. Time, then, is an accident of accidents, an accident of events or occurrences in the present, past, or future. This point is brought out by Lucretius thus: "Time, also, has no separate existence, and it is due simply to

[1] § 72, *l. c.*, p. 24, 12 *sqq.*   [2] §§ 72, 73, *l. c.*, p. 25, 3–10.

events that happen that our mind grasps what has
taken place in the past, and also what is happening
now, and, further, what follows in the future. We
must admit that no one has a perception of time in the
abstract, apart from the movement of events, whether
fast or slow. Further, when men say that events like
the rape of Helen and the conquest of the Trojan
people by the sword have existence, we must be careful that they do not haply force us to admit that these
events have separate existence, on the ground that
the generations of men, of whom these were the accidents, have been carried away by time now gone
by without recall. For whatever may have taken
place may be called an accident, in one aspect, of the
Trojan people,[1] but in another aspect, of the country
itself. Further, if there had been no matter and no
place and room, in which the different processes go
on, never would the fire, kindled by love of Helen's
beauty, have blazed in the heart of Phrygian Paris,
and kindled that famous contest of cruel war; nor
would the wooden horse, unknown to the Trojans,
have set fire to Pergamus by the hand of the Greeks
who came forth from its womb in the night. Hence
you can clearly see that all events from first to last
have no separate existence or being as body has, and
are not terms of the same kind as void is; rather they
are such that you may justly call them accidents of
body and accidents of place in which the different
processes go on." [2]

"Next," Epicurus goes on, "we must consider that
the worlds and every finite aggregate which bears a
strong resemblance to the things we see have arisen
out of the infinite. For all these, whether small or
great, have been separated off from special conglomer-

---

[1] Reading *Teucris* with Munro for *terris*.   [2] I, 459 *sqq*.

ations of atoms, and all things are again dissolved, some faster, some slower, some through the action of one set of causes, others through the action of another. And we must not suppose that the worlds have necessarily one and the same shape. For nobody could prove that in one sort of world there could equally well not be found as be found the seeds out of which animals and plants and all the rest of the things we see arise, and that in another sort of world this would have been impossible." [1]

"Again, we must suppose that human nature, too, has been taught and forced to learn many various lessons by the facts themselves, and that reason subsequently develops what it has thus received and makes fresh discoveries, among some men more quickly, among others more slowly. Hence, even the names of things were not originally due to convention, but in the several tribes under the impulse of special feelings and special presentations of sense primitive man uttered cries. The air thus emitted was moulded by their individual feelings or sense-presentations, and differently according to the difference in the regions which the tribes inhabited. Subsequently whole tribes adopted their own special names in order that their communications might be less ambiguous to each other and more briefly expressed. Some men, we must suppose, who knew about them, tried to introduce the notion of things not visible, and put in circulation certain names for them, which they were compelled to utter, while the others, following their reason as best they could, interpreted them in that sense." [2]

There is no plan in nature, says Epicurus, nothing which can be referred to supernatural will or agency.

[1] § 73, *Epicurea*, p. 25, 11 *sqq.*   [2] §§ 75, 76, *l. c.*, p. 26, 7 *sqq.*

"We are bound to believe that in the heavens revolutions, solstices, eclipses, risings, and settings and the like take place without the intervention or command, either now or in the future, of any being who at the same time enjoys perfect bliss along with immortality. For troubles and anxieties and feelings of anger and favour do not accord with bliss, but always imply weakness and fear and dependence upon one's neighbours. Nor, again, must we hold that ignited globular masses of fire, endowed with bliss, produce these motions at will. Nay, in every term we use we must hold fast to all the majesty which attaches to such notions as bliss and immortality lest the terms should generate beliefs inconsistent with this majesty. Otherwise such inconsistency will of itself suffice to produce disturbance in our minds. Hence, where we find phenomena invariably recurring, the invariableness of the recurrence must be ascribed to the original interception and conglomeration of atoms cut off from the infinite, whereby the world was formed." [1]

This passage, to be fully appreciated, must be read in the light of the antagonistic Stoical doctrine which is so pointedly assailed. The stars, according to the Stoics, were "globular masses of fire," and yet at the same time were rational and supremely happy beings, endowed with life as well as self-motion. Epicurus first points out that the intelligent government of the world is fatal to the immortality of bliss which is the divine prerogative, and then tenders a different explanation of the order and regularity of phenomena. The sun rises and sets regularly only because the combination of atoms evolves that particular change again and again with an approximation to uniformity.

[1] §§ 76, 77, *l. c.*, p. 27, 17 *sqq.*

"We must hold that to arrive at accurate knowledge of the cause of the things of most moment is the business of natural science and that happiness depends upon this and upon knowing what the heavenly bodies really are, and anything else which contributes to exact knowledge in this respect. Further, we must recognise no plurality of causes or contingency in the things of most moment, but must hold that nothing suggestive of conflict or disquiet is compatible with an immortal and blessed nature. And the intellect can grasp the absolute truth of this." [1] By the "matters of greatest moment" Epicurus means the exclusion of the gods or any supernatural agency whatever from the government of the world. This he considers fully established and absolutely certain. No alternative hypotheses or contingencies are admissible on this subject. This is all we know for certain and all we need to know.

"But when we come to subjects for special inquiry there is nothing in the knowledge of risings and settings and solstices and eclipses and all kindred subjects that contributes to our happiness, but those who are well-informed about such matters, and yet are ignorant what the heavenly bodies really are, and what are the most important causes of phenomena, feel quite as much fear as those who have no such special information; nay, perhaps even greater fear when the curiosity excited by this additional knowledge cannot find satisfaction nor subordinate these phenomena to the highest causes. Hence, if we discover more than one cause to account for solstices, settings and risings, eclipses and the like, as we did also in particular matters of detail, we must not suppose that our treatment of these matters fails

[1] § 78, *l. c.*, p. 28, 15 *sqq.*

of accuracy so far as it is needful to insure our tranquillity and happiness. When, therefore, we investigate the causes of celestial and meteorological phenomena, as of all that is unknown, we must take into account the variety of ways in which analogous occurrences happen within our experience; while as for those who do not know the difference between what is or comes about from a single cause and what is the effect of many causes, who overlook the different impression which things make upon us when seen from a distance, and so are ignorant of the sort of matters which leave our tranquillity unaffected, all such men we must treat with contempt. If, then, we believe that an event could happen in one or other particular way out of several which leave our tranquillity unaffected, we shall be as tranquil when we are aware that it actually does come about in more ways than one as we should be if we knew that it happens in only one particular way." [1]

The argument is this: When the same effect is known to have more than one cause, and we are uncertain to which of these causes it is to be referred in a particular case, then if we are sure that the question whether it is to be referred to cause A or to cause B does not affect our tranquillity, we need not carry the investigation any further. The knowledge that of all the causes which bring about this effect there is none that in any way disturbs our tranquillity, conduces to that tranquillity just as much as would the precise knowledge to which of these given causes the effect on a given occasion is due. How this principle works may be seen from the application made by Epicurus himself in the extant letter to

[1] §§ 79, 80, *l. c.*, p. 29, 6.

Pythocles.[1] The fifth and sixth books of the poem of Lucretius traverse the same ground and the same method is there employed. In investigating a phenomenon of the class defined whose cause is unknown, Epicurus, on principle, stops short so soon as he has reached a plurality of causes any one of which is upon analogy judged capable of producing the effect under investigation without calling in supernatural agency. Over the results so obtained, which will appear to some ludicrous, to others lamentable, the friends of the philosopher will prefer to throw a veil.

"There is yet one more point to seize, viz., that the greatest anxiety of the human mind arises through the belief that these heavenly bodies are blessed and eternal, and that at the same time they have wills and actions and causality inconsistent with this belief, and through expecting and apprehending some everlasting evil either because of the myths or because we are in dread of the insensibility of death, as if it had to do with us, and through being reduced to this state not by conviction, but by a certain irrational perversity, so that, if we do not set bounds to our terror, we endure as much or even more intense anxiety than if we held these beliefs. But mental tranquillity means to be released from all these troubles and to cherish a continual remembrance of the highest and most important truths. Hence we must attend to present feelings and sense-perceptions, whether those of mankind in general or those peculiar to the individual, and to all the clear evidence at hand, given by each of the standards of truth. For by studying them we shall rightly trace to its cause and banish the source of disturbance and dread,

---

[1] Diogenes Laërtius, Book X, §§ 84–116; *Epicurea*, pp. 35–55.

accounting for celestial phenomena and the rest of the things which from time to time befall, which cause the utmost alarm to the rest of mankind." [1]

This brings us very nearly to the close of the letter to Herodotus in which Epicurus, as he goes on to say, has given an epitome of his physical theory so adequate and yet so compressed that he recommends his pupil to commit it to memory. Once more, it will be seen, he emphasises the subordination of all physical inquiries to ethical considerations. His sole aim is to banish for ever from the mind those fertile sources of disturbance, superstition, and terror. In so far as these anxieties are due to ignorance, their proper cure is knowledge, and within these bounds the pursuit of knowledge should be encouraged, not for its own sake—far from it—but as the indispensable means to the great end of life, the tranquillity of the individual. In the same spirit Lucretius, who so faithfully reproduces his master's teaching, commences his great task. At the outset of his poem, after he has adduced the sacrifice of Iphigenia as the crowning instance of the evils prompted by religion, he introduces the first of the long series of Epicurean dogmas with these words: "This terror, then, and darkness of mind must be dispelled, not by the rays of the sun and glittering shafts of day, but by the aspect and the law of nature; the warp of whose design we shall begin with this first principle, nothing is ever gotten out of nothing by divine power. Fear, in sooth, holds so in check all mortals, because they see many operations go on in earth and heaven, the causes of which they can in no way understand, believing them, therefore, to be done by power divine. For these reasons when we shall have seen that noth-

[1] §§ 81, 82, *l. c.*, p. 30, 8 *sqq.*

ing can be produced from nothing, we shall then
more correctly ascertain that which we are seeking,
both the elements out of which everything can be
produced and the manner in which all things are
done without the hand of the gods." [1] Master and
pupil are at one in striving for spiritual freedom.

[1] I, 146 *sqq.*

CHAPTER VII

THE EPICUREAN THEOLOGY

It remains to consider the attitude of Epicurus toward religion. We have already seen that he was at once iconoclast and believer. He rejected the national polytheism but substituted for it a polytheism of his own. Ever hostile to false conceptions and utterly disbelieving the old time-honoured legends, which played so great a part in the life and thought and art of his time, he yet retained what he believed to be the essence of religion, and a religion not merely "within the bounds of reason alone," to employ Kant's phrase, but even established on the solid basis of experience. Such an attitude has often been a stumbling block to students of the system, and the difficulties with which it is surrounded required to be unravelled with more than ordinary patience and insight.

Atoms and void were, as we have seen, primary ontological postulates for Epicurus, as they had been for Leucippus and Democritus. If atoms and void are postulated it is possible, they held, to account for all that exists and all that occurs in the infinite universe. Everything follows, said Democritus, by natural necessity. Epicurus agreed, with a single reservation, that, namely, which relates to the swerving of atoms at quite uncertain times and places from an absolutely straight course. Even so, he does not admit any force or power controlling the atoms from outside, since movement is their inherent and inalienable property. There is no room for divine agency so long as that agency is conceived as supernatural, and he emphatically declares that within the universe itself there are no indications of purpose or plan. If, then, anything exists to which the attribute divine can be ascribed, it is certainly not, as the Stoics held, the universe itself, and as certainly it is not conscious beings in any way controlling or interfering with the course of nature. From this it would seem to follow that the existence of gods, as ordinarily understood, must be denied, or at any rate that Epicurus would be justified in taking up an agnostic position as Protagoras had done in the memorable words: "Whether gods exist or do not exist I cannot tell, for there are many things which hinder knowledge, especially the obscurity of the problem and the shortness of human life." But neither Epicurus nor Democritus himself acquiesced in such a conclusion. On the contrary, they affirmed the existence of beings higher than man. As there can be little doubt that on this question the opinion of his great predecessor influenced Epicurus, we may give a short summary of the views of Democritus. As Aristotle expressly testifies, he made no distinction between soul, regarded as the vital principle, and mind or intelligence. Soul in animals and mind in man was simply the most perfect form of matter, and at death the atoms composing the soul were scattered asunder.[1] He accordingly rejected the hypothesis of Anaxagoras that Nous or Mind must be assumed in order to account for the origin of motion in the material universe. Democritus held such an assumption to be both futile and unnecessary, for motion was

[1] Stobæus, *Anthologia*, I, p. 384, 18, Wachsmuth.

eternal and of that which is eternal there can be no beginning.[1] Later writers sometimes speak as if Democritus held the spherical soul-atoms themselves to be a divine element in the universe. But this is an error against which we must carefully guard. No doubt Democritus contrasted the soul with the body as the divine with the human, but soul and body were in his view alike corporeal, and "since the corporeal substances are as various as the form and composition of the atoms of which they consist, it is also possible that one substance may have qualities which belong to no other."[2] The divine element, then, if Democritus used such an expression, must be interpreted, not as a divine being or any being at all, not as a world-soul controlling the material universe from within, but simply as the substance of soul, mind-stuff, the purest and most perfect form of matter wherever it occurs in particular beings. His attitude to popular conceptions of the future life may be gathered from a remarkable fragment preserved by Stobæus: "Some men who do not understand the dissolution of our mortal nature, but are conscious of the misery in human existence, painfully spend their allotted period of life in confusion and fear, inventing lies about the time after they are dead."[3] How closely this fragment agrees with the views of Epicurus the reader will not fail to notice. In a lost work, *On Hades*, Democritus collected and probably criticised the numerous fables current in antiquity about the resuscitation of the dead. In fact, he was the first Greek thinker who in so many words denied the immortality of the soul.

---

[1] See Cicero, *De Natura Deorum*, I, § 120, Diels, *Doxographi*, p. 302.
[2] Zeller, *Pre-Socratics*, Vol. II, p. 262, English translation.
[3] Diels², Fragment 297.

With regard to the divinities of the popular faith he seems to have wavered. Sometimes he treated them as allegorical expressions of ethical or physical ideas.[1] Thus Pallas stood originally for wisdom, Zeus for the sky or ether. Only in later times did these conceptions assume personal existence and become endowed in the popular imagination with a bodily shape. Sometimes he ascribed the origin of religion to man's terror at the awe-inspiring phenomena of nature, thunder and lightning, eclipses of the sun, comets, earthquakes and the like, the phenomena which, according to Epicurus, render the study of nature indispensable, if mental composure is to be assured. Thus the popular gods were converted into natural forces or were made the assumed causes of natural phenomena. But at other times they were reduced to mere dæmons, such as in Greek mythology occupied an intermediate position between gods and men. Democritus assumed that in part the popular faith rested on actual evidence of sense, and that there are in the surrounding atmosphere beings who are similar to man in form, but superior to him in size, strength, and longevity. From these beings, as from all others, emanate streams of atoms, which by contact with the organs of sense, render the beings visible and audible to men and even to the inferior animals. They are erroneously held to be divine and imperishable, although in truth they are not indestructible, but merely slower to perish than man. Of these beings and their images there were two kinds, the one kindly and beneficent, the other destructive and harmful. Hence, Democritus is said to have prayed that he might meet with such images as were kindly and beneficent. He contrived to fit

[1] *Cf.* Diels², Fragments 2, 30.

this assumption to the popular belief in dreams and presages of the future, for the phantom images unfold to us the designs of the beings from which they emanate and reveal what is going on in other parts of the world. Sextus, from whom this information is drawn, expressly says that these dæmons were the only gods whose existence Democritus admitted.[1] Scanty as are the materials, it is abundantly evident that a belief in these superhuman phantoms, gigantic, long-lived, intelligent, is quite compatible with the main principles of atomism. They are products of atoms and of atomic movements, structures, generable, and dissoluble like all the other atomic compounds which we know as particular things. In short, Democritus could believe, not only in man, but in super-man without compromising his fundamental positions, that all takes place by natural necessity, that nothing really exists but atoms eternally moving and the void space in which they move.

Let us now suppose that a materialist sincerely adopting the atomic theory sets about the task of criticising and revising this particular doctrine of long-lived dæmons and phantom images. Where does it require modification ? The starting-point for further inquiry would be the alleged evidence of experience, whether in sense or imagination; and, as these apparitions occur most often by night, the whole province of sleep and dreams must be investigated. A single fragment shows in what a matter-of-fact way the materialist Democritus dealt with these phenomena. The images in question had their seat in the sinews and the marrow when they aroused and played upon our souls, and by means of the veins and arteries and the brain itself they penetrated to

[1] Sextus Empiricus, IX, 19; 42.

the inmost parts of the frame.[1]   If Epicurus had been an original thinker, if the love of knowledge for its own sake had had the smallest weight with him, a very slight advance in psychology would have suggested misgivings.   But with his stereotyped canons of inquiry and his empirical theory of knowledge he had no difficulty in swallowing all that was erroneous in the view of Democritus and contrived to modify it in exactly that direction which brought it into violent conflict with the main principles of atomism. The gods of Epicurus differ from the gigantic phantoms or dæmons of Democritus in three particulars. In the first place, they do not dwell in this or any other world, but in the *intermundia* or interspaces between world and world; secondly, they are not divided into beings beneficent and beings malignant, but are all entirely indifferent to and removed from human interests; thirdly, instead of being merely long-lived, they are indestructible and eternal.   This last characteristic is incompatible with atomism, which can provide no satisfactory answer to the question:

> If all be atoms, how then should the Gods,
> Being atomic, not be dissoluble,
> Not follow the great law?

The best excuse which his champions can offer (and a lame excuse it is) refers us once more to preconceptions, mental impressions, and the canon of truth.   Epicurus, we are told, felt bound to believe that to be true which was attested, or not contested, by experience; felt also bound to hold that no pre-

[1] Hermippus, as quoted by Diels, *Archiv für Geschichte der Philosophie*, VII, p. 155 *sq.*

conception can have arisen except through many previous impressions superposed, and that every impression corresponds to objective reality. All men have the preconception, which implies a multitude of previous impressions, of gods. Out of various attributes ascribed to the gods he selected two as fundamental, and the qualities inferred, blessedness and immortality, must belong to the real object which produced the impressions and consequent preconception. Epicurus thus comes before us as a theologian, indeed as a rationalist in theology. We can trace the steps which led him to his belief in the existence of gods. There is first the universal diffusion of the belief that gods exist. The universality of this belief appeared to him to establish its truth.

This is the argument reproduced by Cicero's Epicurean authority in his treatise on the nature of the gods: "Since the belief in question was determined by no ordinance or custom or law, and since a steadfast unanimity continues to prevail among all men without exception, it must be understood that the gods exist. For we have notions of them implanted, or rather innate, within us, and, as that upon which the nature of all men is agreed must needs be true, their existence must be acknowledged. If their existence is all but universally admitted, not only among philosophers, but also among those who are not philosophers, there is a further admission that must in consistency be made, namely, that we possess a preconception which makes us think of them as blessed and immortal. For nature, that gave us the notion of gods as such, has also engraved in our minds the conviction that they are blessed and eternal." [1]   Here it is important to remember that this

[1] *De Natura Deorum*, I, c. XVII, § 44.

preconception is not an innate idea in Locke's sense
of the term, as something stamped upon the soul at
birth, but is used in its technical Epicurean sense
and denotes a generic type, a permanent deposit,
made by the repetition and superposition of similar
impressions. In the case of the gods these impressions are always impressions upon the mind, for the
emanations from the gods are atom-complexes altogether too fine to affect any sense-organ so as to be
perceived by sense. As Lucretius says: "The fine
substance of the gods far withdrawn from our senses
is hardly seen by the thought of the mind; and,
since it has ever eluded the touch and stroke of the
hands, it must touch nothing which is tangible for
us; for that cannot touch which does not admit of
being touched in turn." [1]

To proceed. If the universal preconception establishes, as Epicurus believes, the existence of gods, it
also establishes the characteristic attributes, perfect
happiness, and immortality, which all men agree in
ascribing to the gods. Epicurus, in the letter to
Menœceus already cited, says: "First believe that
God is a being blessed and immortal, according to the
notion of a god commonly held among men. . . .
For verily there are gods and the knowledge of them
is manifest." Apparently he accepts both blessedness and immortality as characteristics given in the
preconception. From these many other attributes
may be inferred by reason. Both blessedness and
immortality would be impaired by the possession of
bodies of the same dense capacity which belongs to
our own. Hence we can only assign to them a body
analogous to the human, ethereal, consisting of the
finest atoms. They have not body, but quasi-body,

[1] Lucretius, V, 148.

which does not contain blood, but quasi-blood.[1]
As their opponents said jeeringly, they are mere
silhouettes or gods in outline, destitute of solidity.
Again, such bodies as they have could not live in this
or any world without being exposed to the ruin which
would, in time, overwhelm it and them, and in the
meantime they would live in a state of fear, which is
incompatible with perfect bliss. Hence, Epicurus
gave to them as their habitation the spaces between
the worlds. Nor, again, can they be supposed to
take any part in governing the course of events, for
the anxieties and responsibilities of such an office
would be fatal to happiness. "God does nothing,
is involved in no occupations, and projects no works;
he rejoices in his own wisdom and virtue, and is
assured that his state will always be one of the highest felicity eternally prolonged," says the Epicurean
in Cicero.[2]   This being so, men have nothing to fear
and nothing to hope from the gods, and we can now
appreciate the full force of the first golden maxim:
"A blessed and eternal being has no troubles itself,
and brings no trouble upon any other; hence it is
exempt from movements of anger and favour, for
every such movement implies weakness." This
maxim is paraphrased by Lucretius as follows: "For
the nature of gods must ever in itself of necessity
enjoy immortality together with supreme repose, far
removed and withdrawn from our concerns; since
exempt from every pain, exempt from all dangers,
strong in its own resources, not wanting aught of us,
it is neither gained by favours nor moved by anger." [3]
In the letter to Menœceus the belief that the greatest evils happen to the wicked and the greatest bless-

---

[1] Cicero, *De Natura Deorum*, c. XVIII, § 49.
[2] *Ib.*, c. XIX., § 51.   [3] Lucretius, II, 646.

ings happen to the good from the hand of the gods, is reckoned by Epicurus among the false assumptions of the multitude.   In his view, to punish the wicked is to be moved with anger, to reward the righteous is to be moved with favour, and he pronounces both states alike incompatible with happiness.   His gods are entirely indifferent to the whole course of the world, and consequently to the fortunes of humanity.   Beyond these fundamental positions the authority of Epicurus himself does not carry us. But his followers would seem to have somewhat enlarged the picture.   Philodemus speculated freely on the mode of divine existence.   The gods would not need sleep, sleep being a partial death, only required as a means of restoration after fatigue.   They must have nourishment, though this must be adapted to the peculiar constitution of their bodies.   If they could not communicate with each other, they would lose the highest means of enjoyment, and they must therefore employ language, Greek or something like it.   In short, he conceives of the gods as a society of Epicurean philosophers, male and female, who have everything they can desire and full opportunities of converse.   Such gods as these alone inspire no fear in their worshippers, but are reverenced for their very perfection.   Moreover, these gods are innumerable.   If the number of mortal beings is infinite, the law of isonomy, counterpoise, or equal distribution requires that the number of immortals should be not less.[1]

We do not know whether the master would have approved all these fantastic speculations.   Nor are we informed of his conclusions on one other most difficult point.   This is usually described as the

[1] *Cf.* Cicero, *De Natura Deorum*, I, § 49.

physical constitution of the Epicurean gods. The crucial passages in Cicero [1] are tantalising from their obscurity, and it may very possibly be that Cicero himself had only imperfectly apprehended the meaning of the words which he translated. He does, however, commit himself to the statement that the gods, though material, are not firm and solid like the gross bodies of men and visible things, but of a far finer texture, and that they have not numerical or material, but only formal identity. This has been interpreted to mean [2] that the matter of which they are composed, instead of remaining fixed and identically the same through a finite space of time, as is the case with visible and tangible objects, is perpetually and instantaneously passing away, to be replaced by fresh matter. The form or arrangement, of matter alone remains unchanged. Perpetual successions of images, i. e., atom-complexes or films having arisen out of the infinite void, stream to a sort of focus, and there, by their meeting, constitute for a moment the being of the gods; then they stream away in all directions, and upon occasion pass into the material mind of man, bringing with them the notion of the blessed and eternal being whose body they for a moment helped to compose and whose form they still bear. The contrast between material or numerical identity and formal identity can be illustrated by the difference between a standing pond or artificial lake and a river or, still better, a cascade. The water in the artificial lake remains the same for a finite space of time, whereas, though the form of the

---

[1] Cicero, De Natura Deorum, I, §§ 49, 105, 109.
[2] First by Lachelier (Revue de Philologie, 1877, p. 264), who has been followed by W. Scott (Journal of Philology, XII, pp. 212 sqq.) and by Giussani (Lucretius, Vol. I, pp. 227 sqq.).

flowing river and the cascade is constant, the drops of water which compose them are never for one instant materially the same or numerically identical. The water keeps flowing on and away, the form alone persists. Following this clue, the same ingenious interpreters, Lachelier, W. Scott, and Giussani, attempt to gain support for their hypothesis from the doctrine of isonomy (*æquabilis tributio*), which W. Scott expounds as follows: "It is the principle that in infinity all things have their match, *omnia omnibus paribus paria respondent*. By this Cicero seems to mean a law of averages or chances; the law, namely, that of two alternatives equally possible each will occur with equal frequency if an infinite number of cases be taken. In the present case there is a double application of this principle. First, the number of atoms in motion in the universe being infinite, there must, on the whole, be equal numbers of atom-motions tending on the one hand to destroy and on the other hand to feed or maintain composite bodies. Lucretius, though he does not use the word isonomy, lays great stress on the thing in this application. 'Thus neither can death-dealing motions' (*motus exitiales*) 'keep the mastery always nor entomb existence for evermore, nor on the other hand can the motions which give birth and increase to things (*genitales auctificique motus*) preserve them always after they are born. Thus the war of first beginnings, waged from eternity, is carried on with dubious issue.'[1] By the *auctifici motus* we must understand the accretion of constituent atoms to a body in the process of growth; and by the *motus exitiales* their excretion or separation from it in the process of decay. But, again, this balance of opposing tendencies may itself

---

[1] Lucretius, II, 569 *sqq.*; *cf.* also II, 522.

be preserved in two different ways. The processes of growth and of decay, of combination and of dissolution, may either prevail ultimately in each individual object, so that the result on the whole will be a perpetual decay of existing things, accompanied by a perpetual growth of fresh things in their place; or the two processes may go on simultaneously in a given object, so as to produce an equilibrium, the result of which will be eternal duration. Consequently (to apply the principle of isonomy once more), if we take an infinite number of cases (that is, if we consider the whole universe), the alternate and the simultaneous action of the two processes must go on to an equal extent. Now, in our world (and, by analogy, in all the worlds) the first alternative is that which universally prevails; that is, the motions of growth and of decay operate alternately, both on the world as a whole and (at shorter intervals) on each individual within it, thus producing universal death and universal birth. Hence, outside the worlds, or in the *intermundia*, room must be found for the other alternative; that is, the *motus auctifici* and the *motus exitiales* must there work simultaneously and, instead of producing a succession of different beings, must result in the immortality of such beings as exist. We see that the exact point proved by the principle of isonomy is the perpetual continuance in the case of the gods, and in their case alone, of the *auctifici motus;* and that it is on this perpetual continuance that their immortality depends. The Epicurean," in *De Natura Deorum*,[1] "when asked how it is that the stream of matter in the form of images which goes to form the gods never fails, replies at first, that it is because there is an infinite supply of matter

[1] § 109.

to draw upon; but to the objection that this argument would tell equally for the immortality of all *things*, he answers, in effect, that the principle of isonomy determines the supply of the infinite in such a way as to produce death and birth in some beings and immortality in others." [1]   Giussani, the Italian editor of Lucretius, adopts this hypothesis and goes a step further when he affirms that "isonomy was excogitated to prove precisely the perpetuity of the *auctifici motus* in the case of the gods and in their case only." [2]   Giussani assumes that the immortality of the gods is exposed to special danger from hypertrophy or the over-assimilation of nutriment, because they live in the *intermundia* amid an enormous superabundance of food from the atomic ocean surrounding them.   If the gods assimilate more matter than is sufficient for simple preservation, we are justified by Lucretius[3] in inferring that such excessive growth must be followed by a period in which the organism cannot assimilate enough to repair the waste that is going on.   What is the cause of the death of men and animals?   It is the fact that the matter of which they are formed is temporarily persistent.   The matter forming my body, which is, for the moment, my matter, may be so suddenly injured or dispersed by an accident, or it may waste so much faster than slow assimilation of food can restore it, that death must follow.   But no artillery fire, however violent and prolonged, could possibly destroy Niagara, though every shot in its passage through the falls temporarily dislodged drops of water.   For it is the persistence of matter, which preserves a stone in being, that becomes in an organism the cause of

[1] *Journal of Philology*, XII, pp. 222 *sqq.*
[2] Giussani, *Lucretius*, Vol. I, p. 263.   [3] II, 1115-1140.

danger and death. To make it possible for ever-lasting beings composed of atoms to exist, it is not enough, Giussani maintains, that the two processes of waste and assimilation should go on simultaneously and the gain be equal to the loss. For the immortality of such beings an absolute non-persistence of matter is necessary. Such a condition is supplied if the bodies of the gods be supposed to retain identity of form amid perpetual and instantaneous change of matter—in short, if they resemble the cascade or flowing river, and not the pond or artificial lake of the illustration. So far Giussani. All are agreed that in men and animals personal identity is compatible with slow but persistent change of constituent matter. It would seem, then, that, on the hypothesis proposed, the identity of these cascade-like gods would, after all, differ from human identity in degree only and not in kind.

I have thought it right to present to the reader these ingenious speculations as far as possible in the words of the scholars who have put them forward. It is highly improbable that the whole question should not have received full discussion at some time or other, if not in the voluminous works of the master himself, at any rate in those of his faithful disciples who were recognised as authoritative expounders of the system. The buried treasures of Herculaneum included many treatises by Epicurus and by Philo-demus, and now that it has been decided to carry on a systematic excavation of this interesting site, we may reasonably anticipate much additional information on this and other obscure points of Epicurean belief. It may be that such information will corroborate and justify the shrewd conjectures which have been put forward. It may also be that fresh

discoveries will render them obsolete and furnish us
with explanations and solutions not hitherto dreamt
of.   With the evidence which we already possess before them, most scholars who have dealt with Epicureanism have been unable to accept as satisfactory
the hypothesis proposed by Lachelier and in the
main adopted by Scott and Giussani.   They either
give up the problem as insoluable or, like Schömann,
Hirzel, and J. B. Mayor, offer suggestions of their
own which, however, are not more convincing.   It
may be well to point out what its advocates do not
explicitly emphasise that by the hypothesis of Lachelier and Scott the eternity of gods in the past as well
as in the future seems to be implied.   These ideals of
wisdom and virtue must always have existed.   If they
are not perishable, neither are they generable.   In a
universe without purpose or plan, in which everything is brought about by blind physical forces, this
is indeed surprising.   It might well have been thought
that Epicurus, of all men, would be the least likely
to call upon faith to redress the balance of reason and
introduce as articles of belief conclusions rejected by
science.   But if he reasoned in the way suggested
by Scott and Giussani, what he did virtually comes
to this.   Our experience of this world shows us beings generable and perishable.   From this he is supposed to take a gigantic step; to our experience of
this world he adds "and by analogy of all worlds."
There are no immortal beings, then, in any one of the
infinite worlds.   But we have the preconception of
a blessed and immortal being.   Therefore, such is
supposed to be his strange conclusion—we are bound
to believe that immortal beings exist, and, though
the worlds are used up, there still remain the *intermundia.*   Verily, the credulity of a materialist and

an empiricist is not to be surpassed by the imaginative flights of all the idealists. The scoffer might well be excused his frivolous jest that Epicurus pensioned off the gods into the *intermundia*. The Athenian sage may have come to such conclusions on such reasoning, but the cautious inquirer will not commit himself until he receives better evidence than has hitherto been adduced.

However this may be, the letter to Menœceus lays down with clearness and consistency the views of the master on the popular religion. He claims for himself and for all other dissentients from the national faith freedom of conscience, and he further claims that disbelief in the popular theology is yet compatible with true piety. "For verily there are gods," he there says, "and the knowledge of them is manifest; but they are not such as the multitude believe, seeing that men do not steadfastly maintain the notions they form respecting them," the notions, namely, of blessedness and immortality. "Not the man who denies the gods worshipped by the multitude, but he who affirms of the gods what the multitude believes about them, is truly impious." Such a statement reveals the courageous free-thinker. He is not content with criticising the current polytheism, with its immoral fables and lying legends; he is not content with denouncing the doctrine of Providence as false and absurd. He assumes the offensive and brands as impious the acceptance of the beliefs which he rejects. It is the firm conviction that the popular religion was a degrading superstition, enslaving men's minds and causing the greatest evils; it is this which lends to the denunciations of Lucretius their moral earnestness and impassioned fervour. The origin of religion he traced, as Epicurus had done before him, to ignorance and fear. Primitive man, knowing nothing of the true causes of natural phenomena, chose to ascribe them to higher powers and naturally lived in awe and terror, ever dreading the interference of incalculable beings so mighty to harm. Lucretius expands the idea thus:

"They would see the system of heaven and the different seasons of the year come round in regular succession, and could not find out by what causes this was done; therefore, they would seek a refuge in handing over all things to the gods and supposing all things to be guided by their nod. And they placed in heaven the abodes and realms of the gods, because night and moon are seen to roll through heaven, moon, day and night and night's austere constellations and night-wandering meteors of the sky and flying bodies of flame, clouds, sun, rains, snow, winds, lightning, hail, and rapid rumblings and loud threatful thunder-claps. O hapless race of men, when that they charged the gods with such acts and coupled with them bitter wrath! What groanings did they then beget for themselves, what wounds for us, what tears for our children's children! No act is it of piety to be often seen with veiled head to turn to a stone and approach every altar and fall prostrate on the ground, to sprinkle the altars with much blood of beasts and link vow on to vow, but rather to be able to look on all things with a mind at peace. For when we turn our gaze on the heavenly quarters of the great upper world and ether fast above the glittering stars, and direct our thoughts to the courses of the sun and moon, then into our breasts burdened with other ills that fear as well begins to exalt its reawakened head, the fear that we may haply find the power of the gods to be unlimited, able to wheel the bright stars in their varied motion; for lack of power to solve the question troubles the mind with doubts, whether there was ever a birth-time of the world, and whether likewise there is to be any end; how far the walls of the world can endure this strain of restless motion; or whether, gifted by the grace of the gods with an ever-lasting existence, they may glide on through a never-ending tract of time and defy the strong powers of immeasurable ages. Again, who is there whose mind does not shrink into itself with fear of the gods, whose limbs do not cower in terror, when the parched earth rocks with the appalling thunderstroke and rattlings run through the great heaven? Do not people and nations quake, and proud monarchs shrink into themselves, smitten with fear of the gods, lest for any foul transgression or overweening word the heavy time of reckoning has arrived at its ful-ness? When, too, the utmost fury of the headstrong wind passes over the sea and sweeps over its waters the commander of a fleet, together with his mighty legions and elephants, does he not draw near with vows to seek the mercy of the gods and ask in prayer with fear and trembling a lull in the winds and pro-pitious gales; but all in vain, since often caught up in the furious hurricane he is borne none the less to the shoals of death? So constantly does some hidden power trample on human grandeur and is seen to tread under its heel and make sport for itself of the renowned rods and cruel axes. Again, when the whole earth rocks under their feet and towns tumble with the shock or doubtfully threaten to fall, what wonder that mortal men abase themselves and make over to the gods in things here on earth high pre-rogatives and marvellous powers sufficient to govern all things?" [1]

[1] Lucretius, V, 1183 *sqq.*

Clearly, then, no prayers, no vows, no presage of the future ought to find a place in religion as conceived by Epicurus. The worship which alone he approves is such joyous reverence as the human spirit, unmoved by hope or fear, spontaneously and disinterestedly proffers to superhuman excellence and eternal blessedness. If fear is the basis of superstition—as Petronius tersely puts it, "it was fear that first made gods in the world"—then freedom from fear must be the work of enlightenment. It is as the saviour and deliverer of mankind that Epicurus is acclaimed by the Roman poet. "If we must speak as the acknowledged grandeur of the theme itself demands, a god he was, a god, most noble Memmius, who first found out that plan of life which is now termed wisdom, and who by trained skill rescued existence from such great billows and such thick darkness." [1] "Soon as thy philosophy, issuing from a godlike intellect, has begun with loud voice to proclaim the nature of things, the terrors of the mind are dispelled, the walls of the world part asunder, I see things in operation throughout the whole void; the divinity of the gods is revealed and their tranquil abodes, which neither winds do shake nor clouds drench with rains nor snow, congealed by sharp frost, harms with hoary fall; an ever cloudless ether o'ercanopies them, and they laugh with light shed largely around. Nature, too, supplies all their wants and nothing ever impairs their peace of mind. But, on the other hand, the Acherusian quarters are nowhere to be seen, though earth is no bar to all things being descried which are in operation underneath our feet throughout the void. At all this a kind of godlike delight mixed with shuddering awe comes

[1] Lucretius, V, 7 *sqq.*

over me to think that nature by thy power is laid thus
visibly open, is thus unveiled on every side." [1] Epicurus directs his searching glance over the entire
universe. In the tranquil abodes of the divinities
he descries an external heaven, but nowhere can he
find an external hell. The Homeric Olympus was
the creation of the poet's fancy and not the picture
of any mountain summit within his experience. Even
more aloof from all possible, as well as actual, experience is the philosopher's

> lucid interspace of world and world,
> Where never creeps a cloud, or moves a wind,
> Nor ever falls the least white star of snow,
> Nor ever lowest roll of thunder moans,
> Nor sound of human sorrow mounts to mar
> Their sacred everlasting calm.

With the rival school of the Stoics Epicurus agrees
in holding that the true hell is the life of the wicked
here upon earth. The only difference is that the
Stoics emphasised the moral degradation of the
sinner, the feelings of shame, the loss of self-respect,
the consciousness of failure to attain man's proper
end, while Epicurus dwells most upon the boding
fear of punishment and the terror of a guilty conscience. In a fine passage Lucretius at once ridi-
cules and allegorises the current fables of punishment inflicted on the guilty in the unseen world.

"And those things, sure enough, which are fabled
to be in the deep of Acheron, do all exist for us in
this life. No Tantalus, numbed by groundless terror,
as the story is, fears, poor wretch, a huge stone hanging
in air; but in life rather a baseless dread of the gods
vexes mortals: the fall they fear is such fall of luck

[1] Lucretius, III, 14 *sqq.*

as chance brings to each.   Nor do birds eat a way
into Tityos laid in Acheron, nor can they, sooth to
say, find, during eternity, food to peck under his
large breast.   However huge the bulk of body he
extends, though such as to take up with outspread
limbs not nine acres merely, but the whole earth, yet
will he not be able to endure everlasting pain and
supply food from his own body forever.   But he is
for us a Tityos, whom as he grovels in love vultures
rend and bitter, bitter anguish eats up or troubled
thoughts from any other passion do rive.   In life, too,
we have a Sisyphus before our eyes, who is bent on
asking from the people the rods and cruel axes, and
always retires defeated and disappointed.   For to ask
for power which, empty as it is, is never given, and
always in the chase of it to undergo severe toil, this is
forcing uphill with much effort a stone which, after
all, rolls back again from the summit and seeks in
headlong haste the levels of the plain.   Then to be
ever feeding the thankless nature of the mind, and
never to fill it full and sate it with good things, as the
seasons of the year do for us, when they come round
and bring their fruits and varied delights, though
after all we are never filled with the enjoyments of
life, this, methinks, is to do what is told of the
maidens in the flower of their age, to keep pouring
water into a perforated vessel which, in spite of all,
can never be filled full.   Moreover, Cerberus and
the furies and yon privation of light are idle tales, as
well as all the rest, Ixion's wheel and black Tartarus
belching forth hideous fires from his throat: things
which nowhere are nor, sooth to say, can be.   But
there is in life a dread of punishment for evil deeds,
signal as the deeds are signal, and for atonement of
guilt, the prison and the frightful hurling down from

the rock, scourgings, executioners, the dungeons of
the doomed, the pitch, the metal plate, torches; and
even though these are wanting, yet the conscience-
stricken mind through boding fears applies to itself
goads and frightens itself with whips, and sees not,
meanwhile, what end there can be of ills or what
limit, at last, is to be set to punishments, and fears
lest these very evils be enhanced after death. The
life of fools at length becomes a hell here on
earth." [1]

The Epicureans were never tired of arguing against
the conception of God as either Creator or Providence,
against divine interference with the course of nature,
either to create, to sustain, or to destroy. On these
points their chief antagonists were the Stoics, but
they argued just as fiercely against the Peripatetics,
who denied Providence, upheld the eternity of the
world, and yet maintained that nature in all her
operations is unconsciously working to an end. On
the analogy of any product of human ingenuity, the
work of creation implies tools, levers, machines,
agents, and materials. How, it is asked, could air,
fire, water, and earth have been obedient and sub-
missive to the architect's will? Besides, if this work
began at any point in time, why did the Creator refrain from creating until just that instant, and what
was his motive for starting then? What delight
can the Creator find in the variety of his work? And
if it be a delight, why was he able to dispense with
it for so long? If the work was undertaken for the
sake of man, it has failed in its object, so far, at least,
as the unwise majority of men are concerned.[2]
Lucretius puts these arguments as follows:

---

[1] Lucretius, III, 977 *sqq.*
[2] Cicero, *De Natura Deorum*, cc., VIII, IX.

"To say that for the sake of men they have willed to set in order the glorious nature of the world, and, therefore, it is meet to praise the work of the gods, calling as it does for all praise, and to believe that it will be eternal and immortal, and to invent and add other figments of the kind, Memmius, is all sheer folly. For what advantage can our gratitude bestow on immortal and blessed beings, that for our sakes they should take in hand to administer aught? And what novel incident should have induced them, hitherto at rest, so long after to desire to change their former life? For it seems natural he should rejoice in a new state of things, whom old things annoy; but for him whom no ill has befallen in times gone by, when he passed a pleasant existence, what could have kindled in such a one a love of change? Did life lie grovelling in darkness and sorrow until the first dawn of the birthtime of things? Or what evil had it been for us never to have been born? Whoever has been born must want to continue in life so long as fond pleasure shall keep him; but for him who has never tasted the love, never been on the lists of life, what harm not to have been born? Whence, again, was first implanted in the gods a pattern for begetting things in general as well as the preconception of what men are, so that they knew and saw in mind what they wanted to make? And in what way was the power of first-beginnings ever ascertained, to know what could be effected by a change in their mutual arrangements, unless nature herself gave the model for making things? But if I did not know what first-beginnings of things are, yet this, judging by the very arrangements of heaven, I would venture to affirm, and, led by many other facts, to maintain that the nature of things has by

no means been made for us by divine power, so
great are the defects with which it is encum-
bered." [1]

Philosophic criticism of the popular faith was no
new thing in Greece. It began with Xenophanes,
was rampant in the age of the sophists and was indorsed by Plato, Aristotle, and the Stoics. As a
rule, the ancients were remarkably tolerant in matters
of religious belief. The prosecutions of Anaxagoras,
Protagoras, and Socrates at Athens were primarily
political, and in succeeding centuries even avowed
atheism entailed little personal risk. The Epicureans were not unwilling to join in the services of the
national religion, and did not hesitate to claim that
their views were more consistent with true piety than
those of their rivals the Stoics. Their polytheism,
at any rate, was sincere, and they could dispense
with the artifices and allegorical interpretations by
which the one living universe was converted into a
hierarchy of personified natural forces. At the same
time, they were free to maintain their negative attitude, to denounce and ridicule as superstitious whatever in the current beliefs was inconsistent with their
own fundamental assumptions.

It is not easy to determine precisely the standing
and influence which this school of free-thinkers obtained in the Greek world. It is quite certain that
Epicurus, in his own lifetime, succeeded in awaken-
ing public interest and winning wide popularity, that
after his death his adherents grew and multiplied, and
that the question why there were so many Epicureans
was constantly propounded and variously answered.
We hear of jealousy and enmity between them and
rival schools, but only once or twice is there any

[1] Lucretius, V, 156–159, 165–186, 195–199.

suggestion of persecution on religious grounds. At the beginning of the second century B. C. it is asserted that some Epicureans who had taken refuge at Lyttos, in Crete, were banished by a decree, which denounced them as enemies of the gods, men who had invented a womanish, ignoble, and disgraceful philosophy. The decree went on to threaten any of them who dared to return with a horrible death by torture. At Messene a similar decree outlawed the Epicureans as defilers of the temples and a disgrace to philosophy through their atheism and indifference to politics. They were ordered to be beyond the borders of Messene before sunset and the magistrates were directed to purify the city and shrines from all traces of the heretics.[1] It is highly probable that these are isolated cases of political rancour, and that the chief count in the indictment was not atheism, but indifference, that is, refusal to become the subservient tools of some political faction, the *odium theologicum* being invoked by the winning side against irreconcilable foes. At Rome, where politics was so closely bound up with religion, the profession of Epicureanism never exposed any one to pains or penalties. The circle of Cicero's friends included several convinced Epicureans, who enjoyed universal esteem. Such were his correspondent Atticus and Cassius, one of the conspirators against Cæsar. The poem of Lucretius, again, exerted a powerful influence, as is seen in the evident leaning of both Virgil and Horace toward the system which he had so passionately advocated. Two centuries later Lucian gives us a vivid narrative of events in Paphlagonia, which show the Epicureans of that district to have been as fearless enemies of superstition as Epi-

---

[1] Suidas, *Lexicon*, *s. v.* "Epicurus."

curus or Lucretius himself could have desired.[1] A certain Alexander laid claim to prophetic powers and established his oracle at Abonuteichos. The fame of his responses, his growing power and influence, which extended even to Rome, the tricks and impostures by which he deluded those who consulted him and the violent measures which he took to put down all opposition may be read in the pages of Lucian and formed the subject of one of Froude's "Short Studies." The enemies with whom Alexander waged relentless war were the Christians and the Epicureans. Both alike he denounced as atheists, excluding them from his oracle and from the festivals which he had founded. Moreover, by his orders on a public occasion, the golden maxims of Epicurus were burnt and their ashes flung into the sea. The claims of this impostor were tacitly recognised by the Neo-Platonists, Neo-Pythagoreans, and Stoics, and, as Lucian shrewdly observes, his knaveries would have imposed upon any man who was not an intrepid inquirer after truth. Among philosophers a Democritus, Epicurus, or Metrodorus would alone have been his match, because the suspicions which such pretensions to the miraculous naturally excite would, in their case, have been fortified by the reasoned conviction that the laws of nature are invariable and admit of no capricious interference. Lucian, as his writings show, was an adherent of no philosophical school. His satire is directed against all impartially and his testimony to the important services rendered by Epicureans in the cause of truth and honesty is all the more valuable on this account. He hated charlatans as heartily as Voltaire. From some details which he mentions it may be inferred that Alexander's in-

[1] Lucian, *Alexander Pseudomantis.*

fluence was at its height during the reign of Marcus
Aurelius, and while the Stoic emperor was engaged
in his campaigns against the Marcomanni, 170–175
A. D.

Curiously enough, recent excavation has furnished
indisputable evidence of Epicurean activity during
the same century in another part of Asia Minor.
In the year 1884 two French scholars, Holleaux and
Paris, discovered inscriptions on the walls of the
market-place of the obscure Pisidian town Œnoanda.
They were copied in 1889 and again in 1895, and by
publication since have been made generally accessible to scholars.[1] They reveal a striking story.
Diogenes of Œnoanda was a zealous Epicurean
teacher, who seems to have devoted his life to the
exposition of his system.   When advancing years and
the premonitions of disease warned him of his approaching end he determined, as he tells us, to make
one last appeal to his countrymen in a permanent
form on behalf of the cause which he had so much at
heart.   His motives were twofold.   In the first
place, he had a genuine desire to benefit humanity
at large, not only his contemporaries, but posterity
and the casual strangers who might visit the place.
But we will quote his own words: "This writing
shall speak for me as if I were present, striving to
prove that nature's good, viz., tranquillity of mind,
is the same for one and all.   There is another reason
for my setting up the inscription.   Old age has now
brought me to the sunset of my life and on the verge
of departure; while acclaiming with a pæan the con-

---

[1] *Bulletin de Correspondance Hellénique*, Vol. XVI, pp. 1–76; Vol.
XXI, pp. 346–443; an annotated edition was published by Teubner in
1907, under the title *Diogenis Œnoandensis Fragmenta ordinavit et
explicavit Johannes William.*   See also the commentary of Usener, in
Rheinisches Museum, Vol. 47.

summation of my pleasures, I wish now, before it is
too late, to succour the discerning. If it were one
or two or three or four or five or six or as many as you
like of such, but not too many, who were in evil
plight, I might have visited each individually and
tendered them the best advice as far as in me lay.
But the vast majority of men suffer from the plague
of false opinions and the number of victims increases
—for in mutual emulation they catch the contagion
one from another, like sheep. Moreover, it is right
to succour those who shall come after us, for they,
too, belong to us, though as yet unborn; and it is
also a dictate of humanity to help the strangers who
sojourn among us. Since, then, the succour of an
inscribed writing reaches a greater number, I wish
to make use of this portico to exhibit in a public
place the remedy which brings salvation. For thus
I banish the vain terrors which hold us in subjection,
eradicating some pains altogether and confining such
as are due to nature within very moderate bounds
and reducing them to the smallest dimensions." [1]
He had a further motive which the course of the
inscription makes sufficiently obvious, viz., to put
on record an effective answer to all the adversaries
of the Epicurean system. He proceeds to refute in
detail the views of Socrates, who is taken as a type
of all who declined to study natural science, the
Heraclitean doctrine of flux and universal relativity,
the early Ionians, Empedocles, Anaxagoras, Democritus, and finally the Stoics. The reader is en-
treated not to be content with a casual glance at the
inscription, but to give it an attentive study. The
author's enthusiasm and honesty of purpose are
obvious, but his scholarly attainments were hardly

[1] *Diogenis Œnoandensis Fragmenta*, Fragment I (William).

adequate to his design, or he would never have fallen into the mistake of attributing to Aristotle himself the universal relativity which that philosopher refutes as a doctrine of Heraclitus. Even in regard to the system which he professed he seems to have been misinformed on some minor points. It was the ethical theory which he apprehended best and valued most. The circumstances under which his singular intention was formed and carried out are sufficient proof that in his day Epicureanism had its propaganda and was a living force, and that here, as elsewhere, it was promulgated first and foremost as a rule of life, a means of escape from human misery.

CHAPTER VIII

SCEPTICISM IN THE ACADEMY: CARNEADES

The word "sceptic" has a history of its own. In its original meaning, harmless enough, it denoted an inquirer, but even then, as people do not inquire about that which they already know, it implied some degree of uncertainty. Again, inquirers are often confronted with difficult problems which by no amount of study can be definitely solved. Certain data point to one explanation, certain other data to another and quite different explanation. In such cases the inquirer, after weighing the evidence, may still be in a state of suspense or indecision, unable to make up his mind. Thus the term acquires a negative meaning; the sceptic becomes by easy stages a doubter. When his doubts extend to conclusions which most other men regard as true, he is apt to be set down by them as a disbeliever, and the term scepticism, as ordinarily applied both in philosophy and religion, has come nowadays to imply a measure of disbelief which is not part of its original connotation. The scepticism of antiquity busied itself with the problem of knowledge. But when compared with cognate inquiries in modern philosophy, it appears in its scope and range almost ludicrously tentative, jejune, and superficial. That the object of cognition was external reality, nay more, that it was material reality, was not in that age seriously questioned. No one ever challenged the existence of a

312

real world of things lying behind the phenomena of which we are conscious. Confronted by dogmatists who maintained that they had certain knowledge of the truth of things, ancient scepticism started like its opponents with the assumption that things exist and that there is a truth to know, thus at the outset begging the question which causes the modern thinker his greatest perplexity. Its function, then, is purely negative and largely polemical, yet, even thus circumscribed, it allowed greater activity to thought than did the rival dogmatic systems. The impulse to pure speculation, to seek knowledge for its own sake, was, as we have seen, depreciated and almost stifled both by the Stoics and by Epicurus. But it survived, stunted and warped, it is true, but not quite extinct among those independent critics who refused allegiance to these and all other dogmatic systems.

The ancient Sceptics fall into three groups. To the first belong Pyrrho and his disciple Timon, with whom negation had its modest beginnings. The next group comprises the Sceptics of the Middle and New Academy; its protagonists are Arcesilas and Carneades. It developed the theory of probabilism, which led up to eclecticism, and the logical consequence of eclecticism was the renunciation of scepticism altogether. This final step was taken by the later Academic Antiochus. The last group, the most advanced in their scepticism, includes Agrippa, Ænesidemus, and Sextus Empiricus, who are generally known as the later Sceptics. The works of Sextus Empiricus have come down to us, while those of his predecessors are mainly lost; indeed, most of them wrote nothing, and of those who did little has survived.

Pyrrho of Elis accompanied Alexander's march as far as India, and thus became acquainted with Anaxarchus, a Democritean philosopher who took part in the same expedition. After his return home he lived to an honoured old age in his native city of Elis, in poor circumstances, which he bore with characteristic repose of mind. His disciple Timon of Phlius, after winning a competency by lecturing at Chalcedon, gravitated to Athens where he spent the remainder of his days and wrote much both in prose and verse. His most celebrated work was a satirical poem entitled *Silli*, of which considerable fragments remain. It consisted of three books. In the first he spoke in his own person; the others took the form of a dialogue between the author and the ancient philosopher Xenophanes of Colophon, Timon asking questions and Xenophanes answering them at great length. By this device he secured an unbounded field for satire in a sarcastic account of all philosophers, living and dead. Timon's wit is incisive; he gives no quarter and his mock-heoric style is enlivened with telling burlesques of Homer. It is indirectly through this disciple, who was more of a poet than a philosopher, that we derive the only definite notice of Pyrrho's teaching. According to Timon, then—and the report comes from the philosopher Aristocles, who lived centuries afterward [1]— there are three questions which the seeker after happiness must consider: (1) What is the nature·of things? (2) What ought to be our attitude to things? (3) What will be the result if we take up this attitude? Things, Pyrrho declared—and it is obvious that by things he meant external reality—are all equally indistinguishable, incalculable, and unaccountable, and

[1] In Eusebius, *Pr. Ev.*, XIV, 18, 2.

therefore sensations and opinions are neither true
nor false. This being so, the proper attitude is not
to trust them [1] but to preserve unwavering neutrality,
free from prejudice or inclination to either side, and
to say of any single object that it "no more is than is
not" or it "both is and is not" or it "neither is nor
is not" this or that.   According to another authority,[2]
Timon explained the formula "not more this than
that" as a refusal to define or to assent to a definition
of what a given thing is. Thus refusal to speak
(aphasia) is sometimes found as an equivalent. The
result of this attitude Timon affirmed to be mental
repose or imperturbability,[3] a tranquil and self-
centred indifference to a world of which we can know
nothing. For their unwarranted judgments about
objects betray men into desire, painful effort, and
disappointment. Thus the end sought by the dogmatists through the vain pursuit of knowledge is,
after all, more easily secured by the renunciation of
knowledge, and this end is a state of mind which,
as both Stoics and Epicureans agreed, is one constituent mark of true happiness.   For whether happiness consisted in pleasure or in virtue, the rival schools
concurred in the belief that its realisation insured to
its possessor mental composure, serene and undisturbed.

It is not a little remarkable that this concise summary of the sceptical position should have been
ascribed to Pyrrho on the evidence of his disciple
Timon. We are informed that Pyrrho himself wrote
nothing on philosophy. Moreover, Cicero frequently
mentions Pyrrho, but always as an austere moralist,
one might say an ascetic, who went even beyond the

[1] In Eusebius, *Pr. Ev.*, XIV, 18, 3.   [2] Diog. Laërt., 75, 76.
[3] Ataraxia. See Eusebius, *Pr. Ev.*, XIV, 18, 3.

Stoics in the attitude which he recommended toward all external things. The Stoics held that we should regard all objects except good and evil as indifferent to us; Pyrrho, according to Cicero, held that the wise man is actually insensible to these objects,[1] and many stories were told or invented in antiquity exaggerating his alleged indifference to his environment. Besides, Cicero has discussed the problem of knowledge at some length, but in this connection he nowhere mentions Pyrrho, nor does he seem to be aware that he was a sceptic. It may be argued that Cicero was not a man of wide reading and got his information at second hand, but this, if true, would imply that the compilers of the handbooks which Cicero certainly consulted were equally silent upon the point of Pyrrho's scepticism. They must have regarded him, as Cicero does, in the light of a dogmatic moralist. These facts would seem to justify the conclusion that in Pyrrho's teaching the sceptical element was not much developed. He may have learned from Anaxarchus the Democritean tenet that knowledge obtained through the senses is untrustworthy; he may have developed empirically this one side of Democritean teaching, while rejecting altogether the other side, namely, the assumption of atoms and void as sole realities, an assumption reached through the intellect alone and not through sense. Pyrrho was chiefly concerned to combat perceptions of sense. This he did empirically without the aid of dialectic. He was pre-eminently an ethical teacher; he based ethics, as Democritus had done, on quietism or calm retirement from the world. His aim was to realise that tranquil repose whereby the soul lives calmly and steadily, undisturbed by superstition,

---

[1] Cicero, *Acad. Pr.*, II, 130; *De Fin.*, IV, 43, 49.

fear, or any other emotion. The systematic form given to his teaching by Aristocles is perhaps to be ascribed to subsequent developments. Certain it is that the later Sceptics ranged themselves under his banner and gloried in the name of Pyrrhoneans, while they looked askance at, if they did not actually disown, the New Academy with which we have next to deal.

The school which Plato founded in the Academy had many vicissitudes of fortune in its long and romantic history. For some seventy years after Plato's death the heads of that school were dogmatists who by degrees came to concentrate their attention upon ethics. The school at this period is known as the Old Academy. Under Arcesilas of Pitane, in Mysia, who died in 241 B. C., a great change was made. He retained dialectic, the method of oral instruction instituted by Plato, but broke with the traditions of his predecessors by treating every proposition as an open question. In his own lectures he laid down no definite views, but refuted those of other philosophers and trained his pupils in arguing indifferently for and against any given thesis. The Stoics were the opponents with whom he came chiefly into collision, and the controversy turned on the question whether knowledge could be attained through the senses by the Stoic criterion. This, as we have seen, was an apprehensive presentation which, on their view, guaranteed its own truth and the reality of its object by the conviction of immediate certainty. Arcesilas himself admitted no standard of truth, but he was willing to meet the Stoics on their own ground and refute them from their own premisses. The certain apprehension for which they contended consists in the assent of the mind to the peculiar kind of presentation called apprehensive. This apprehension of certainty was, they declared, not peculiar to the wise man whose every intellectual act is knowledge, but is also to be found in the great majority of unwise mankind with whom, however, it takes the form of opinion. Arcesilas fastened on this as an inconsistency. Apprehension of objective reality must, he affirmed, be either scientific knowledge in the sage or mere opinion in the unwise. On Stoic principles, he contended, there is no room for any intermediate state of mind in which both classes of men share. This amounts to calling simple apprehension a logical abstraction; so much the Stoics might safely concede. But their opponent went further. First he challenged the possibility of giving assent to a presentation; he argued that the object of assent was a proposition, not a perception. It is not sensations we approve but judgments of the reason. Arcesilas next appealed to reason. He denied that there was such a thing as a perception which in Stoic phrase apprehends objective reality. By various arguments he endeavoured to show that none of our perceptions possess this guarantee of their own truth, for the same certainty of conviction might accompany a false perception. If, then, we can never be sure that a presentation is true, we can never be sure that by assenting to it we are apprehending objective reality and are forced to conclude that the world of real objects remains incognisable. From this conclusion necessarily followed suspense of judgment, and in his controversy with the Stoics Arcesilas could enforce this by an *argumentum ad hominem*. The Stoics, as we have seen, did not uphold all affirmations of the senses, but laid down conditions which must be fulfilled before the evidence of the senses could be accepted. If these conditions were not satisfied, the Stoic sage had no option; he must perforce withhold assent. For, if he yields assent without sufficient evidence, he descends from the high ground of scientific knowledge to mere fallible opinion, often shown by subsequent experience to be erroneous. Arcesilas with much ingenuity readily adopted the Stoic tenet that the sage will never opine. He trusted to his dialectical skill to convince his opponents that, as they would never be in a position to do aught else but opine, they must, if consistent, fall back into his own attitude of suspended judgment.[1]

Cicero sums up the controversy between the dogmatist and the sceptic as follows: "It appears to Arcesilas possible to refrain from opining, and not only possible but indispensable that the sage should do so. Such behaviour was quite in keeping with the character of the sage. Very likely he asked Zeno what would happen if it were neither possible for the wise man to apprehend with certainty, nor becoming in him to opine. Zeno, I dare say, replied that the wise man would not opine because there was an object capable of being known and apprehended. What, pray, was that object? A presentation, to be sure. Of what sort, then? Zeno, I imagine, gave his definition as follows: 'A presentation impressed, stamped, and engraven upon the mind, a presentation which comes from a real object and represents that object as it is.' And did this hold, was the rejoinder, even if a true presentation were indistinguishable from a false one? This question brought home to a man of Zeno's shrewdness that if a presentation of a real object was indistinguishable from that of an unreal object, it was impossible for any presentation

[1] Sextus Emp., *Adv. Math.*, VII, 153 *sqq.*

to be apprehended and known. Arcesilas made no objection to his adding to the definition the qualifying clause 'such as could not come from an unreal object.' We cannot know what is false: neither can we know what is true if the true is everywhere indistinguishable from the false. He threw his whole energies into the task of proving that there is no presentation of a real object that is not indistinguishable from a false presentation of an unreal object." [1]

In Arcesilas we seem to discern a somewhat different phase of scepticism from that of Phyrro, and this impression is confirmed by the fact that Arcesilas was one of the philosophers whom Pyrrho's pupil Timon satirised in the *Silli*. There he is described as a sort of chimera or fabulous creature of triple form:

> Plato the head of him; Pyrrho the tail; midway Diodorus. [2]

Pyrrho had combated popular opinions, popular customs, and popular beliefs on empirical grounds. Arcesilas, a learned philosopher, combated a scien-

---

[1] Cicero, *Acad. Pr.*, II, 77.

[2] Diogenes Laërtius, IV, 35. The line is a parody of Homer, *Iliad*, VI, 181, where the Chimera is said to be "in front a lion and behind a serpent and in the midst a goat." Diodorus Cronus of Iasus in Caria, one of the last adherents of the Megarian school, was a pupil of Apollonius, himself a pupil of Eubulides. Like the other Megarian philosophers, he was an acute dialectician and the inventor of sophistical puzzles on the impossibility of motion and change, which have come down to us. The surname Cronus, which was also borne by his teacher Apollonius, alludes to his argumentative skill; "crooked-counselling Cronus" is a stock epithet in Homer. There is no evidence that Arcesilas had ever been ostensibly a pupil of Diodorus any more than of Pyrrho. He had been a disciple of Theophrastus until Crantor gained him for the Academy. But the later Megarians had a great reputation, and their sophistical puzzles enjoyed wide popularity. Arcesilas, we may be sure, would not fail to profit by the example of such masters in the art of polemical controversy. *Cf.* p. 325.

tific system and an infallible criterion by means of dialectic. A consideration of the contradictions in our ordinary perceptions and notions led Pyrrho to deny that there could be any truth in them. Arcesilas was not concerned to deny that conceivably our perceptions might contain the truth, but to maintain that any truth they might conceivably contain could not be known by us. Hence there is nothing in Pyrrho's position inconsistent with the search after truth. Like Socrates, he has been foiled hitherto, but he can invite us again and again to renew the search and set out on the investigation of opinions. Arcesilas is not in a position to search for truth. We may even already possess it, but at any rate we cannot distinguish it with any certainty from error. He is not stating a fact but settling a question of principle. The Pyrrhoneans report that truth has not yet been found, but they are willing to seek it. Arcesilas believes that not only is truth not yet found but that it is impossible to find it, true presentations being indistinguishable from false. Arcesilas left nothing in writing, and we really know very little of his views. But it would seem that even in the region of practice he diverged altogether from Pyrrho. So far from recommending men to be insensible to their environment and to regard all objects with indifference, Arcesilas fell back upon opinion, which he maintained to be a sufficient guide for action. There was no need to wait for absolute knowledge; a reasonable probability was adequate. For, if happiness was the end, the degree to which this end was realised could be measured by the successful result of our conduct, whether absolute knowledge or mere opinion, whether certainty or probability formed the basis of that conduct.

A century later Carneades of Cyrene (213–129
B. C.) won the admiration of his contemporaries and
of succeeding generations by his commanding elo-
quence and genius for polemical controversy. Like
Socrates, Pyrrho, and Arcesilas, he himself left nothing in writing, but the results of his inquiries were
transmitted to posterity by the industry of his favourite pupil Clitomachus, the author of some four hundred
treatises. When Carneades became the head of the
Academy he soon restored its reputation, which had
suffered since the death of Arcesilas. Before this he
had learned the Stoic logic under Diogenes the Babylonian, the successor of Chrysippus, and he made the
writings of Chrysippus himself his chief philosophical
study. Throughout his career he acknowledged his
obligations to that master of acute and subtle argument whose constructive work it was the task of his
lifetime to overthrow. "But for Chrysippus, where
should I have been?" was his parody of the current
saying, "But for Chrysippus, where had been the
Porch?" Later Stoics, on the other hand, professed
to discover a design of Providence in the fact that
Chrysippus lived midway between Arcesilas and
Carneades; according to them Chrysippus not only
repelled the attacks already made, but demolished
by anticipation the arguments of the yet more formi-
dable assailant who was to follow. The personal
influence of Carneades was as remarkable as his skill
in controversy. Such was the charm he exercised
that some of his rivals quitted their own class-rooms
to attend his lectures. The force of his polemic may
be measured by the modifications and innovations
which, for a time at least, it was fashionable to introduce into Stoicism in order to meet his criticisms.
Unquestionably he was the greatest philosopher of

Greece in the four centuries from Chrysippus to
Plotinus; indeed, in ability and depth of thought
he surpassed Chrysippus.   Plato's transcendent genius overshadowed all his successors, but in the
illustrious roll of his disciples Carneades is not unworthy of a place beside Aristotle and Plotinus.
It was, however, on the negative and destructive
not the positive and constructive side that he assimilated the spirit and method of Plato.   With the
ideal theory and with Plato's sanguine hope of re-
generating mankind the apostle of agnosticism had
nothing in common.   Scepticism with him had a
wider range and a higher aim than with his predecessors.   His task was twofold, to refute all existing
dogmas and to evolve a theory of probability which
might serve as a basis for action.   This last is the
more original contribution, although, as we shall see,
it ultimately led to the abandonment of the sceptical
position.

We have first, then, to summarise the negative and
destructive criticism which Carneades directed against
the epistemology, the ethics, the teleology, and natural theology of contemporary schools and primarily
of the Stoics.   If certainty is attainable, as the dogmatists hold, there must be a standard or criterion,
whether it be reason or the senses or an infallible presentation, by which we can discriminate truth from
falsehood.   In denying the possibility of any such
standard of truth Carneades restated and reinforced
the general argument of Arcesilas.   There could be
no such standard for sense-perception since presentations or impressions of sense were frequently
found to be deceptive.   This consequence is inevitable so long as we adhere to the Stoic doctrine of what
presentation to sense really is, namely, a modification

or change in the soul which furnishes information, not merely about itself, but about the external object which caused it. For this external cause is known by its effects alone, and wherever these conflict we have no means, so far as present sensation is concerned, of deciding which of them are true and which of them are false. Certainty of conviction, if the Stoics make this their criterion, attaches to presentations which are afterward discovered to be false. It is not, then, in the nature of presentation as such, but only in the true presentation that a standard can be sought.

Carneades then proceeded to state that (1) there are false presentations; (2) such false presentations may pass for true; (3) if two presentations present no distinguishing marks, they cannot be regarded, the one as true, the other as false; (4) there is no presentation by the side of which cannot be placed a false presentation, which is, notwithstanding, indistinguishable from the true. The first proposition was never disputed except by Epicurus; the third was allowed on all hands. It was on the second and fourth propositions that the stress of controversy turned. Carneades and Clitomachus expended their whole ingenuity in proving them, defining and analysing with wearisome minuteness, and pressing into their service the abnormal phenomena which are always in favour when psychology is in an imperfect state. In dreams and trances we are moved by unreal presentations as powerfully as if they were true. Sane men may be subject to hallucinations and mad men are the prey of delusions. But if impressions of sense are fallible, it is in vain to look to the understanding for a remedy since general notions, on the Stoic view, are based on experience.

They are elaborated from sense-impressions and require constantly to be verified by reference to sense. Moreover, it has been the work of logic to develop and work out a system of notions and concepts, and yet logic is honeycombed with fallacies and sophistical problems for which no solution can be found even by Chrysippus. Such were the Mentiens or Liar, the Electra and similar puzzles which the ingenuity of the Megarian sect excogitated to disturb the repose of unwary reasoners in all ages.[1] Such was also that favourite but dangerous instrument of Chrysippus, the Sorites, or chain-argument, which showed how hard it was to define and draw exact limits, in quantitative distinctions especially, for, when asked whether three are few or many, even he borrowed a weapon from the armoury of the Sceptics by suspension of judgment and refusal to answer. In addition there was the contradiction inherent in the very nature of knowledge which the Sophists exposed when they asked how learning was possible, since some previous acquaintance with the thing to be learned was presupposed.

But Carneades was not content with a formal denial that knowledge was possible. An abstract proposition of this kind could never carry much

---

[1] *E. g.* some one (let us hope a Cretan) says: "I am telling a lie." Is this proposition true or false? Logicians are asked to decide. This is the problem called The Liar. Again, Orestes disguised meets his sister Electra. Does she or does she not know her brother? This is the Electra. Six of these fallacies or sophistical puzzles are ascribed to the Megarian Eubulides, Diog. Laërt., II, 108, but some of them at least were current before his time. They are: (1) The Mentiens or Liar; (2) the person disguised or hidden under a veil; (3) Electra (a variety of the last); (4) Sorites, "How many grains make a heap?" (5) Cornutus, some one asks: "Have you shed your horns?" a categorical answer Yes or No being required; (6) The Bald Man (a variety of the Sorites). *Cf.* Grote, *Plato*, III, 482–490.

weight. Students of the sciences pursue their researches unremittingly and derive satisfaction from watching the continuous growth of their acquisitions, even if they are sensible that as the circle of knowledge widens its circumference also widens and the margin where the known abuts upon the unknown must, in consequence, be always growing greater. Carneades felt it incumbent upon him to examine the results of all previous investigations and to demonstrate their worthlessness. If the scientific method of his time was, as he contended, unsound, its conclusions must be invalid and it was his business to show this in detail. Here again, as in the formal theory of knowledge, his chief adversaries were the Stoics. Their most notable achievement, their ethical system, afforded many opportunities for attack. It was inconsistent, he argued, to refuse the name of good to the objects of natural desire, while at the same time maintaining virtue to be nothing but an activity directed to the choice of them. It is said that his polemic on this point led Antipater and other heads of the school to modify the traditional formula for the end of action. For some time, in what is called the middle period of Stoicism, the attempt was made to bring the objects of natural desire into closer relation to morality, the end being defined as doing all things for the sake of obtaining the primary objects of natural desire. Cicero affirms that whereas the earlier Stoics had declared reputation, especially posthumous fame, to be a thing absolutely indifferent, the vigorous onslaughts of Carneades forced their successors to concede it a place among things preferred.

But if the science of the Stoics was subordinate to their ethics they nevertheless declared it to be a self-contained system impregnable to attack. It culminated in the teleological theory of the universe, the doctrine of the existence and nature of God, and his providential care for man, of which the divinely ordered course of events, including the means of prophecy and divination, was the outcome. Fortunately the ample materials preserved by Cicero[1] and by Sextus Empiricus[2] enable us to reproduce, with tolerable accuracy, the Academic criticism of these doctrines. Cicero's spokesman in the dialogue on the nature of the gods first examines the evidence adduced by the Stoics for the divine existence. They had appealed, like Epicurus, to the *consensus gentium*, the universal belief that gods exist. If, replied their opponent, the belief is universal and necessary, it is worse than useless to attempt to rest it upon argument, which simply raises doubts as to the validity of the belief. But is there such an universal belief? It was easy to reply that, in the sense required by the argument, it neither was nor could be universal. The sight of the starry heavens may strike multitudes, even Kant himself, with awe, but it failed to convince the Epicureans that nature or the universe is a living, rational being. On the contrary, they denied that either the stars or the universe have life. Besides, urges Carneades, it is strange to commit the question to the judgment of the ignorant multitude, when the Stoics tell us that the majority of mankind are fools. As to the alleged appearances of the gods in human form to men of old, the Academic asks for evidence, and until this is forthcoming he dismisses them as rumours and old wives' fables. Then again the Stoics appealed to divination and the manner in which portents and prophecies came true. To this the reply is that, if all is foreordained,

[1] Cicero, *De Nat. Deor.*, III.   [2] Sextus Emp., *Adv. Math.*, IX.

the knowledge of futurity is not advantageous, but harmful to men, while the mistakes of diviners throw discredit on the whole art of divination. If it were really an art, it would rest on rational principles, like the art of medicine, but, as practised in antiquity, divination was merely a matter of routine and tradition. The belief in the gods, no doubt, arose in part from awe-inspiring natural phenomena.

This proposition Carneades was as little inclined to dispute as Epicurus, but he is careful to point out that the question of the origin, as distinct from the validity, of the belief is irrelevant. For what are the Stoics concerned to prove? Is it that men believe in the gods or is it that the gods really exist? If the former, their argument is sound; if the latter, it is worthless. Zeno, in treating of the divine nature, had reasoned thus: What is rational is more excellent than what is irrational. Nothing is more excellent than the universe, therefore the universe is rational and exercises reason. Here, as the Academic points out, there is an ambiguity in the term "excellent." The universe may be beautiful, it may be adapted to our convenience, and hence we may pronounce it excellent. But this is no ground for declaring it to be wise or to exercise reason. Before that can be inferred it must be proved to be animate, otherwise there is just as much ground for inferring that the city of Rome, or the universe itself, is musical, mathematical, or philosophical. Nor can the regularity of the celestial movements prove the divinity of the stars, for there are certain terrestrial phenomena, such as the tides, the tertian and quartan fevers, which are also regular in their recurrence. Are they, therefore, divine? Chrysippus, again, had argued that what man is not able to produce must have been produced by a higher being, *i. e.*, by deity. But this inference is open to the same objection, namely, that by the term "higher" two different points of view are confounded. There may, indeed, be a being higher than man, but why must this being be rational and man-like? Why not nature herself? What grounds are there for an anthropomorphic conception of nature? Nor is there any more force in another argument of Chrysippus. The sight of a beautiful house, he says, suggests the idea of the owner for whom it was built. As every house was destined to be inhabited, the universe must be intended for the habitation of God. If the universe were a house, is the rejoinder, it might be so, but the very point at issue is whether the universe is a house or not, whether it has been constructed for a definite purpose, or whether it is simply an undesigned result of natural forces. Socrates had asked: Whence comes the rational soul of man if there is not a rational soul in the universe? If there is not, Carneades replies, the human mind and its faculties are merely spontaneous products of nature acting according to her own laws. Again, Chrysippus had insisted [1] on the organic unity of the world and the correlation and mutual interdependence of all its parts. Suppose this granted, there would still be no reason to accept his inference that the cause of all this harmony is a divine spirit or Pneuma which permeates and gives life to all things and connects them together in one organic whole. For the coherence and permanence of nature may be due to natural forces and not to the gods.

It will be seen from the foregoing that Carneades assailed the real cardinal dogmas of Stoic theology. It was not for him to call in question the existence

[1] Cicero, *De Nat. Deor.*, II, 19.

of the gods, but to criticise the belief in an eternal
world-soul or universal reason and the doctrine of
providence. The attitude of the critic must not be
misunderstood. He was a pure agnostic. Ostensibly he put forward no positive view; his object is
merely to show that the Stoic conceptions were untenable; that in attempting to define the nature of the
gods they merely succeeded in proving their non-existence. The attributes assigned to the Stoic deity were
contradictory, and the critic proved this from Stoic
premises, but, as we shall see, this acute thinker
used arguments which go much further than this
and bring to light the fundamental difficulties in
any conception of God, whether He be conceived as
personal or impersonal, finite or infinite, or veiled
under some abstraction as the absolute or the un-
conditioned. In the audacity of his excursion into
this region of thought Carneades has never been
surpassed. Hume and Mansel do but restate his
arguments adapted to modern conditions.[1] In the
ordinary view, if not by the Stoics, God is regarded
as at once an infinite and an individual being. But
we cannot, it is said, apply to Him the characteristics
of personal existence without limiting His nature.

Carneades, as we learn from Sextus,[2] started by
proving what the Stoics never denied, that God is an
animate being, since what is animate is better than
what is inanimate. From this he develops the logical
consequences implied in our conception of such a
being and derived wholly from experience. An animate being is body possessed of soul, and within our
experience every animal possesses sensation. The

---

[1] Hume, *Dialogues Concerning Natural Religion;* Mansel, Bampton
Lectures on the *Limits of Religious Thought,* esp. Lect. VII; *Cf.* Sextus
Emp., IX, 152–181.   [2] Sextus Emp., *l. c.,* IX, 152.

body of an animal must be either simple or composite, *i. e.*, it must consist of a single element or be a compound of several elements. Of the first alternative we have no experience, while in composite bodies, just because each element tends to fly apart to its proper sphere, decomposition is inevitable. Whatever, then, is corporeal is discerptible and therefore perishable. Body, as we know it, is everywhere liable to disintegration; none being indivisible, all bodies must be dissoluble and liable to be broken up into their component parts. Again, whatever is composed of changing elements is itself liable to change and therefore perishable; therefore all animals are mortal. We have seen how the Stoics, following Heraclitus, met these objections, affirming the present order of the universe to be perishable while its substance remains eternal. But the Stoic deity, though corporeal, is endowed with life and soul. The succeeding arguments turn on these attributes. Whatever is animate is capable of feeling and susceptible to external impressions, and therefore liable to destruction, for if it is susceptible to impressions it must be affected by them and suffer from them. If it suffers from them it must be liable to disruption and disintegration, and therefore perishable. Again, every animate being, if capable of feeling, is susceptible of pleasure and pain, but whatever experiences pain is also mortal. These objections assume the Stoic theory of sensation, a presentation as defined by Chrysippus being nothing more than a modification or change in the soul, and sensation without the feeling of pleasure or pain being inconceivable. But whatever is liable to change is liable to deterioration, and whatever is liable to pain, which is caused by deterioration, is liable to suffer, to be disintegrated and destroyed. Again, the Stoics taught that every animal has an instinctive desire for what is in harmony with its nature, an instincitve dislike of what is contrary to its nature. But whatever is contrary to the nature of a being is destructive of its life Moreover, the very things which normally produce sensation, things hot and cold, pleasant and painful, are, when in excess, destructive to life. Hence everything that lives is exposed to annihilation.

Some of the foregoing arguments, it may be noted, are equally applicable to the Epicurean gods. Against the Heraclitean and Stoic identification of deity with warm breath or fiery ether, the following objection was taken: There is no reason to suppose that fire is more akin to divinity than the other elements. It is not more essential to life than they are; if it is the cause of feeling in man, it must, on Stoic grounds itself, be susceptible of feeling and therefore liable to destruction; moreover, fire is not self-existent but needs fuel for its support.

But God, to the Stoics, is a rational being endowed with all excellence. It is easy to show that virtue, as we understand it, is incompatible with this idea of the divine nature. Every virtue supposes an imperfection, in overcoming which it consists. To be brave, a man must be exposed to danger; to be magnanimous, he must be exposed to misfortunes. To be temperate, he must resist pleasure; to display endurance, he must conquer pain. Take the four cardinal virtues in detail. Shall we attribute to God wisdom, which consists in a knowledge of good and evil and of things morally indifferent? What need has a being in whom there is not and cannot be any evil to discriminate between good and evil? And what need has he of reason or apprehension, which we employ for the purpose of obtaining by means of the evident a knowledge of the obscure, whereas to God nothing can be obscure? As for justice, the virtue which assigns to each his due, how is it appropriate to the gods? For it was the product, the Stoics maintain, of human fellowship and association. Temperance consists in foregoing sensual pleasures; but is this a virtue compatible with the divine nature? And how can God be conceived of as brave? Is he so in respect to pain or labour or danger, not one of which things affects him? And yet, if these four virtues are excluded, how can we conceive of a God who exercises neither reason nor virtue.[1] Or how conceive of a being in perpetual bliss who is capable of feeling pleasure but incapable of feeling pain? Pleasure can only be known by contrast with pain, and the possibility of heightening and augmenting life always supposes the possibility of lowering and diminishing it. Nor is it otherwise with the intelligence displayed in the adaptation of means to an end. He alone is thus intelligent who always discovers what will subserve his purpose. If, however, he must discover it, it cannot have been previously known to him. Hence this intelligence can only belong to a being who is ignorant about much. Such a being, then, has his limitations. He can never feel sure whether sooner or later something will not cause his ruin. He will therefore be exposed to fear. A being susceptible of pleasure and exposed to pain, a being who has to contend with dangers and difficulties, and who feels pain and fear, must inevitably, so thought Carneades, be finite and destructible. If, therefore, we cannot conceive of God, except in this form, we cannot conceive of him at all.

[1] Cicero, *De Nat. Deor.*, III, 38 *sqq.*

Nor do the difficulties diminish when we pass from the divine nature to divine providence, the second cardinal dogma of Stoic theology. As we have seen, their world-soul or immanent reason works by final causes and ordains all events for the good of the several parts and especially for the benefit and welfare of the rational creature man. In support of this belief the Stoics pointed to evident marks of adaptation and design. Carneades could easily show that the evidence was inconclusive. Whence, he asks, so many pernicious and destructive agencies on land and sea? Why, for instance, if the world was made for the safety of man, were poisonous snakes created? But, it may be urged, man is, after all, a rational being, and God's providential care is manifest in the bestowal of this supreme endowment. Carneades rejoined boldly that the gift of reason is rather an injury than a benefit. Experience shows that the great majority of mankind only use it to make themselves worse than brutes. So far, then, as they are concerned, what becomes of divine providence? Again, right reason alone is beneficial to its possessor, and right reason is so rare that it cannot be derived from God, who would never have been guilty of partiality in his dealings with men. The objection is not met by the rejoinder that these evils arise from man's abuse of reason. The deity must have foreseen that the bare gift of reason was liable to abuse and that such abuse could only be prevented by making reason infallible.

Pressing still further the inconsistency between the two Stoic doctrines of divine providence and universal folly and depravity, Carneades asks: How can it be said that man is the especial favourite of Heaven if it be true that lack of wisdom is the greatest of all evils and that all men lack wisdom? If God really cared for men, he ought to have made all men good or at least to have rewarded the righteous and punished the wicked. Suffering virtue and triumphant vice is inconsistent with any scheme of moral government. To maintain that piety is regularly rewarded and impiety regularly punished is to shut our eyes to the numerous negative instances, and even such imperfect retribution as we may then discover in this world is the natural result of human agency. Intentional neglect is a great fault in a human ruler, and in a divine ruler there can be no such thing as unintentional neglect. The special pleading of Chrysippus meets with little mercy. When, adapting the legal maxim *de minimis non curat lex*, he urged that *minora dei neglegunt* the reply was that life and liberty are not *minora*. To the Stoic, it is true, all external things are *minima* in comparison with virtue; but then it is just these external things which are at the disposal of Heaven. Virtue the Stoic sage must win for himself; it is the one thing which is always in his own power. Consequently it is himself, not God, that he credits with it. If it be argued that vice is punished in the descendants of the guilty person, what should we say to such justice in a human ruler? Moreover, how can God punish if He be incapable of anger? If His power is not equally exerted in helping the good, it must be that He lacks either the will or the knowledge to do this. If His care does not extend to individuals, what reason is there for believing that it extends to nations or to humanity at large? The practice of divination, however, implies a particular supervision extending to the minutest details of each inidivdual's life.

To return, however, to the main problem. We

have seen the reasoning by which Carneades endeavoured to prove that neither of the contradictory attributes, destructible or indestructible (or, in other words, mortal and immortal), can properly be applied to God. How stands the case if the question be raised, Is He finite or infinite? or the further question, Is He corporeal or incorporeal?[1] If a thing exists, it is either finite of infinite. God is not infinite, for then He would be immovable and inanimate. For if that which is infinite moves it must move through space; it must move from place to place, and therefore be in place, and being in place it is limited or finite. If, then, there is anything infinite, it does not move, or, if anything moves, it is not infinite. And similarly that which is infinite is inanimate or without soul. For if permeated by a soul, this soul holds it together from centre to circumference and from circumference to centre. But that which is infinite has neither centre nor circumference. Hence that which is infinite is inanimate. But we ordinarily think of God both as moving and as endowed with soul. It follows, then, that God is not infinite. But neither is He finite, for that which is finite is part of that which is infinite, and, since the whole is superior to the part, the infinite is superior to the finite. But it is absurd that anything should be superior to God or to the divine nature. Again, if a thing exists, it is either corporeal or incorporeal. God is not incorporeal, since that which is incorporeal is inanimate, devoid of life and sensation and incapable of activity. Nor, again, is He corporeal, since all that is corporeal is liable to change, and therefore destructible, whereas, that which is divine is held to

[1] Sextus Emp., *Adv. Math.*, IX, 148-151, 180, 181; *cf.* Cicero, *De Nat. Deor.*, III, 29-34.

be indestructible. Or otherwise thus, if God is corporeal, He is either a compound of simple elements or consists of a single simple element. If a compound, He is destructible, for every formation resulting from the union of elements must be destroyed by the dissolution of those elements. But if He is a single elementary body, whether fire, air, water, or earth, He is without life and without reason, which is absurd. It appears, then, that neither of the contradictory attributes can be predicated of the subject, neither infinite nor finite, neither corporeal nor incorporeal. The conclusion is that there can be no subject for predication. All the forms under which we think of God being impossible, His existence cannot be asserted.

Here we may be allowed to pause and offer a few remarks upon this vigorous polemic. First, it is curious to observe how far Carneades has anticipated much of subsequent metaphysic; his reasoned objections when translated into English run almost insensibly into modern philosophical language. The argument from design, as it is commonly called, goes back to Socrates; even before the Stoics took it up it had been so clearly stated by Xenophon, Plato, and Aristotle that it is no wonder Carneades felt it incumbent upon him to criticise it. In doing this he placed himself at the level of his opponents. He shared their imperfections; he was no better able than they were to detect the errors in the popular science of the day. Nor had he either the capacity or the inclination to undertake physical research. Many of his objections are little better than fallacies of a transparent kind. He saw more acutely than the Stoics the difficulties of the problem, and secured many a dialectical triumph by pointing to the ab-

surdities in the details of their anthropomorphic
scheme. But his method of criticism necessarily implied that, at least provisionally, he accepted the
anthropomorphic conception himself. The deity he
rejects is, after all, only a magnified and non-natural
man with more than a man's might and much of a
man's caprice. With him, as with the Stoics, the
divine differs from the human in degree, not in kind.
He never rises above this conception and hence falls
far short, not only of Plato's ideal of absolute perfection, but even of Aristotle's transcendent First Cause.
The Greek intellect had already made great strides
toward a purer conception of deity from the age when
Xenophanes denounced Homer and Hesiod together
with the whole fabric of lying legends and polytheistic
immoralities down to the time when Aristotle realised the impossibility of ascribing human virtues
to God, and carefully eliminated as many attributes
as possible from his First Cause. Carneades, it
would seem, failed utterly to appreciate this advance.
He appears not to have comprehended even the
higher side of pantheism, the doctrine of a spirit of
law and order working in the world, apostrophised
by Cleanthes as "Nature's great king, who by thy
just decree controllest all." Otherwise he would
never have supposed that he had answered the Stoics
when he proposed to substitute Nature for God.
In comparison with the gross confusion of God and
matter which degraded the divine without raising the
material, his dim perception of a natural growth
apart from any divine providence is attractive, we
may even say lofty. But for the most part it was the
lower side of Stoic pantheism that he chose to attack,
and his ingenious syllogisms enabled him to score a
series of fruitless argumentative victories.

To give some further details. It is objected that
God cannot possess virtue because virtue is above its
possessor and there can be nothing above God.[1]
This objection, resting as it does on a confusion of the
abstract with the concrete, can hardly have been
meant to be taken seriously, for in arguing against
the Stoic deification of abstractions Carneades is
careful to point out that the virtues are but qualities
of the human agents in whom they reside. So,
again, the anthropomorphic conception suggests the
inquiry whether speech and language can be ascribed
to the deity.[2] To deny this attribute was opposed to
the general belief; to affirm it can be shown to lead
to the grossest absurdities. Speech, as we understand
it, implies the possession of vocal organs, and we are
straightway landed in the cruder anthropomorphic
details of Epicurean theology. The use of speech
implies conversation, and the language employed
must be that of some particular nation, either Greek
or a foreign tongue. If Greek it must be some particular dialect, Attic or Æolic or some other. But why
should a preference be given to one dialect over
another? Moreover, if the language employed be
Greek, a foreign tongue would have to be acquired
presumably by instruction. Every one of these sup-
positions teems with absurdities. Once more, Carneades was not less concerned to attack than his
opponents to defend the ordinary polytheism. As
we have seen, the Stoics regarded the many gods of
the popular faith as manifestations of one supreme
power. In any case, polytheism was a witness to the
universal belief and was entitled to respect in so far
as it rested upon usage and tradition, and formed part

---

[1] Sextus Emp., *Adv. Math.*, IX, 176.
[2] Sextus Emp., *l. c.*, IX, 178; Cicero, *De Nat. Deor.*

of the established social order. The method of attack chosen was by sorites or chain-syllogisms which,
as we are informed, were greatly admired and often
quoted by Clitomachus.[1] Here are some specimens.
If Zeus be a god, his brother Poseidon is a god; if
Poseidon, Achelous; if Achelous, the Nile; if the
Nile, any river; if any river, then any mountain tor-
rent. But mountain torrents are not gods; then
neither is Zeus a god. Again, if the sun is a god,
then his appearance above the horizon, which we call
day, is a god; if the day, the month; if the month,
the year, which is a series of months; and similarly
with morning, noon, evening, and other parts of
time. But the year is not a god, then neither is the
sun a god. Obviously, then, the popular belief has no
distinctive mark by which to separate the divine from
that which is not divine. It is refuted when the essential dissimilarity between the two is established. It is
characteristic of the sceptical Academy that in spite
of this trenchant criticism Carneades never openly
broke with the popular theology as Epicurus had done.
There is no reason to doubt that he accepted the belief in the gods as an opinion more or less probable
and useful for practical purposes. He claimed the
Sceptic's privilege of abstaining from pronouncing a
decided opinion for or against it. He neither, like
Plato, cherished the kernel of truth disguised but not
wholly concealed under mythology, nor like Zeno did
he attempt to allegorise and rationalise it as permanently valuable from its old associations and present
influence. He as far as possible disregarded it, except where he was concerned for controversial purposes to refute the Stoic system of interpretation of
the myths by personification of material elements.

[1] Sextus Emp., *Adv. Math.*, IX, 182 *sqq.*

So much for the negative and destructive criticism on which the fame of Carneades chiefly rests. But when he passed from theory to practice, the positive side of his teaching was no less remarkable. It was designed to meet the reproach which in all ages the dogmatists have levelled at their opponents, namely, that the convinced sceptic, if consistent, is reduced to inaction. If the moment we examine any impression of sense we find that the arguments for its trustworthiness or untrustworthiness exactly balance each other, what grounds are there for action? Why give the preference to any one of our impressions over another, and by acting upon it abandon the only safeguard against error, suspension of judgment? Pyrrho's quietism or absolute insensibility to environment seemed justified by such considerations, but even Pyrrhonists, perceiving the absurdity of carrying it to all lengths, since complete inactivity would mean death, permitted men to follow appearances, as it was called, and be guided by custom in the various conjunctures of ordinary life. But could no better basis for action be found than the compulsion of circumstances; than habit, instinct, or association? If the arguments for and against a particular judgment of sense exactly balanced each other, suspension of judgment would be the right attitude. But experience shows that as a rule the scales do incline decisively in one direction or the other. Thus probable judgments are formed, and though certainty is unattainable their probability admits of varying degrees. In order to introduce and establish such a calculus of probability it was necessary to make a new classification of presentations; in other words, of impressions and ideas.[1]

[1] Sextus Emp., *Adv. Math.*, VII, 166–189 (the most accurate account); Cicero, *Acad. Pr.*, II, 64–146, more especially 98–11.

A presentation as defined by the Stoics was (1) a mental change or impression in the subject (2) caused by an external object. It therefore can be considered under a double aspect from a twofold point of view. In relation to the object the presentation is true when it agrees with the object, false in the contrary case. But in the absence of a criterion of truth this distinction leads to no result, and we have already seen how decisively the Stoic criterion was rejected by Carneades. In relation, however, to the subject who has the presentation there is the really valuable distinction between presentations which appear to him true and those which appear to him false. The former we call probable, the latter improbable. Being necessarily ignorant of the relation of ideas to the objects they represent, we are reduced to judging them by their relation to ourselves, by the appearance of truthfulness, the greater or less clearness they have for us. Among those which appear true there are some which seem so only in a slight degree; the object may be small or too far off or our senses may be weak and present it only in a confused manner. These may be dismissed, as well as all which appear false; we have no use for them. Others, again, seem very probable the more we examine them. They may be false, but the chance of error does not hinder us from according them our assent; it is by them we regulate our judgment and action. The first condition, then, of acceptance is that a presentation should be probable in itself, *i. e.*, should excite a belief in its own truth apart from any extraneous support. But presentations to sense do not occur in isolated fashion; they form a chain, a connected series. If I see a man I see him as part of a sensible *continuum*, I perceive his figure, height, colour, movement, speech, dress, and shoes; I am aware of the air, light, time of day, sky, earth, and the friends which form the accompaniments of his environment. The absence of any of these accompaniments awaken suspicion of the presentation. Thus Menelaus, having left a phantom Helen on board ship, cannot believe his eyes when he sees the true Helen at Pharos. The previous false impression is a hinderance to the acceptance of the true one. When, on the contrary, all the concomitants are present, this is so far a guarantee of truth. The second condition, then, if we are to assent to the presentation, is that it should be unimpeached, that nothing in the series to which it belongs should distract or hinder us from attending to it. When a presentation stands in connection with and is confirmed by other presentations it reaches this higher grade of probability, which for most practical purposes is sufficient; in other words, the impression is confirmed by the agreement of related ideas.

Lastly, there is a third and higher grade by which we may, if necessary, approximate still more closely to the certainty which is beyond our reach. The more important concerns of life require a closer attention and more than ordinary precaution. We may consider each of the concurrent presentations in detail and subject them to a severe scrutiny. Thus we examine the subject which has the presentations: Is he in health? of sound mind? The medium: Is the air thick? the distance great? Is the time or the place suitable? The ordinary course of things seldom allows of all these precautions being taken. Suppose you see a coil of rope, which at first sight is taken for a serpent. The first impulse is to run away. On second thoughts you return and examine it; it is motionless. Probably it is not a serpent. But in

winter all snakes hibernate. Give it a knock with a
stick; if this has no effect you conclude that it is a
coil of rope. Thus the effect of probable conviction
is strengthened by cumulative evidence. Separate
presentations may be false without our being able to
detect the falsehood. All that we can do is to attach
a tolerably accurate value to the "perhaps" since
unconditional "yes" or "no" is beyond the reach
of our faculties, and the more important the decision
the more accuracy should we endeavour to attain.
Higher and yet higher grades of probability approximate to certitude as an asymptote to its curve without
ever reaching it. Or we may put it thus: Carneades,
like a true Sceptic, refuses altogether to make any
assertion about the thing in itself, but having distinguished the objective point of view from the subjective as clearly as any of the moderns, he substitutes
for objective certitude a relative and qualified assent
to the appearances or impressions of sense. He
claims the right to speak and act like other men, provided it be always understood that such speech and
action implies no belief in the objective truth of impressions.

Closely connected with this theory of probability
is Carneades' defence of human freedom in opposition
to the Stoic determinism.[1] If all events were connected by a chain of cause and effect necessity would
be supreme. What, then, would be in our power?
Clearly he assumes that something is in our power,
namely, to give or refuse our assent to an appearance
of sense. This was, in fact, universally assumed.
The Stoics started by laying down: (1) that every
event and all movement has a cause—a physical
principle; (2) that every proposition, whether about

[1] Cicero, *De Fato, passim.* Only part of this treatise is preserved.

the present or the future, is true or false—a logical axiom. From this it seems inevitably to follow (3) that every event is determined by previous events and, if so, is determined beforehand, is therefore certain and can be predicted. But if destiny is the universal law every event is necessary and there is no place for liberty. But none of the contemporary schools went so far. Thus Epicurus refuses to admit that when the atom swerves aside there is any cause for its declination or that a proposition relating to the future (e. g., Hermarchus will be either alive or dead to-morrow) is either true or false. The Stoics, on the other hand, were driven to accept determinism by a variety of impelling forces: by their physics, their support of divination, their theory of the organic unity of the world and the mutual inter-connection or "sympathy" between all its parts. They were bound, therefore, to accept the *nexus* of cause and effect in the endless chain of phenomena. Still, even they had not the least intention of denying that something is in our power. Hence Chrysippus, in order to save freedom (in his own restricted sense of the term), is obliged to excogitate a difference between destiny and necessity. There is, he maintains, the logical possibility of an event not happening although it is certain to happen. It can be predicted and yet at the same time be contingent. How was this position to be made good? His expedient was a subtle distinction between primary or principal and proximate or subsidiary causes; a distinction analogous to the old Platonic and Aristotelian anithesis between cause and condition as explained, e. g., in the *Phædo*.[1] According to Chrysippus, the preceding links in the chain of causation, are indeed, causes of the events which they con-

---

[1] Cicero, *De Fato*, 41; *cf*. Plato, *Phædo*, 98 C–99 D.

dition, but they are only auxiliary or proximate, not principal causes. We see an object, desire of it ensues. Our assent is the principal cause, but the presentation or appearance is a secondary, proximate cause, the occasion, if you like, on which the true cause acts. External agency sets the roller in motion, but it rolls of its own inherent nature. So, too, the external agency of presentation supplies the initial impulse, but individual assent and choice are the result of man's own nature. And, as Cleanthes had said, man is "free" to obey the universal law.

Carneades profited by the weak points in such a theory. By a sorites he proved that it was impossible to admit destiny without denying liberty. If all events follow from antecedent external causes, all events are necessarily connected by a chain of causation. If so, necessity is the cause of all events. If so, nothing is in our power. But we are conscious that something is in our power, whereas if all happens by destiny all is due to antecedent external causes. Hence all does not happen by destiny.[1] To maintain this conclusion it is not, he thought, necessary with Epicurus to deny that every event has a cause[2] or to dispute the logical validity of the disjunctive proposition relating to the future. It is sufficient to say that not every event is the result of antecedent external causes. Our will does not depend on such antecedent causes. When we say that a man's actions have no cause, we mean they are done without antecedent external cause, and not that they are done absolutely without a cause. The cause resides in the will, in the man's individual nature. Epicurus should have said that the atom swerves in obedience to the law of its own

---

[1] Cicero, *De Fato*, 31.   [2] *Ib.*, 23.

nature by its own weight. In other words, alongside of the series of causes connected by natural necessity, causes are admitted which do not depend upon any antecedents—*causæ fortuitæ non inclusæ in rerum natura atque mundo*—accidental causes, not of necessity subsisting in the nature of things and in the world. To this class belong the causes which render the proposition "Cato will come into the senate" true. The action of such causes cannot be foreseen or predicted; only the event discovers that Philoctetes will be left at Lemnos or that Œdipus will turn parricide. Carneades, then, holds that every future proposition is true or false, but not that there are eternal and immutable causes which prevent things from happening otherwise than they do happen. Past events are true because certified by experience; future events are true because they will hereafter be realised in experience. The future, then, is just as immutable as the past because it is true, and this without resort to destiny or necessity. Thus, while Carneades grants the truth of the disjunctive proposition relating to the future, he denies that it can be foreseen, for, in his judgment, causality is not the same as invariable succession. He draws a distinction between matters of speculation and the ordinary affairs of human life, and in the latter he holds with Butler that "probability" is our guide. It will be seen that his arguments have a far wider bearing than on the Stoics whom he was immediately attacking.

The whole of ethics as treated by Carneades is coloured by his theory of probability, but of the precise manner in which it was applied we have little information. Here as elsewhere he is first and foremost a critic. To the conception of an end in itself he made no opposition. The art of living cannot any more than any other art dispense with a moving principle, and therefore an ideal is requisite to give to action first an impulse and afterward consistency. Carneades begins [1] by laying down two requisites essential in his opinion to the concept of the highest good: (1) it must be accordant with, not opposed to, nature, and (2) it must be capable of exciting an impulse or a craving in the mind. He finds only three ends, or rather motives, which satisfy these conditions. They are pleasure, freedom from pain, and the primary objects of natural instinctive desire. The last phrase, as we have already seen, includes such things as self-preservation, bodily health, sound senses, beauty, and mental aptitudes. Again, each of the three ends proposed can be viewed in a double aspect, according as its mere attainment or the effort to attain it is regarded as the highest good. This would seem to furnish a table of six possible ideals of life. But as no one ever proposed the effort to attain either pleasure or painlessness as an end in itself distinct from the result attained, the list of six possible ideals is reduced to four. To these four must be added three others, for in place of a single and simple highest good a composite ideal of life may be proposed by the union of two simple ends. This scheme of classification of all possible ends or ideals of conduct had a great vogue. The dogmas of contemporary schools and of all moralists in the past could, without much violence, be adjusted to it. Thus the Cyrenaics and Epicurus, in spite of the great difference of their principles, were included under the first head as making pleasure the end. Freedom from pain, though it might with more reason have been claimed for Epicurus, was assigned to the

[1] Cicero, *De Fin.*, V, 16 *sqq.*

Peripatetic Hieronymus. The activity directed to the primary natural objects as distinct from their actual attainment was equated with the highest good proposed by the Stoics, or, in plain terms, with virtue and morality. Again, the complex ends, the union of virtue with pleasure or virtue with painlessness had actually found adherents in Callipho and Diodorus.[1] Finally, by a *tour de force*, the most celebrated ethical doctrines of the past, the views of Plato and Aristotle and the schools they founded, the Old Academy and the Peripatetic, were relegated to the last place on the list as recognising in the highest good the union of primary natural advantages with virtue or the activity directed to their attainment.

It is evident that the choice of an ideal will greatly modify our whole theory of right and wrong. The Epicurean conception of justice is wholly different from that of the Stoics. Intellectual goodness and speculative activity hold a very different place in the systems of Aristotle and of the Stoics. Carneades contented himself with classifying all possible ends and pointing out the results which follow from the selection of any one of them. But he declined to commit himself. He did not dogmatically assert what was the nature of the highest good. Indeed, his favourite disciple Clitomachus professed himself entirely ignorant of his master's real opinions on the subject. It can only have been for controversial purposes that, as we are told, he warmly defended at one time the attainment of primary natural advantages and at another time Callipho's union of virtue and pleasure as the end of life.[2] He even con-

---

[1] Cicero, *De Fin.*, V, 21.

[2] Cicero, *Acad. Pr.*, II, 131, 139; *cf. De Fin.*, II, 35, V, 20; *Tusc. Disp.*, V, 84.

tended that on the theory of good there was no essential difference between the Stoics and Peripatetics. The point at issue was not anything of fundamental importance but merely verbal quibbling and a change of terminology. Whatever his motive in making this assertion, it was often repeated by his followers and led to strange perversions of historical fact. In declining to make any particular choice among the conflicting ends, he acted in conformity not only with his own principles, but also to some extent with the temper of the age. Men had become far less confident that a strictly defined course of life would secure the happiness of the individual. Every species of end, it seemed, had already been proposed and it was not felt that any of these ends had conferred the anticipated benefit. Strict conformity to the letter had betrayed all sects into extravagance. From a position of neutrality, Carneades had the best opportunity for criticising the extravagance of each in turn with sanity and moderation. The Stoics might accuse him of sapping the true grounds of morality, the Epicureans of putting forward a scheme of life which was poor in theory and impossible in practice. Yet something might fairly be said for a popular moral philosophy of which the two cardinal points were the belief that man's happiness does not depend upon any ethical theory, and the assertion that all received ethical theories do not go beyond probability. Holding such an intermediate position, Carneades could afford to be humane on questions where the Stoics were bound to be rigorously ascetic, and, if Chrysippus professed to find a cold consolation for the ills of life in the thought that no man is free from them, his critic, with more good taste and feeling, urged that to all but the malevolent the universality of suffering is its saddest aggravation.[1] The conviction that the human faculties had but a limited range was, it is true, an outgrowth of Scepticism, but it was obvious that it might be so applied as to impair the rigid exclusiveness of rival systems and to favour the reaction to Eclecticism.

It is a pity that we do not know more of the constructive side of the philosophy of Carneades, that his destructive criticism has tended to obscure the other features of his system. The New Academy had begun with the Socratic profession of ignorance and the Socratic mode of examining opinions; it had employed the Pyrrhonean weapons merely as serviceable in assailing the Stoics and all who claimed absolute certitude. Such a procedure had its dangers; it might easily lead to consequences which the Academics had not foreseen and would not have indorsed, the dogmatic assertion that knowledge is impossible and the self-contradiction which this implies. If Carneades, as we have seen, despaired of any certainty to be derived from physical investigations; if neither the senses nor the understanding furnished knowledge; if he compared logic to a polypus which devoured its own limbs; and if he fixed upon no good as the highest, did he, then, despair of philosophy? Such a conclusion, though apparently favoured by his negative polemic and his appeal to the fact that philosophers were hopelessly divided and that nothing had been settled by the controversies of the schools, must nevertheless be rejected. But if knowledge, in Hume's language, is resolved into probability, what precisely is the function which philosophy can retain? It remains as a formal science but not as a means of discovering truth. Its

---

[1] Cicero, *Tusc. Disp.*, III, 59.

task is to classify presentations and the general notions formed from them. The method of philosophy, then, is a method of testing and arranging concepts, a result which strikingly agrees with Herbart's definition.[1] We cannot expect to reach to certainty; we can but register and compare concepts according to the standard of probability. It is easy to see that this, though a scientific theory, is somewhat sterile and barren of result. The Academics did not always see that the reasonings used to support an alleged fact are often false while the fact alleged is true. But it is their conspicuous merit that least of all the philosophers of the time they regarded speculation as a means to an end.

[1] *Die Bearbeitung der Begriffe.* Of course Herbart's conception is in content wholly different from that of Carneades.

CHAPTER IX

ECLECTICISM

In the middle of the second century B. C. an impartial observer and student of history, reflecting on the tendencies of the time so far as they affected philosophy, would have been most anxious to know how the struggle between dogmatism and scepticism, then at its height, would develop. He would seemingly have been justified in recalling the similar position in the fifth century when the progress of pre-Socratic speculation was arrested, and those celebrated lecturers the Sophists succeeded in diverting public attention from philosophy, of which they despaired, to humanism; that is, to the study of literature, rhetoric, and practical politics. If our observer leaned to dogmatism, he might be pardoned for remembering with pride that in the hour when the Sophists carried all before them, Greece was on the eve of its greatest philosophical triumphs; that the reaction against scepticism spread victoriously from its humble beginning in Socrates to Plato's heights of idealism and Aristotle's encyclopædia of the sciences. So now, he might have inferred, agnosticism, even when bolstered with probabilism, would fail in the long run to satisfy men, and he might have anticipated, not unreasonably, that a reaction would follow in the wake of the New Academy, perhaps even a reaction to idealism. For such a reaction the world had long to wait. The creative impulse

seemed exhausted. Instead of the rise of a new
system, what actually followed was a period of uncertainty and readjustment, in which almost all existing schools were tentatively and sensibly modified,
and a gradual fusion and approximation of sharply
opposed theories set in. In this, the period of eclecticism, the independence of every system was threat-
ened; in the effort to ward off renewed assaults the
very foundations were sapped and shaken from
within. The most powerful solvent was undoubtedly
the negative criticism of Carneades. The vigour of
his onslaught made him the terror of his contemporaries. It was one thing to maintain the abstract
thesis that knowledge is unattainable; he had es-
sayed the harder task of proving by argument that it
had not been attained. But there was another influence at work. The very fact that controversies
prolonged for generations, had brought the dogmatists themselves no nearer to agreement must have
led some of the disputants to doubt whether their
principles expressed the whole truth in a complete
and final form. Where there was room for such
misgivings a tendency to modification of doctrine and
mutual accommodation began to show itself in spite
of the obstinacy with which each of the disputants
clung in turn to his favourite tenets. The change
was in the air, but it affected the different schools very
unequally. The Epicureans never diverged from the
principles of their founder. That the Peripatetics
suffered considerably is clear from the treatise *De
Mundo*, which, though it has come down to us
among Aristotle's works, was certainly written after
his death and contains a remarkable fusion of Stoicism with the principles of his philosophy. Evidence
quite as startling is furnished by two short ethical

treatises: *De Virtutibus et Vitiis*, attributed to Aristotle, and *De Affectibus*, attributed to Andronicus of Rhodes, a leading Peripatetic, and by the summary of Peripatetic news or ethics furnished by Stobæus. The rise of neo-Pythagoreanism, another testimony to the eclectic spirit, must be dismissed as more properly belonging to a later period. Our attention is demanded by the changes introduced into the two other most important schools, the Stoics and the Academics.

After the prosperous careers of Carneades and Clitomachus Plato's school met with vicissitudes. Its next head was Philo of Larissa, who came to Rome and taught there in the Mithridatic war, about 88 B. C. Up till that time he had professed allegiance to the principles of Carneades, but later he published a book which provoked strong opposition in the school. He was charged with wilful misrepresentation of the facts.[1] The precise nature of his innovations has been the subject of much discussion, but that he attempted to put a new complexion on the sceptical teaching of Arcesilas and Carneades is all but certain. He may have argued—at least this seems the most plausible conjecture[2]—that the Academic leaders, in refuting the Stoic criterion, did not express their own views, but merely adopted a justifiable, polemical expedient, and he may even have set up a contrast between the exoteric and the esoteric doctrines of the Academy, though his opponents asked in vain what the latter were. However this may be, the opinions with which Philo is credited on good authority show a considerable divergence from the uncompromising scepticism of Carneades.

[1] Cicero, *Acad. Pr.*, II, 12 and 18.
[2] *Cf.* the edition of Cicero's *Academica*, by Prof. J. S. Reid, *Introd.*, pp. 58 *sqq.*

Things, he contended, were in their own nature
knowable, though not by the standard of knowledge
which the Stoics proposed.[1] If he held such an opinion, it was natural that he should endeavour to interpret the teaching of his predecessors in conformity
with it. We are not, then, surprised to find on unim-
peachable authority[2] that Philo and Metrodorus of
Stratonice affirmed that Carneades had been misunderstood by everybody. The point at issue was
whether the probable opinions to which Carneades
gave utterance were or were not to be regarded as
assertions of a positive conviction. Clitomachus, of
course, who was best qualified to speak, denied this,
and the counter-statements of two dissentient disciples is wholly inadequate to shake our belief in the
genuineness of the master's scepticism, supported as
it is by the unanimous testimony of his opponents
the dogmatists. But there is no reason to doubt that
the positive teaching which Philo tried to fasten on
his master was held by himself; in other words, from
the admission of probability as a guide for action
Philo had come to apply it dogmatically in the
theoretical sphere, wilfully oblivious of the very
clear distinction which Carneades laid down between
the absolute and the relative in the matter of assent
and suspension of judgment. If Philo had begun to
compromise with the enemy, his pupil, Antiochus of
Ascalon, the next head of the school, openly capitu-
lated. For years he had maintained the old struggle
against the Stoics, and refuted their claims to set up
an infallible criterion. At last, worn out by con-

[1] Sextus Emp., *Pyrrh. Hyp.*, I, 235; *cf.* Numenius, cited by Eusebius,
Pr. Ev., XIV, 9, 1.
[2] *Ind. Herc. Acad. phil.* (A list of the adherents of the Academy found
at Herculaneum and edited by Bücheler, Greifswald, 1869.) *Cf.* Cicero,
Acad. Pr., II, 78. Augustinus, *Contr. Academicus*, III, 41.

troversy, he recanted his agnostic errors and declared
knowledge not only to be possible, but possible
through the very criterion which he had so long refused to recognise.[1] But his surrender on this all-
important issue was only a typical instance of his
complete change of front. His later opinions, thanks
to Cicero, who knew him and heard him lecture, are
as well known to us as those of any philosopher after
Plato, and a strange medley they are. From his
chair in the Academy he taught Stoic logic, Stoic
physics, and an ethical theory which was only not
orthodox Stoicism because it was fatally wanting in
the unity, coherence, and consistency which even
opponents admired in the Stoics. With a singular
disregard of internal probability, Antiochus was not
content with borrowing almost all his new-found
dogmas from the Stoics, but coolly claimed them for
his own rightful inheritance. With a strange per-
version of the historical sense, he charged Zeno with
having originally stolen the characteristic principles
of Stoicism from the old Academy. To that term
he gave a liberal interpretation. By an effort of the
imagination he made the old Academy embrace the
critics and opponents as well as the followers of
Plato, all united in one harmonious school of doctrine.
He claimed for it not only Speusippus, Xenocrates,
Polemo, Crates, and Crantor, but also Aristotle and
Theophrastus, and even Zeno himself, for was not
he, too, like Arcesilas, a disciple of Polemo? That
the old Academy and the Peripatetics were, in Cicero's
words,[2] one single school, differing in their nomen-

---

[1] Cicero, *Acad. Pr.*, II, 69; *cf.* Numenius, cited by Eusebius, *Pr. Ev.*,
XIV, 9, 2; Augustinus, *Contr. Acad.*, II, 6, 15, III, 18, 41.

[2] Cicero, *Acad. Post.*, I, 17, 18. This assumption runs through the whole
exposition, *Acad. Post.*, I, 19 to 46; see esp. 24 *sqq.*, 30 *sqq.*, 33, 35, 40,

clature while they agreed in substance, was asserted
by this singular authority with so much vehemence
that he might have turned even wiser heads than
Cicero's. Here, then, we have eclecticism with a
vengeance. If we may judge by the procedure of
Antiochus, its privilege is arbitrarily to fit together
various parts of different systems into a more or less
incongruous whole at the caprice of the individual
eclectic. Poor as was the performance, it sufficed.
The scepticism of the Academy died out in the first
century B. C. Almost its last representative in literature was Cicero, and Cicero, as we shall see, was himself an eclectic.

Though he made no independent contributions to
philosophy, Cicero, by his writings, did much to
render the subject familiar to his countrymen. He
had good opportunities for becoming acquainted with
all the schools; he had heard most of the leading men
lecture, and his wide reading was directed by the
ambition of adding a new department to Latin
literature. His procedure in compiling his numerous
treatises was very simple. As he ingenuously con-
fesses, he did the work of a translator.[1] He would
select some acknowledged authority of repute for the
views he wished to expound, and reproduce the gist
of the argument, putting it into the mouth of some
Roman of eminence. The setting of the dialogue,
a judicious sprinkling of historical illustrations, and
the proems or introductions were all that was required
to adapt Clitomachus or Antiochus, Panætius or
Posidonius to the needs of Roman readers. This

---

46. The system expounded under Plato's name is simply the eclectic
construction of Antiochus; see also *De Fin.*, IV, 14–45, 56 *sqq.*, 60 *sqq.*

[1] *Epp. ad Atticum*, XIII, 52, *apographa sunt: minore labore fiunt:
verba tantum adfero, quibus abundo.*

much Cicero could easily furnish himself, while his real gift for exposition, combined with his enthusiasm for his subject, enabled him to turn out in rapid succession a series of readable dialogues dealing with many of the most controverted topics of the day. A professed adherent of the New Academy, he valued highly the privilege of criticising all opinions without being committed unreservedly to the defence of any, a privilege which a barrister above all men would appreciate. When he comes to questions of law and morality, Cicero makes a singular use of his freedom to hold whatever opinion seems probable. He wholly dissociates himself from the negative views of Carneades, with which he had no more sympathy than with the utilitarian ethics of Epicurus.[1] A violent reaction against both led him at first to accept the eclecticism of Antiochus, but gradually he approximated more closely to the Stoics whose rigid consistency and moral idealism had a fascination for him as for other Romans in spite of the hard criticism which at other times he passed upon them. Hence in reviewing his opinions we have to distinguish the pupil of Carneades in the *Academica, De Natura Deorum, De Divinatione*, and *De Fato*, from the pupil of Antiochus in *De Legibus* and *De Finibus*; and from the defender of Stoic Ethics in the *Tusculan Disputations* and *De Officiis*. We can never be sure, however, whether any opinion advanced in Cicero's works is really his own, and he protests emphatically that he is not bound by previous utterances and that it is a mistake to fasten upon himself the inconsistencies of his different writings.[2] In this conspicuous example of a professed sceptic we see the havoc which the

---

[1] See, for instance, *De Legibus.*, I, 39.
[2] *Tusc. Disp.*, V, 33, 82.

disintegrating spirit of eclecticism had wrought upon the symmetry and consistency of all systems of thought. More than a century afterward the same arbitrary acceptance of different philosophemes characterised the otherwise interesting contribution of the historian Plutarch of Chæronea to the controversial literature of the schools. This eclectic also was, like Cicero, a professed Academic, but he differed from Cicero, not only in the range of positive doctrines that he embraced, but still more in the unsparing severity with which he directed his harsh and unsympathetic criticism against Stoics and Epicureans alike.[1]

In the history of Stoicism it is usual to distinguish three periods. In the first the doctrine was elaborated. The two centuries following upon the death of Chrysippus form the middle period, a period of transition, during which the older doctrines were modified, simplified, and occasionally relaxed in an eclectic spirit. To the last of the three periods belong the Roman Stoics of the Empire, such as Seneca, Musonius, Epictetus, and Marcus Aurelius. With the death of Chrysippus the energy of the school relaxed. His immediate successors, Zeno of Tarsus, Diogenes of Seleucia (often called the Babylonian), Antipater of Tarsus, were men of no originality though not without ability. On the two last named fell the brunt of the conflict with Carneades. When Stoicism emerged from this conflict, the physical basis of the system remained unchanged but was neglected. Problems of interest bearing upon psychology and natural theology continued to be dis-

---

[1] Against the Stoics in *De Communibus Notitiis* and *De Stoicorum Repugnantiis*, against Epicurus in *Adversus Coloten* and *Non posse suaviter vivi secundum Epicurum*.

cussed. But all original research, all lively interest
in that department ceased. We hear that Diogenes
expressed doubts as to the cycles of the world's
existence and that his disciple Boëthus renounced
the belief in the universal conflagration. His doctrine of a deity not immanent in but distinct from the
inanimate universe, which he superintends from without, was a compromise between Stoic and Peripatetic
teaching.

In the department of ethics the Stoic teachers were
occupied in elaborating their conception of the good,
and in particular they endeavoured to bridge the
gulf which separated the objects of natural and instinctive desire from the rational end of human action.
We meet with several glosses or interpretations of the
formula of Chrysippus which were current at this
time and it is impossible to mistake the controversial
aim of such alterations. Thus Antipater distinguished between the mere attainment of primary
natural ends and the activity directed to their attainment, accepting Carneades' identification of this
activity with virtue. But earlier still, Diogenes had
defined the end thus: "To calculate rightly in the
selection and rejection of things according to nature."
Archedemus, a contemporary of Diogenes, put this
in plainer terms still. "The end," he said, "is to live
in the performance of all fitting actions," *i. e.*, of all
relative duties (Kathēkonta). Now it is highly improbable that the earlier Stoics would have sanctioned
such interpretations of their definitions. The mere
performance of relative or imperfect duties, they
would have said, is something neither good nor evil;
the essential constituent of human good is ignored.
And this, we know, is the criticism which in a later
age was actually passed by Posidonius. His words

are: "This is not the end, but only its necessary concomitant; such a mode of expression may be useful for the refutation of objections put forward by the Sophists"—more precisely, by Carneades—"but it contains nothing of morality or well-being." [1] He saw clearly that the concessions extorted by the assaults of the adversary went perilously near to sacrificing the essential dogmas of Stoic ethics. The rigour and consistency of the older system were sensibly modified by the increased importance and fuller treatment which from this time onward fell to the lot of external duties.

To this result another important factor contributed. The picture of the impeccable sage had embodied that enthusiasm for righteousness which breathes with Semitic earnestness through all the teaching of the earlier Stoics. But the sage had become an ideal. Men in earnest about right living felt the need of practical precepts, of rules for the daily conduct of life. They could not always imitate the sage, but they could at least learn to appreciate the importance of the "external" duties required of all men, wise or unwise. The central figure in this middle period of Stoicism was a remarkable man. Born at Rhodes about 185 B. C. Panætius was a citizen of the most flourishing of Greek cities, and almost the only one which still retained vigour and freedom. Yet he lived for years in the house of Scipio Africanus the younger, at Rome, accompanied him on embassies and campaigns, and was perhaps the first Greek who in a private capacity had any insight into the working of the Roman state or the character of its citizens. Later in life, as head of the Stoic school at Athens, he achieved a reputation

[1] Galen, *De Plac. Hipp. et Plat.*, p. 470, Kühn.

second only to that of Chrysippus. He is the earliest
Stoic author from whom we have, even indirectly,
any considerable piece of work, as Books I and II of
the *De Officiis* are a *réchauffé*, in Cicero's fashion, of
Panætius "Upon External Duty."

The introduction of Stoicism at Rome was the
most momentous of the many changes that it saw.
After the first sharp collision with the jealousy of the
national authorities, it found a ready acceptance and
made rapid progress among the noblest families. In
Greece its insensibility to art and the cultivation of
life was a fatal defect; not so with shrewd men of the
world desirous of qualifying as advocates or jurists.
It supplied them with an incentive to scientific research in archæology and grammar; it penetrated
jurisprudence until the belief in the ultimate identity
of the *Jus Gentium* with the law of nature modified
the prætor's edicts for centuries. Even to the Roman
state religion, with its narrow conceptions and burden-
some rites, it became in some sort a support. Scæ-
vola, following Panætius, explained that the prudence
of statesmen had established this public institution
in the service of order midway between the errors of
popular superstition and the barren truths of en-
lightened philosophy. Soon the influence of the
pupils reacted upon the doctrines taught. For abstract discussions the ordinary Roman cared little or
nothing. He was naturally an eclectic, for, indifferent to the scientific basis or logical development
of doctrines, he selected from various writers and
from different schools what he found most serviceable. All had to be simplified and disengaged from
technical subtleties. To attract his Roman pupils
Panætius would naturally choose simple topics susceptible of rhetorical treatment or of application to

individual details. He was the representative, not
merely of Stoicism, but of Greece and Greek literature, and would feel pride in introducing its greatest
masterpieces. He had a particular admiration for
the writings of Plato. The classic style, the exquisite
purity of the language, the flights of imagination appealed to him no less strongly than the philosophy.
He marks a reaction of the genuine Hellenic spirit
against the narrow austerity of the first Stoics. Zeno
and Chrysippus had introduced a repellent technical
terminology; their writings lacked every grace of
style. With Panætius the Stoic became eloquent;
he did his best to improve the uncouth words in
vogue, even at some slight cost of accuracy.

To Roman society, then, Panætius came as the
missionary of Hellenic culture. The philosophy he
inculcated was Stoicism, it is true, but a broad-
minded and liberal Stoicism, tolerant and concilia-
tory. He himself diverged from orthodoxy on several
important points. Like Boëthus, he abandoned the
doctrine of a periodic conflagration of the universe.
This involved the further consequence that he renounced the limited immortality hitherto accepted in
the school, for, according to the first founders, the
souls of the wise, and of the wise alone, retained a
separate existence until the end of each world-cycle
and the consummation of all things in the general
conflagration. He rejected the old Stoic doctrine of
divination. In these deviations it is easy to trace the
influence of Carneades. But the eclectic tendencies
of the time are more significantly betrayed by his
innovations in ethics, which were delicately adjusted
to the susceptibilities of men of the world. It may
be too much to say that he introduced and expounded
a twofold standard of morality. But he certainly

divided virtues into two classes, theoretical and practical; that is to say, he recognised in Prudence an intellectual faculty co-ordinate with the three cardinal
virtues, Justice, Courage, and Temperance, which
were practical, and, without altogether abandoning
the aspiration after perfect wisdom and virtue, he
never forgot that his business was with those who
had set out on the road to virtue and were a long way
removed from the ideal sage. This in itself impairs
the rigid consistency of an ethical system which starts
from the proposition that all virtue is one and is essentially knowledge. In the first book of his celebrated treatise on appropriate action or external duty
Panætius dealt with moral good; in the second book
with expediency or utility. His translator, Cicero,
complains with justice that he omitted to treat the
cases in which a conflict of motives is conceivable,
where one line of conduct is dictated on grounds of
morality and a different line of conduct suggested by
considerations of expediency. This omission Cicero
himself endeavours to the best of his ability to supply
in his own third book, *De Officiis*. Here even more
than in the other parts of the treatise the reader cannot fail to note that relaxation of the moral standard
which seems inevitable when problems of every-day
life are discussed in a spirit of casuistry. A few examples will suffice. It is disputed whether the vendor
is bound to disclose defects in an article submitted for
sale; whether in a storm at sea the owner should
make jettison of worthless slaves or of valuable cargo.
No dialectical quibbles can blind us to the fact that
in these problems we are concerned with a second-
rate morality, a conventional code which has the
public opinion of the day for its ultimate sanction.
Its embodiment is the honest man, the respectable

citizen, *vir bonus*, whose judgment Panætius and Cicero endeavour to enlighten as best they can.

Passing over other disciples of Panætius, of whom Hecato is the most conspicuous, we come to Posidonius (130–46 B. C.), who carried on among the Romans of the next generation the work his master had begun. By birth a Syrian of Apamea, he spent many years in travel and scientific researches in Spain and Gaul, Africa and Sicily, Liguria and the regions to the east of the Adriatic. When he settled as a teacher at Rhodes his fame attracted numerous scholars. He became known to many eminent Romans, among them Marius, Rutilius, Pompey, and Cicero. He was, without doubt, the most learned man of his age. He was the last Stoic who took an interest in physics and busied himself with the positive sciences, as his contributions to geography, natural history, mathematics, and astronomy sufficiently attest. He sought to determine the distance and magnitude of the sun, to calculate the diameter of the earth and the influence of the moon on the tides. Judged from the modern stand-point, he may appear uncritical or even credulous, but at the time his spirit of fearless inquiry provoked the criticism of his contemporary Strabo, who deemed it altogether alien to the Stoic school,[1] and almost Peripatetic. Add to this that he was a competent historian who wrote a narrative of his own times from the fall of Corinth to the Mithridatic war, in fifty-two books. This, like his numerous other writings, proved a mine of information to subsequent writers. The wavering and want of finality characteristic of eclecticism is well seen when we compare his philosophical tenets with those of Panætius. The master and the pupil alike took

[1] Strabo, II, 3, p. 104.

the liberty of diverging from Stoic orthodoxy, but in different directions. Posidonius fell back upon the old belief in divination, and the series of world-cycles, each ending in a general conflagration. But in return he broke more completely than any one before him with the psychology of his school. Finding it impossible to explain the emotions as judgments or the effects of judgment, in short, as morbid states of the one rational soul, he gave up the unity of the soul. To account for the emotions he postulated, like Plato, an irrational principle, including a concupiscent and a spirited element, although he subordinated all three as faculties to the one substance of the soul lodged in the heart. This heterodox conclusion he did not scruple to avow in the definition which he gave of the end of action, namely, "to live in contemplation of the reality and order of the universe, promoting it to the best of our power, and never led astray by the irrational part of the soul." Strange language this, in the mouth of a Stoic. He also maintained the immortality and very probably the pre-existence of the rational soul, and we learn without surprise that his admiration for Plato led him to write a commentary on the *Timæus*.

Other evidence might be adduced, but from what has been said it is clear that Panætius and Posidonius, the two most eminent Stoics of the middle period, handled the traditional doctrines with remarkable freedom. If their innovations had, in the long run, little permanent effect it was because in the last period of Stoicism men ceased to take an interest in such questions. Their whole attitude had become changed. Their attention was concentrated upon ethics, and even in this department they regarded the scientific basis, the interlacing network of theories, as matter of curiosity rather than of edification. Epictetus and even Seneca, for the most part, professed a general allegiance to the first founders. Untroubled by critical doubts, they acquiesced in the doctrines of Zeno and Aristo, Cleanthes and Chrysippus. When Seneca, for example, does touch upon the theoretical side of Stoicism, it is in the hope of finding some novelty to interest his readers and almost in the spirit of antiquarian research. To be over-curious on speculative questions is generally regarded as reprehensible, as diverting the attention of the individual from the all-important task of his own moral improvement. The Roman Stoic of imperial times addressed his appeal to the reason and conscience of men, but it was no part of his ambition to become a speculative thinker himself or to make thinkers of others. Indifference to exact scientific theory and willingness to accept good moral teaching from any quarter, from Plato and Epicurus as readily as from Chrysippus, is not peculiar to Seneca; it is the common characteristic of all the later Stoics. Philosophy in their view is the healer to whom men come from a sense of their weakness and disease, whose business is "with the sick, not with the whole." The wisdom by which she heals is not a matter of long dissertations or dialectical subtleties, but rather a continual meditation and self-discipline. To endure and to renounce, to bear and to forbear, is the watchword of Epictetus. The way to virtue, says Seneca, is not hard to find, but the life of one who treads it is a continual struggle, a campaign in which there is no repose. By constant effort alone can we emerge victorious from the conflict and build up a fixed habit and rational character.

An apology is due to the reader for this hasty and

inadequate glimpse at a great philosophical system in the last stages of its development. It long continued to exert a profound influence upon adherents who had become professedly indifferent to its theories, if for no other reason because this system alone offered satisfaction to the deepest longings of earnest and strenuous natures. The Roman empire enjoyed external prosperity; the accumulation of material wealth, the growth of luxury and frivolity, went on unabated. The most eminent Stoics were usually found in the ranks of the opposition, carrying on against the Cæsars the hopeless struggle to which as a party and a sect they had been committed by Cato of Utica. But whether in opposition like Thrasea or in office like Seneca, the principles of a Stoic brought him sooner or later into collision with the government, and under the early empire, at any rate, the victims of tyranny included not a few martyrs to philosophy. In this respect Stoicism stands apart from other ancient schools; if we except the occasional outbursts of local fanaticism against the "godless" Epicureans, there was no other sect before the rise of Christianity of sufficient importance to be persecuted.

It has been shown that the unsettling ferment of eclecticism began among contending schools at Athens, was fostered by the powerful polemic of Carneades, and gained a remarkable impetus when philosophical issues were presented to the phlegmatic, matter-of-fact Roman temper. As the movement progressed, the Academy ceased to be sceptical, the Peripatetics made compromising concessions; the Stoics of the middle period suffered doubts and scruples to lead them now in this direction, now in that in the path of innovating reform, while in their successors eclectic tendencies were just as completely, if unconsciously, manifested by that concentration upon practical ethics which involved the almost total neglect of all other parts of the system. To this general disintegration of dogmatism the rise of the later Sceptics gave a finishing, satirical touch.

CHAPTER X

ÆNESIDEMUS AND THE REVIVAL OF
PYRRHONISM

The connection between medicine and philosophy, it is now generally recognised, was much closer in ancient than in modern times. The long series of medical writers, from Hippocrates to Galen, abound in allusions to the problems of science in general and to the opinions of contemporary thinkers. For some two centuries before Galen's advent the condition of medicine was by no means satisfactory. Great discoveries had been made, but their meaning was not fully apprehended. Amid the controversies of rival schools there was nowhere an established or accepted authority which commanded respect, no one system entitled to universal recognition. The practitioner might well feel justified in holding, as a matter of experience, that in his own department, at any rate, there was no such thing as certainty. It is not surprising that such a conviction should bias his general outlook on the world. At all events it is a significant fact that many of the later Sceptics belonged to the medical profession and in particular to the empirical school; the coincidence between opposition to dogmatism in medicine and in philosophy can hardly be fortuitous. By a fortunate accident the writings of one eminent physician and sceptic, Sextus Empiricus, have been preserved. To his zeal and industry we are indebted for a very complete summary of the sceptical position as he understood it, and as he drew freely on his predecessors we are introduced to the arguments and opinions of thinkers more eminent than himself, who but for his work would be little more than names to us. Sextus was in his day the head of the sceptical school, if school it can be called, which he denied. He lived about 200 A. D., and spent at least part of his life at Rome. As a physician he belonged, in spite of his name, to the school of medicine opposed to the Empirics and known as the Methodics. He wrote *Pyrrhonean Outlines* (Hypotypōseis), in three books; *Against the Dogmatists*, in five books, which deal successively with Logic, Physics, and Ethics, and lastly six books in which he combated the special sciences of Grammar and Rhetoric, Geometry and Arithmetic, Astronomy and Music. The two last are properly distinct treatises; they are usually cited, however, as parts of a single treatise, *Adversus Mathematicos*, in eleven books. These writings, of which the *Pyrrhonean Outlines* are at once the earliest and the best, are a storehouse of information respecting the latest phase of sceptical teaching. Not only are the position and aims of Pyrrhonism clearly defined, but the arguments by which it was supported are given in full with constant reference to the counter-arguments of the different dogmatic schools. When Sextus has set forth his own position and guarded it from attack on every side, he, of course, assumes the offensive. The bulk of his writings then becomes polemical, and almost every system of philosophy is in turn examined and refuted to his own satisfaction. As he proceeds with his task certain features in his method arrest our attention. An enormous advance has been made in the precise formulation and systematisation of the argument. Though dissociating himself from the Academics, Sextus has taken good care to incorporate whatever he could find in Carneades and Clitomachus available for his own purpose, notably the rejection of formal logic, including demonstration, syllogism, induction, definition, division, and every other logical instrument.[1] The impression he makes is that of a diligent and clearsighted compiler with not much originality. For an historian of philosophy his equipment was certainly defective. The only dogmatic system he was thoroughly versed in was that of the Stoics. He was but imperfectly acquainted with Plato; his knowledge of Aristotle is so slight that it was probably gained at second hand; even Epicurus he had studied none too well. The amount of material he has amassed is not always well arranged, and he is sometimes lacking in internal coherence. Still, he is conspicuous for clearness and good sense. His acknowledgments to his predecessors are frequent. Accordingly it is to these predecessors that we must direct our attention. Sextus makes it abundantly evident to whom the merit of the teaching he advocates and expounds is really due. Besides scepticism in this elaborate and comprehensive form had been inculcated long before his time. Diogenes Laërtius has preserved a list of sceptical teachers, beginning with Pyrrho and ending with Saturninus the pupil of Sextus, who is made the fourteenth in the succession.[2] But he impartially mentions the statement of Menodotus, the eleventh

---

[1] Sextus Emp., *Pyrrh. Hyp.*, II, 134–259.

[2] Diog., Laërt., IX, 115, 116. The names are (1) Pyrrho, (2) Timon, (3) Euphranor, (4) Eubulus of Alexandria, (5) Ptolemæus of Cyrene, (6) Heraclides, (7) Ænesidemus, (8) Zeuxippus, (9) Zeuxis, (10) Antiochus of Laodicea, (11) Menodotus, (12) Herodotus of Tarsus, (13) Sextus Empiricus, (14) Saturninus.

on the list, to the effect that Pyrrho's school died out after Timon, who left no disciples. On this point there can be no reasonable doubt that Menodotus was right. When we examine the list we may, with perfect confidence, accept the last eight links of the chain, from Ænesidemus the seventh to Saturninus the fourteenth. Undoubtedly these were all Pyrrhonists or later Sceptics standing to each other in the relation of master to pupil. When we go further back there is room for caution. Quite apart from the plain statement of Menodotus, there are chronological difficulties in continuing the chain, as the list of Diogenes does, backward to Timon. The names are too few to bridge over two centuries. On the other hand a motive for the extension of the list is easily suggested, namely, the desire to represent the later Sceptics as affiliated by unbroken tradition to the master whom they venerated and whose name they chose to revive.

We assume, then, the genuineness of the list from Ænesidemus onward to Sextus and Saturninus, and, in common with all recent historians of philosophy, it is to Ænesidemus that we attribute the resuscitation of Pyrrhonism in the permanent form which it maintained for at least two centuries.[1] Of the personal history of this remarkable man little is known; even his birthplace is variously given as Cnossus in Crete and Ægæ in Achæa. A list of his works and a sketch of their contents is preserved by Photius.[2] There is besides a passing mention of him by Aris-

---

[1] Eusebius, *Pr. Ev.*, XIV., 18., 22., citing Aristocles, Bk. VIII., *De Philosophia*, states this explicitly. But Diog. Laërt., IX, 115, cites Menodotus to the effect that the revival of Pyrrhonism began somewhat earlier with Ptolemæus, the fifth on the list given in the last note.

[2] *Bibliotheca (Myr. Cod., 212)*, p. 169b, 18 *sqq.* (Bekker).

tocles.[1] For the rest we depend upon the copious references of Sextus, who was more indebted to him than to any of his predecessors. That he taught at Alexandria and originally belonged to the Academy seems certain. His teacher Heraclides probably belonged to the same section of the Academy as Cicero, and, like him, resented the capitulation of Antiochus to the Stoics. Ænesidemus himself went further. He attributed this fatal declension to inherent weakness in the position of the sceptical Academy throughout, from Arcesilas and Carneades to Clitomachus and Philo of Larissa. They had, he maintained, all along been dogmatists in disguise. They had announced their negative conclusions too confidently, and denied the possibility of knowledge without reserve. This statement, we may remark in passing, though often repeated by the later Sceptics, would have been flatly contradicted by the Academics themselves, as it is by Cicero. It was necessary, then, to make a fresh start and go back to Pyrrho. Accordingly, Ænesidemus wrote a treatise in eight books and called it *Pyrrhonean Discourses*. In the first book he sketched the principles of Pyrrhonean as distinct from Academic scepticism, and his reasons for dissenting from the latter, which are essentially the same as those given by Sextus. The remaining books of this treatise were chiefly polemical, and in them he subjected the procedure of all the schools, especially the Stoic, to thorough-going criticism in the three departments of logic, physics, and ethics. Here again his example is faithfully followed by Sextus. The work was dedicated to Lucius Ælius Tubero, a prominent Roman statesman, and this fact furnishes the best clue to its date. It has re-

---

[1] Eusebius, *Pr. Ev.*, XIV, 18, 3, 8 *sqq.*, 22.

cently been proved that Philo of Alexandria was acquainted with and made use of the treatise. It is therefore not impossible that the Tubero in question was the well-known statesman who was Cicero's friend and contemporary. Even if, as has sometimes been assumed, though quite unnecessarily, he was a different individual belonging to the same family and bearing the same name, he cannot have lived many decades later. The silence of Cicero, both as to the revival of Pyrrhonism and the work dedicated to Tubero, nay, the very existence of its author, would be most naturally explained if the work itself was not written or at any rate not published until after Cicero's death, B. C. 43. In another work, his *Outline Introductory to Pyrrhonism*, Ænesidemus undertook to arrange the whole material at the disposal of the Sceptic in his contention against the dogmatic position under ten heads or tropes.[1] The word trope properly denotes procedure; the ten tropes were intended to contain the means of refuting dogmatism in all possible forms, and to provide directions for stating every line of available argument which could lead to negative conclusions and paralyse assent.

The first trope starts with differences in the constitution of different animals and in their modes of perception. Some animals have one sense highly developed, some another. In the sense of smell many are superior to man. The second trope applies this line of argument to the individual differences be-

---

[1] Sextus Emp. *Pyrrh. Hyp.*, I, 35–164; Diog. Laërt., IX, 79–88. The ten tropes are expressly attributed to Ænesidemus by Sextus Emp., *Adv. Math.*, VIII, 345; Diog. Laërt., IX, 78, 87; Aristocles, cited in Eusebius, *Pr. Ev.*, XIV, 18, 11. The latter, if the text is correct, speaks of nine, not ten, tropes; *cf.* Philo of Alexandria, *De ebriet.*, pp. 383–388, Mang., also Von Arnim, *Philo und Ænesidem, Quellenstudien zu Philo von Alexandria* (Berlin, 1888), pp. 53–100, esp. pp. 56 *sqq.*

tween man and man. For example, Demophon, the steward of Alexander, is said to have felt warm in the shade and to have shivered in the sun; Andron the Argive was scarcely sensible of thirst; and there was no lack of other well-known instances of abnormal development to appeal to. The third proceeds from the variety in the constitution of the sense-organs, showing that the same object appears under different aspects according to the senses to which it is presented. An apple is yellow to the sight, sweet to the taste, fragrant to the smell; had we more senses, the Sceptic argues, we might discover other qualities. The fourth proceeds from the variability of our physical state and mental mood and the effect of such conditions as sleep, waking, joy, grief, hunger, thirst, etc. When the state of the percipient is so variable, how are we to decide which is the proper state for the perception of external things ? He who offers a standard or criterion must be prepared to prove its validity, and this will be found to be impossible. If so, it is impossible to form any judgment on external things. The fifth [1] adduces the diversities of appearance due to the position and distance of objects. Thus the dove's neck exhibits kaleidoscopic colours in the sun's light, square towers in the distance appear round, straight sticks in the water bent. The sixth proceeds from the mode and mechanism of sense-perception. Thus visible objects are not seen directly, but always through a medium, whether air, water, vapour or fog. The instrument, the eye, is liable to water and to be covered by films. So, too, with the ear, the

---

[1] In Diog. Laërt., IX, 85, this trope appears as the seventh. Similarly what is given in the text as the seventh is in Diogenes made the eighth; the eighth of the text is in Diogenes the tenth, and the tenth of the text is in Diogenes the fifth.

nose, the tongue, the skin; all the instruments of
sense are subject to alterations, which form fresh
barriers between us and knowledge of the external
object as it is. The seventh proceeds from variation
in quantity and the modes in which objects are presented, as temperature, colour, motion. For instance, while the scrapings of goats' horn appear
white, the horn itself appears black, but silver filings
appear black while a mass of silver looks white.
The eighth proceeds more generally from the relativity of all phenomena. All external things are
relative, not only to the perceiving subject, but also
to one another. Thus the same man is in one relation son, in another father, in another brother. The
ninth proceeds from the strength of association,
pointing out that impressions familiar to us cause no
surprise, while what is novel and strange for that very
reason excites wonder. The tenth proceeds in a
similar manner from the diversity in manners and
customs, law and religion, beliefs and opinions in
general among different nations, pointing out, *e. g.*,
how widely the standard of right and wrong has differed in different ages and countries. It has been
well observed that these ten tropes scarcely merit the
reputation they acquired in antiquity. It is difficult
to detect any order in their arrangement or thread of
connection between them. Sextus dilates upon them
and loads them with illustrations. In his view the
first four relate to the judging subject, the seventh
and eighth to the object judged, the remainder to
both subject and object. But the fact is, they all
enunciate more or less indirectly the relativity of
human knowledge.[1] They do not contain anything

---

[1] *Cf.* Lotze, *Logic*, Bk. III, c. 1., § 310. "The ten tropes, or logical
grounds of doubt, all come to this, that sensations by themselves cannot

that had not been at least as well said before, either by
the sophists or the New Academy, and they do not
atone for their lack of novelty by any precision of
scientific arrangement.   As we have seen, the order in
which they are enumerated by Sextus differs from that
of Diogenes Laërtius.   In many of the later heads we
find practically repeated the substance of the former.
The inference is obvious that the table was drawn up
quite empirically to satisfy no other requirements
than the convenience of polemical controversy.

Subsequently an attempt was made to reduce the
number of the tropes or rather to make a new list.
Five sceptical tropes attributed to Agrippa[1] are as
follows: The first is based on the discrepancy of
human opinions, the second on the fact that every
proof itself requires to be proved which implies a
regressus ad infinitum, the third on the relativity of
our knowledge which varies according to the constitution of the percipient and the circumstances in
which he perceives, the fourth is really a completion
of the second and forbids the assumption of unproven
propositions as the premisses of an argument.   The
fifth seeks to show that reasoning essentially involves
a vicious circle inasmuch as the principle adduced in
proof requires itself to be supported by that which
it is called in to prove.   The first and third of these
tropes cover the same ground as the more famous ten,
which consist in the main of arguments derived from
the fallibility of the senses; the remaining three are
new and attack the possibility of demonstration.   Unless the premisses of demonstration are assumed with-

discover to us what is the nature of the object which excites them." For
Lotze's examination of the tropes and of the sceptical position in general
see *Ib.* §§ 310–312 (II, 193–199.   English translation).
[1] Sextus Emp., *Pyrrh. Hyp.*, I, 164–178; Diog. Laërt., IX, 88 *sqq.*

out proof, the dogmatist will find himself committed either to an infinite regress or to a vicious circle. A further attempt at simplification was made by reducing the tropes to two only:[1] (1) Nothing is self-evident, for if things were certain of themselves men would not differ about them; (2) nor can anything be made certain by proof, because we must either arrive in the process at something self-evident or we must involve ourselves in an endless regress.

In the ten tropes the Sceptic confines himself to the well-worn story of the contradiction revealed by sensible phenomena. Agrippa's list of five tropes presents in addition the difficulties inherent in all attempts at logical demonstration. Here, no doubt, the influence of the sceptical Academy can be traced. But it is not on the tropes with which we have been dealing hitherto that the claims of Ænesidemus to a place among speculative inquirers should be based. His reputation for originality is due rather to a series of arguments concerned with truth, with causality and with signs, all of which, as they were understood by the dogmatists, he seeks to overthrow. We pass then, under the guidance of Sextus,[2] to the first of these, the argumentation against truth. Ænesidemus maintains that there is no such thing as truth, and skilfully adapts to his purpose the current distinction between objects of sense and objects of thought, between things sensible and things intelligible.

If truth exists it is one or other of these: it is either something sensible or something intelligible, or it is at once both sensible and intelligible or it is neither sensible nor intelligible. Now every one of

---

[1] Sextus Emp., *Pyrrh. Hyp.*, I, 178–180.
[2] *Adv. Math.*, VIII, 40–48; *cf. Pyrrh Hyp*, II, 80–97.

these alternatives is impossible. Truth is not sensible, for sensible things are either generic or specific. Things generic are the resemblances common to several individuals, like man and horse, found in every man and in every horse. Things specific are the qualities peculiar to this or that individual, to Dion or Theon. If, then, truth is a sensible thing it must be either generic or specific; now it is neither generic nor specific. Furthermore, that which is visible can be perceived by sight, that which is resonant by hearing; in general, whatever is sensible can be similarly perceived by the aid of some one sense, for sensation, in and for itself, is devoid of reason, while truth cannot be perceived without reason. Truth, then, is not a sensible thing. Nor, again, is it intelligible, for then no sensible thing would be true, which is absurd. Further, it would then be either intelligible for all at once or for some individuals alone. But it is impossible that it should be known by all simultaneously, nor is it known by some particular individual, for this is improbable and is, in fact, the point at issue.

Lastly, truth is not at once both sensible and intelligible. For if so, we shall have to say either that everything sensible and everything intelligible is true or else that not every sensible thing, but certain sensible things, not everything intelligible, but certain intelligible things, are true. Now it cannot be said that everything sensible and everything intelligible is true, for sensible things are in contradiction with sensible things and intelligible things with intelligible things and reciprocally sensible things are in contradiction with intelligible things and intelligibles with sensibles. And it will be necessary, if all is true, that the same thing both is and is not, is true and false at the same

time. Nor can it be that some of the sensible things
are true or some of the intelligible things, for that is
precisely the point at issue. Besides, it is logical to
say that all sensible things are either true or false, for
quâ sensible they are all similar; one is not more sensible, the other less so. And so, too, with things intelligible; they are all equally intelligible. Yet it is
absurd to say that every sensible thing or every intelligible thing is true. If, then, this reasoning holds,
truth does not exist.

This reasoning implies that truth and sensible
things and intelligible things—in other words, the
qualities of being true, of being sensible, and of being
intelligible are severally realities. All three are regarded as positive and intrinsic properties possessed
by the objects that are called true or sensible or intelligible. Common speech and even the language of
philosophers lends support to such a view. The
Stoics actually defined truth as a corporeal thing, a
body. But upon reflection it will be seen that a thing
does not contain in itself the property of being true.
Two terms are necessary, the thing which exists and the
thought to which it is presented. Aristotle had long
ago made this perfectly plain.[1] "Falsity and truth"
he says "are not in things, but in thought; it is not
as if the good were true and the bad were in itself
false. The cause, then, of that which *is* in the sense
of being true or false is an affection of thought; it is
related to the remaining genus of being and does not
indicate any separate class of being. That which *is*
in the sense of being true or *is not* in the sense of being
false depends on combination and separation. The
combination and the separation are in thought and
not in the things, and that which is in this sense is

[1] *Metaph.* E., IV, 1027, b. 18-33.

a different sort of 'being' from the things that are in the full sense. The true judgment affirms where the subject and predicate really are combined and denies where they are separated, while the false judgment predicates the contradictory of this. We think things together and apart in the sense that there is no succession in the thought but they become a unity." He went further, affirming that "in regard to simple concepts and essences, falsity and truth do not exist, even in thought." It is not surprising, then, that after conceiving as a thing in itself what can only be conceived as a relation, the sceptic should end by disproving its existence. It is quite certain that truth does not exist if we mean a reality independent of all thought. And the same thing may be said of what is sensible and what is intelligible, for in these terms, too, relations are implied. "But," the Sceptic may reply, "whether a relation or a thing in itself is meant makes little difference, provided you grant that where the relation expressed by the term sensible is found there is also found the relation expressed by the term truth. And this you do grant, if you say that what is true is sensible, as you must do unless you maintain that what is true is intelligible, and then the same question will arise under a slightly different form." Here we discern a second ambiguity. The Sceptic takes in an absolute sense identities which are only admitted in a partial or relative sense. We admit without misgiving that what is true is either sensible or intelligible. But what do we mean? Simply that there are true things[1] which are either sensible or intelligible. These two qualities, true and sensible or true and intelligible can coexist in the

[1] The content or subjects of Aristotle's true thoughts, judgments or propositions.

same object. A thing true under one aspect is sensible under another, and both at once. The thing is sensible, but it is not solely and essentially sensible; it is sensible without losing its own nature; it is at once, in Plato's words, the same as that which is sensible and yet different from it. The Sceptic, however, takes the terms literally. "You admit," he will say, "that the true is sensible; this means that what is true and what is sensible are the same thing, or, in your own language, that where the relation expressed by the term true is found there we necessarily, also, find the relation expressed by the term sensible." Thus, where we understand two things elsewhere distinct are united and coexist in the same object and are in this sense identical, he understands that they form an absolute identity. According to him a thing is not at once sensible and true, but because it is sensible it is no longer true. He makes the bond which unites the two terms analytic not synthetic.[1] This misconception of predication follows inevitably when relations are confused with things in themselves. When the true and the sensible are taken for things in themselves, to say that the one is the other is to identify them completely and in essence. A thing can have several relations with other things, but it cannot be in itself several things. All sensible things are sensible in virtue of one relation, and in addition certain of them are in certain relations true as well. To this the Sceptic demurs: "Logic requires that all sensible things should be true or false, since _quâ_ sensible they are all identical, one is not more so than the other." This is the old plea which

---

[1] Compare the remarks of Mr. G. E. Moore, _Principia Ethica_, pp. 9 _sqq._, on what he terms the "naturalistic fallacy," _e. g._, since something else (pleasure) is good, _ergo_, good is that something else (pleasure).

loses its force when once it is understood that the identity expressed in predication is not absolute but partial and contingent.

Ænesidemus next treats of causality: "There is no such thing as cause, for a body (corporeal thing) is not the cause of a corporeal thing. In fact, either this corporeal thing is not generated, like the atom of Epicurus, or it is generated like ordinary bodies; it is either perceptible by the senses, like iron, or it is imperceptible, like the atom; in both cases it can produce nothing, for if it produces something it does so either by remaining in itself or by uniting with something else. But by remaining in itself it can produce nothing but itself, it can produce nothing that is not in its own nature. Nor by uniting with something else can it any more produce a third thing which did not exist before, for it is not possible that one should thus become two or two become three. If one thing could thus become two, each of the two units thus produced would, in its turn, become two, and there would be four of them, and then each of the four in its turn doubling itself there would be eight units, and so *ad infinitum*. Now it is quite absurd to say that from a unity there proceeds an infinity of things, and it is no less absurd to say that from a unity there arises a multiplicity. Again it is absurd to say that from the union of a given number of things there can arise a numerically greater number. For if one unit being added to another unit produces a third unit, this latter by being added to the former two will produce a fourth unit, this fourth a fifth unit, and so *ad infinitum*. Thus we have shown that body cannot be the cause of body; one corporeal thing cannot produce another. By the same reasoning, the non-corporeal cannot be the cause of the non-corporeal, for plurality can never come from unity, nor from a given plurality a numerically greater plurality. Further, what is not corporeal, being incapable of contact, can neither do nor suffer, neither act nor be acted upon. But again, just as the incorporeal never generates the incorporeal, so a body cannot produce what is not corporeal nor the non-corporeal a body; for body does not contain in itself the nature of the non-corporeal nor does the non-corporeal contain in itself the nature of body. Plane-tree never gives birth to horse, nor horse to plane-tree, because the nature of horse is not included in that of plane-tree; horse never gives birth to man because the nature of man is not included in that of horse. So, too, from body there never arises the non-corporeal, because the nature of what is not corporeal is not in the nature of body. Conversely from the incorporeal there never arises body. Nay, more, if one of the two were in the other it will never be engendered by the other, for if each of the two exists, it does not arise from the other, but possesses reality already; being already existent it cannot be generated, for by generation or becoming is meant a process or advance toward being. Hence, body not being the cause of the non-corporeal nor the non-corporeal the cause of body, we conclude that there is no such thing as cause." [1]

This reasoning of Ænesidemus was completed by the enumeration in the fifth book of his *Pyrrhonean Discourses* of eight tropes [2] specially intended to refute those who believed in the existence of causes. The list as preserved by Sextus is couched in some-

---

[1] Sextus Emp., *Adv. Math.*, IX, 218–227; *cf.* Diog. Laërt., IX, 97–99. Contrast the more cautious attitude of Sextus himself, *Pyrrh.*, *Hyp.*, III, 13–29.

[2] Photius, *Biblioth.*, 170, b, 17 *sqq.*; Sextus Emp., *Pyrrh. Hyp*, I, 180–184.

what obscure terms. These eight tropes differ from the ten tropes, both by their purpose, and the manner of their presentation. Ænesidemus is not concerned here to oppose to each other opinions of equal value which are contradictory, but merely to indicate various modes of false reasoning about causes, so that the word trope is employed in a new sense. The list which Ænesidemus gives is, truth to say, a list of sophisms, of errors perpetrated in the search for causes. Among such errors the eight which follow are conspicuous: (1) Resorting to a cause which is not evident and which is not attested by another thing which can be called evident; (2) stopping short at one single reason, when we have the choice of several good explanations equally plausible; (3) when things follow in a regular order, calling in causes which disregard this order; (4) supposing that the things which we do not see come about like the things which we do see, although they may conceivably come about otherwise; (5) explaining everything, as most philosophers have done, by the aid of elements which they have assumed instead of following the common notions admitted by everybody; (6) disregarding, as many philosophers do, all causes but those which conform to their own hypotheses, and passing over in silence those which are contrary to these hypotheses, in spite of the fact that these latter causes are also probable; (7) calling in causes which are contrary not only to appearances but even to principles previously adopted; (8) employing for the explanation of doubtful things causes equally doubtful. Ænesidemus went on to remark that it can happen that in affirming causes philosophers have been mistaken in various other ways which may be subsumed under those already given.

Again we pause to make a few obvious comments. It is hardly necessary to point out that the idea of cause, when analysed, is easily seen to imply a relation, and that in a twofold aspect. A thing can only be conceived as cause in relation to its effects. Ænesidemus seems not to have touched on this point, and the later Sceptics hardly realised it. Again the act of thought by which a thing is known in itself is not the same as that by which it is known as a cause. The thing is at first conceived in itself in its essence; then it is looked upon as a cause; causality is a relation which is superadded to the idea that we have of the thing without destroying it and without being confounded with it. But the Sceptic does not take it so. Here again, authorised, we must admit, by language and by custom, he considers causality as a real objective quality belonging to the thing; he makes of it a thing in itself. Further, this property is identified with the thing itself in which it is suppposed to exist; do we not say that one thing is the cause of another? And, consequently, if a thing is a cause, it is so absolutely and by its essence in its intimate nature. Once this is done it becomes necessary to comprehend how this determinate essence can produce something other than itself. But the question so stated is absurd. A thing once given and defined in its essence can only remain what it is. To say it is a cause is to say that it is something other than itself; this would be a contradiction. In modern parlance, from the idea of a thing will never be derived, analytically, the idea of something else, and this remains true if in place of a single essence we consider several united in juxtaposition. In other words, as Hume and Kant have shown, causality is a synthetic rela-

tion. The two terms posited as cause and effect are
not given to our thought as identical, but only as
having a certain connection under a category, *sui
generis*, which we call causality. Ænesidemus understood this, and this is why it is right to see in him
a precursor of Hume and Kant. We are in a position now to determine what truth and falsehood the
reasoning of Ænesidemus contained. So long as a
cause is considered as a thing in itself his reasoning
is unassailable. It loses all validity the moment we
consider a cause as a relation established by thought
between different objects. Such a relation connects
the objects without modifying their true nature.
They are at first what they are in themselves, and besides this they are looked upon as connected with
other things by certain laws. If this much be pre-
mised, there is no contradiction; in this way, what is
corporeal may be connected with what is corporeal,
what is incorporeal with what is incorporeal; we may
even consider the corporeal as the cause of the incorporeal, the incorporeal as the cause of the corporeal.

But Ænesidemus was not content with disproving
the existence of cause. He attacked the doctrine of
signs, which in his day was the recognised method
of research and scientific discovery. Ignorance of
cause may debar us from the direct method of explanation, from descending from the cause to the
effects; but is not an indirect method possible, may
we not ascend from effects to causes ? Such a method
implies that certain phenomena, the effects, are signs,
and certain others, the causes, are the things signified
by these signs. Ratiocination would then be the
means which the mind possesses for rising to the explanation of things. Such was precisely the thesis

of both the Stoics and Epicureans which Ænesidemus undertook to overthrow. According to Photius,[1]
Ænesidemus, in the fourth book of his treatise, declared that there are no visible signs which disclose
invisible things, and those who believe in their existence are the dupes of a vain illusion. This testimony
is confirmed by a more explicit passage in Sextus.[2]
If phenomena appear in the same way to all observers who are similarly constituted, and if, further,
signs are phenomena, then the signs must appear in
the same way to all observers similarly constituted.
This hypothetical proposition is self-evident; if the
antecedent be granted the consequent follows. Now,
continues Sextus, (1) phenomena do appear in the
same way to all observers similarly constituted. But
(2) signs do not appear in the same way to all observers similarly constituted. The truth of proposition (1) rests upon observation, for though, to the
jaundiced or bloodshot eye, white objects do not
appear white, yet to the normal eye, *i. e.*, to all observers similarly constituted, white objects invariably
do appear white. For the truth of proposition (2) the
art of medicine furnishes decisive instances. The
symptoms of fever, the flush, the moisture of the
skin, the high temperature, the rapid pulse, when observed by doctors of the like mental constitution, are
not interpreted by them in the same way. Here
Sextus cites some of the conflicting theories maintained by the authorities of his age. In these symptoms Herophilus sees a mark of the good quality of
the blood; for Erasistratus they are a sign of the
passage of the blood from the veins to the arteries;
for Asclepiades they prove, too great tension of
corpuscles in interspaces, although both corpuscles

[1] *Biblioth.*, 170, b. 12.   [2] *Adv. Math.*, VIII, 215 *sqq.*

and interspaces, being infinitesimally small, cannot be perceived by sense but only apprehended by the intellect. Sextus, having borrowed this argument from Ænesidemus, has developed it in his own fashion, and is probably himself responsible for the medical instances which he has selected. He uses it to establish that signs are not, as the Epicureans maintain, sensible things. From his first hypothetical proposition, coupled with propositions (1) and (2), Sextus infers that signs are not phenomena. We have no right, then, to call any phenomenon a sign, and, if this be so, reasoning from effects to causes is invalid.

It remains, then, to prove that neither do they belong to the domain of things intelligible, as was the view of the Stoics; in other words, that they cannot be apprehended by reason or intellect. This proof Sextus undertakes to furnish. But there is no evidence that Ænesidemus himself ever dreamed of doing so. He must have confined himself to demonstrating that there are no "signs" in the sense of things visible disclosing what is invisible, i. e., no signs among sensible things; or, in the words of Photius, "There are no signs, manifest and obvious, of what is obscure and latent." Sextus himself reminds us that he has slightly modified the argument of Ænesidemus by taking the term phenomena, or appearances, as the equivalent of sensible phenomena, appearances to sense.[1] It is highly improbable that Ænesidemus had already made the distinciton familiar to the later Sceptics between two classes of signs. According to Sextus,[2] there are signs which act, as we

---

[1] *Adv. Math.*, VIII, 216.

[2] *Pyrrh. Hyp.*, II, 100; *cf.* the context, 99–102; *Adv. Math.*, VIII, 148–158.

should say, by the law of association, reminding us that in past experience two phenomena were conjoined, as smoke with fire, a scar with a wound, a stab to the heart with subsequent death. If afterward one of the two phenomena is temporarily obscured and passes out of immediate consciousness, the other, if present, may serve to recall it; we are justified in calling the one which is present a sign, and the other, which is temporarily absent, the thing signified. With the term "sign," as thus understood, the sign commemorative or reminiscent, Sextus has no quarrel. By its aid prediction is justified; we can infer fire from smoke, the wound from the scar, approaching death from the fatal stab, for in all these cases we proceed upon past experience. Sextus reserves his hostility for another class of signs which we may call the sign demonstrative. When one of the two phenomena assumed to be the thing signified never has occurred in actual experience, but belongs wholly, by its own nature, to the region of the unknown, the dogmatists nevertheless maintained that, if certain conditions were fulfilled, its existence was indicated and demonstrated by the other phenomenon, which they called the sign. For instance, according to the dogmatists, the movements of the body indicate and demonstrate the existence of the soul; they are its sign. It is "sign," then, in this latter sense, the indicative or demonstrative sign, whose existence Sextus disputes and undertakes to refute. To make this distinction implies a clear grasp of the method of observation as opposed to the logical or dialectical method, in short, to the high *priori* road. His eight tropes incline us to credit Ænesidemus with a scientific turn of mind. They show a tendency to interpret the data of experience impartially, without pre-

conceived ideas.   And yet, as we have seen, they are,
after all, the work of a logician rather than of an observer of nature; nor is there any extant authority to
warrant us in attributing the distinction in question
to Ænesidemus rather than to Sextus.   The distinction which Ænesidemus undoubtedly made between
signs presented to sense and signs presented to intellect is not the same as that made by Sextus between
signs commemorative and signs demonstrative, for
the Epicureans, who admitted none but signs presented to sense, nevertheless believed in the possibility
of the inductive leap, as we should call it, from the
known to the unknown.   Indeed, there are extant
fragments of a treatise on signs and inference by
Philodemus, a later Epicurean, which are interesting
because the inferential method recommended bears
a distinct analogy to that of modern inductive logic.
The foregoing considerations are apparently confirmed by passages in Sextus where he seems to have
followed Ænesidemus and to have inadvertently adduced as a demonstrative sign one which upon examination turns out to be unmistakably a sign belonging to the other class.[1]

The theory of signs, so far as we have good evidence
for attributing it to Ænesidemus, comes to very
little.   It is manifestly incomplete.   Some, indeed,
have seen in it nothing more than a particular form of
the tenth trope.   Others, however, are inclined to
believe it had for Ænesidemus a wider bearing, and
to see in him a precursor of J. S. Mill, if, indeed, he
is to be credited with the arguments adduced by
Sextus.   When he is treating of reminiscent signs
Sextus does, indeed, describe induction in terms not
unworthy of Mill.   The reminiscent sign is a phenom-

[1] *Pyrrh. Hyp.*, II, 106; *Adv. Math.*, VIII, 252.

enon which has been clearly observed at the same time as the thing of which it is a sign. If it presents itself again after the latter has been obscured, it reminds us of the thing which was observed simultaneously with itself, but is no longer actually in evidence; thus smoke makes us think of fire. We have often seen these two phenomena together or coexisting; as soon as we perceive one of them, memory suggests to us the idea of the other, namely, the fire not now actually visible. So, too, with the scar which shows after the wound and the stab to the heart which is followed by death. On the sight of the scar, memory suggests to us the wound which preceded it; on seeing a man stabbed in the heart, we predict his approaching death. What the Sceptic combats is the theory of demonstrative signs, that is to say, the theory according to which there is a necessary and constant connection between phenomena, a causal nexus such, in short, as is still maintained by dogmatists to-day. It is agreed that from their own point of view the sceptical arguments are unassailable. If we adhere to the data of experience, to phenomena alone, it is impossible to see in induction anything else than an association of ideas founded on habit and, like it, variable. Thus Mill, while trying to establish his scientific theory of induction, admits that induction cannot be absolutely valid. It only holds for our world, and there may be systems in which phenomena are not submitted to any laws or uniformities. We do not claim that Ænesidemus got as far as that; there is nothing in the Greek texts to authorise such a statement. He stopped short of explaining in what sense and how far there can be such a thing as experimental science without the casual nexus. But he understood and proved that there is no such thing as science in the absolute sense of the dogmatists. There is, indeed, no science, no demonstration, unless ideas are linked together by a necessary band or connection, but there is no true necessity unless relation can be rationally determined or, in modern parlance, determined *a priori*. Now, given a fact, or, as the Stoics call it, a sign, let us try to determine *a priori* the nature of the thing signified. Here, just as when we were dealing with cause, it is obvious that we never can succeed, and if we never succeed, there will be no demonstration. This is what Ænesidemus meant, and he is unanswerable.

We can now assign Ænesidemus his place in the sceptical school. Sextus seems to oppose him to the later Sceptics, of whom Agrippa appears to have been one of the first. His originality cannot be seriously questioned. It was he who really resuscitated Pyrrhonism, and in the main it retained the form he gave it, though some modifications were bound to occur in the course of two centuries. Ænesidemus distinguished himself as a dialectician. Metaphysical paradoxes and dialectical subtleties at once too absurd for refutation and impossible to refute were his stock-in-trade. If there was any proposition which he withdrew from universal doubt, it was the dictum of Heraclitus, the identity of all contradictions in the absolute, which is a metaphysical and transcendental thesis. But before making an imputation so gravely affecting his consistency as a Sceptic, we ought to be sure of our ground. Sextus, who carefully distinguished scepticism from systems which might be confused with it, starts with that of Heraclitus. In the course of his remarks he makes the plain statement that Ænesidemus and his followers declared scepticism to be a path to the philosophy

of Heraclitus.   There are other passages in which
Sextus mentions, usually without indorsing them,
opinions of Ænesidemus, such as that time is real,
the primary corporeal thing, or to be identified with
air; that phenomena are of two kinds, specific and
generic; that motion may be divided into spatial and
qualitative, that thought or intellect is "outside" or
independent of the body.[1]   Some of these opinions
are ascribed by Sextus to Ænesidemus "according to
Heraclitus," a phrase which hardly suggests that the
opinion in question belonged properly to Heraclitus
and was disowned by Ænesidemus as it would be by
Sextus himself.

Some scholars, indeed, refuse to accept the plain
statement of Sextus, and think the whole difficulty
may be removed by the assumption of a misconception on his part.   But it is very unlikely that Sextus
failed to distinguish the opinions of Heraclitus
reported by Ænesidemus from those of Ænesidemus himself, whereas, if the Pyrrhonean Sceptic
who had broken with the Academy did in the end
himself follow the path to Heraclitus, his opinions at
this stage of his philosophic development could be
conveniently cited as those of "Ænesidemus according to Heraclitus."   A further question remains.
Were these opinions put forward dogmatically, or did
Ænesidemus by becoming a Heraclitean still not
cease to be a sceptic and put them forward merely
as what appeared to him?   In the absence of further
evidence the question can hardly be decided.   But
it is at all events easy to discriminate him from his
successors.   They were for the most part, as we have
seen, medical men.   To speculation, which they de-

[1] *Pyrrh. Hyp.*, III, 17; *Adv. Math.*, X, 233; *ib.*, VIII, 8; *ib.*, X, 38;
ib., XII, 349.

clared futile, they opposed their art, a practical
science, which they held to be legitimate and necessary.
Scepticism was an end in itself to Ænesidemus; his
successors made of it an introduction to the medical
art.   If later Sceptics believed in anything it was
solely in empirical sequences of phenomena discover-
able by observation apart from any theory.   In this
direction Ænesidemus influenced them but little.
If he was a metaphysician they tended to become
positivists.   But again there is no evidence that they
ever actually took this decisive step.   Coexistences
and sequences of phenomena might be to them all
that we can know, but they still talked glibly of things
in themselves, in the very act of refusing their assent
to them.   The function of thorough-going scepticism
is invariably critical, though the Sceptics themselves
seldom see this   If Hume's scepticism was, as Kant
supposed, a *reductio ad absurdum* of thorough-going
empiricism, it may also be said that the scepticism of
the Pyrrhonists was a *reductio ad absurdum* of those
assumptions of crude realism and materialistic empiricism which were the common property of all the
post-Aristotelian schools which the Sceptics themselves shared with their opponents the Stoics and
Epicureans.   In justice, however, to the Sceptics we
must defend them from the charge of inconsistency
so frequently brought against them by modern critics.
How, it is asked, can universal doubt be reconciled
with the attitude of practical men taking part in
everyday life.   The answer given by Sextus is clear
and explicit.   The Pyrrhonist does not deny phenomena, for they are the only criterion by which he
can regulate action, and inactivity implies death.
In his daily life he sometimes obeys the guidance of
nature, at other times the compulsion of his feelings;

sometimes the tradition of laws and customs, at others the teaching of the arts.   But in all these ways he is merely following appearances or phenomena.[1]   This attitude has been wittily described as the philosophy of the dinner-bell, and it is easy to sneer at Sextus for not comprehending the effects of his own work as a whole or realising that in the attempt to subvert all established principles he was cutting away the ground on which he stood.   The critics have not really thought out the sceptical position.   They have not faced the consequences of general uncertainty.   The calmness and self-possession of the Pyrrhonist favours the inference that he considered his own attitude reasonable, as if in a world of unreason and a chaos of unrelated phenomena there could be such a thing as a reasonable attitude.   He might fairly be charged with inconsistency if he admitted consistency in experience and in the universe.   But this is just what he declines to affirm.

Upon this charge let Hume, the greatest of sceptics, answer for his brethren of antiquity.   He has told us that it is only by forgetting his own arguments that he can recover cheerfulness.   "Most fortunately it happens, that since reason is incapable of dispelling these clouds, nature herself suffices to that purpose, and cures me of this philosophical melancholy and delirium, either by relaxing this bent of mind, or by some avocation and lively impression of my senses, which obliterates all these chimeras. . . . I may, nay I must yield to the current of nature in submitting to my senses and understanding; and in this blind submission I show most perfectly my sceptical disposition and principles.   But does it follow that I must strive against the current of nature, which

[1] Sextus Emp. *Pyrrh. Hyp.*, I, 23, 24.

leads me to indolence and pleasure; . . . and that I must torture my brains with subtilities and sophistries, at the very time that I cannot satisfy myself concerning the reasonableness of so painful an application, nor have any tolerable prospect of arriving by its means at truth and certainty? . . . These are the sentiments of my spleen and indolence; and, indeed, I must confess that philosophy has nothing to oppose to them, and expects a victory more from the returns of a serious, good-humour'd disposition than from the force of reason and conviction.   In all the incidents of life we ought still to preserve our scepticism.   If we believe that fire warms or water refreshes, 'tis only because it costs us too much pains to think otherwise.   Nay, if we are philosophers, it ought only to be on sceptical principles, and from an inclination which we feel to the employing ourselves after that manner." [1]   This is the attitude of the ancient Sceptic, and the fact that other men denounce it as irrational or inconsistent is part of its justification.

[1] *Treatise of Human Nature*, Bk. I, Pt. IV, *sub fin.*   (Works, ed. Green and Grose.   Vol. I, p. 548 *sqq.*)

SELECT BIBLIOGRAPHY

For the Stoics the general reader may consult:

Grant, A. The Ancient Stoics. Essay VI, prefixed to The Ethics of Aristotle. London (1856), 4th ed., 1884.

Long, G. The Thoughts of the Emperor M. Aurelius Antoninus. London (1862), 1886.

Long, G. The Discourses of Epictetus, with the Encheiridion and Fragments. Translated with a Life of Epictetus and a view of his philosophy. London (1877), 1891.

Rendall, G. H. Marcus Aurelius Antoninus to Himself; an English Translation with Introductory Study of Stoicism and the Last of the Stoics. London, 1898.

Martha, C. Les moralistes sous l'empire romain, philosophes et poètes. Paris (1864), 1881.

Dill, S. Roman Society from Nero to Marcus Aurelius. London, 1904.

For the Epicureans:—

Wallace, W. Epicureanism. London, 1880.

Martha, C. Le poème de Lucrèce, morale, religion, science. Paris, 1869.

Masson, J. Lucretius, Epicurean and Poet. London: Murray, 1907, and A Complementary Volume, 1909.

Munro, H. A. J. Translation of Lucretius. New edition. London: Bell, 1908.

The following list of books has been drawn up for the use of those who make this epoch of philosophy a special study:—

I. INDISPENSABLE COLLECTIONS OF MATERIAL

Pearson, A. C. The Fragments of Zeno and Cleanthes, with Introduction and Explanatory Notes. London, 1891. [The best introduction to the Stoics.]

Von Arnim, J. Stoicorum Veterum Fragmenta. Vol. I, Zeno et Zenonis discipuli, 1905. Vol. II, Chrysippi fragmenta logica et physica, 1903. Vol. III, Chrysippi fragmenta moralia. Fragmenta successorum Chrysippi, 1903. Leipzig, Teubner.

Diels, H. Doxographi Græci. Berolini, 1879.

Stobæus. Anthologii Libri Duo Priores qui inscribi solent Eclogæ Physicæ et Ethicæ, recc. Wachsmuth et Hense. Berolini, apud Weidmannos, 1884.

Usener, H. Epicurea. [The first edition out of print.] Lipsiæ: Teubner, 1887.

II. WORKS OF REFERENCE

Bonhöffer, A. Epictet und die Stoa. Untersuchungen zur stoischen Philosophie. Stuttgart, 1890.

Bonhöffer, A. Die Ethik des Stoikers Epictet. Anhang: Exkurse über einige wichtige Punkte der stoischen Ethik. Stuttgart, 1894.

Brochard, V. Les Sceptiques grecs. Paris, 1887.

Dyroff, A. Die Ethik der alten Stoa. Berlin, 1897.

Guyau, M. La Morale d'Epicure et ses rapports avec les doctrines contemporaines. Paris, 1878.

Heinze, M. Die Lehre vom Logos in der griechischen Philosophie. Oldenburg, 1872.

Hirzel, R. Untersuchungen zur Cicero's philosophischen Schriften. 3 vols. Leipzig, 1882. The second volume has for subtitle: Die Entwicklung der stoischen Philosophie.

Krische, A. B. Forschungen auf dem Gebiete der alten Philosophie. I. Bd. Die theologischen Lehren der griechischen Denker. Eine Prüfung der Darstellung Cicero's. Göttingen, 1840.

Maccoll, N. The Greek Sceptics. London: Macmillan, 1869.

Masson, J. The Atomic Theory of Lucretius. London, 1884.

Natorp, P. Forschungen zur Geschichte des Erkenntnissproblems im Alterthum. Protagoras, Demokrit, Epikur und die Skepsis. Berlin, 1884.

Ogereau, F. Essai sur le système philosophique des Stoiciens. Paris, 1885.

Patrick, M. M. Sextus Empiricus and Greek Scepticism. London: Bell, 1899.

Ravaisson, F. Essai sur le stoicisme. Paris, 1856.

Saisset, E. Aenésidème. Paris, 1840.

Schmekel, A. Die Philosophie der mittleren Stoa in ihrem geschichtlichen Zusammenhange. Berlin, 1892.

Siebeck, H. Die Umbildung der peripatetischen Naturphilosophie in die der Stoiker. (In Untersuchungen zur Philosophie der Griechen. Zweite, neu bearbeitete und vermehrte Auflage.) 2 ed. Freiburg, i. B., 1888.

Stein, L. Die Psychologie der Stoa. 1 Band. Metaphysisch-anthropologischer Theil. Berlin, 1886. (Berliner Studien für klassische Philologie und Archäologie. 3 Band.)

Stein, L. Die Erkentnisstheorie der Stoa (2 Band der Psychologie). Berlin, 1888. (Berliner Studien, 7 Band.)

Wilamovitz-Möllendorff, U. v. Antigonos von Karystos. (Philologische Untersuchungen von Kiessling und Wilamovitz-Möllendorff, 4 Heft). Berlin: Weidmann, 1881.

Woltjer, J. Lucretii Philosophia cum fontibus comparata. Specimen Litterarum quo inquiritur quatemus Epicuri Philosophiam tradiderit Lucretius. Groningæ, 1877.

Zeller, E. Nacharistotelische Philosophie I. (Philosophie der Griechen III, 1.) Vierte Auflage. Leipzig, 1909. [This posthumous edition appeared too late for use in the present volume.]

III. EDITIONS

Seneca. Texts of the Epistles, by Hense, Leipzig, Teubner, 1898, and the Naturales Quæstiones, by Gercke, 1907.

Epictetus (transcribed by **Arrian**). Text by Schenkl, Lipsiæ, 1894. The last complete annotated edition is: Epicteteæ Philosophiæ monumenta ad Codd. Mss. fidem recensuit, Latina versione adnotationibus, indicibusque illustravit Io. Schweighäuser. 5 Tom. Lipsiæ, 1799–1800. [The last two of the five volumes contain the Commentary of Simplicius on the Encheiridion.]

M. Aurelius Antoninus. Text by Stich, Lipsiæ, 1882. Gataker's valuable edition has for title: Marci Antonini Imperatoris de rebus suis, sive de eis quæ ad se pertinere censebat, Libri XII, Locis haud paucis repurgati, suppleti, restituti: Versione insuper Latinâ novâ; Lectionibus item variis, Locisque parallelis ad marginem adjectis; Ac Commentario perpetuo, explicati atque illustrati; Studio operâque Thomæ Gatakeri, Londinatis, Cantabrigiæ, 1652.

Cicero. De Finibus. By J. N. Madvig. Editio altera. Hauniæ, 1869.

    De Natura Deorum. By J. B. Mayor. 3 vols. Cambridge, (Eng.), 1880.

    Academica. By J. S. Reid. London: Macmillan, 1885.

    De Officiis. By H. A. Holden. Cambridge (Eng.), 1886.

Plutarch. The Four Tracts:—De Stoicorum Repugnantiis; De Communibus Notitiis adversus Stoicos; Non posse suaviter vivere secundum Epicurum; Adversus Coloten;—in Wyttenbach's edition of the Moralia, Oxonii, 1795 (Lipsiæ, 1796).

Timon. Sillographorum Græcorum Reliquiæ. Recogn. et enarrav. Curtius Wachsmuth. Præcedit commentatio de Timone Phliasio ceterisque sillographis. Lipsiæ, 1885.

Sextus Empiricus. Opera Græce et Latine. Notas addidit J. A. Fabricius. 2 vols. Lipsiæ, 1718. Editio emendatior, Lipsiæ, Kuhn, 1840-1841.

Galen. De Placitis Hippocratis et Platonis libri novem. Text by Ivan Müller. Lipsiæ, 1874.

Metrodorus. Metrodori Epicurei Fragmenta collegit A. Körte. Leipzig, 1890. (In Jahrbücher f. classische Philologie, Supplementband XVII, pp. 529-597.)

Lucretius. With Notes and a Translation, by H. A. J. Munro. Fourth edition finally revised. Cambridge (Eng.), 1886.

 Revisione del Testo, Commento e Studi Introduttivi di Carlo Giussani. 4 vols. Torino, 1896-1898. Also a Supplement, Note Lucreziane. Torino, 1900. [It is to be hoped that this edition will appear in an English dress.]

 Edited by W. A. Merrill, Ph.D., New York, American Book Company, 1907.

Diogenes of Œnoanda. Diogenis Œnoandensis Fragmenta ordinavit et explicavit Johannes William. Lipsiæ, 1907.

INDEX

Academy, New or Sceptical, 7, 340, 351, 359, 369, 375, 379; generally, 317–358.

Academy, Old, 317, 349, 357.

Accident, non-essential quality, 221, 241, 242, 270–272.

Ænesidemus, 373 *note*, 374–397; writings, 375; probable date, 375, 376.

Agrippa, Pyrrhonean Sceptic, his five tropes, 379.

Alcmæon of Croton, 62.

Alexander of Abonuteichos, 308.

Alexander the Great, 3, 314.

Anaxagoras of Clazomenæ, 19, 204, 219, 283, 306; refuted by Epicurus, 244, ; cited, 244, 245.

Anaxarchus, 314.

Anaximenes of Miletus cited, 20.

Anima in Lucretius, 267, 268.

Animus or mens, in Lucretius, 267, 268.

Antigonus Gonatas, king of Macedonia, 5.

Antiochus of Ascalon, Eclectic, 356–358, 375.

Antipater of Tarsus, sixth head of Stoic school, 326, 360, 361.

Antisthenes, founder of the Cynic school, 88.

Apollonius of Cyrene, Megarian philosopher, 320 *note*.

Appetitus, 66.

Aratus of Soli, pupil of Zeno, author of an astronomical poem, 6, 14.

Arcesilas of Pitane, 317–323, 375.

Archedemus, eclectic Stoic, 111, 112, 361.

Aristippus, 164, 165, 210.

Aristo of Chios, heterodox pupil of Zeno, 6, 90, 368; cited, 86.

Aristocles, 314, 317.

Aristotle, his dualism and transcendent First Cause, 19, 20, 22, 39, 338; his influence on the Stoics, 13, 28, 32, 41, 62; criticised by Chrysippus, 54; his ten categories revised by the Stoics, 56; contrast between them in psychology, 64, 65, 105, points of contact with Stoic ethics, 3, 91, 112; general, 205, 213, 256, 258, 272, 283, 311, 323, 337, 349, 353, 357, 382.

Aristotle, works formerly ascribed to *De Lineis Insecabilibus*, 212; *De Mundo*, 354; *De Virtutibus et Vitiis*, *De Affectibus*, 355; his *Ethics* cited, 54, 112, 164.

Aristoxenus, 267.

Arrian, published Discourses and Encheiridion of Epictetus, 113, 124.

Asclepiades, physician, 390.

Assent, 64, 65, 72, 73, 315, 318, 344, 346.

Atom, meaning of, 220; of Democritus, 207; of Epicurus, 24, 25; terms for, 220, 221; how described, 218, 222; shapes, 223; motion of; 224–227, 255–264; systems of atoms, 233; unchangeable qualities, 240–242; minimal parts or minima, 248–251; declination, 255–264, 345.

Atomic theory of Leucippus unpopular in antiquity, 205; adopted by Epicurus, 207.

Atomists, 174, 219, 256; problems of, 204; their materialism, 205, 206; contrasted with Eleatics, 207; theory of hearing, 239.

Atticus, an Epicurean, 307.